THE INFLUENCE
OF
JOHN DONNE

THE INFLUENCE
OF
JOHN DONNE

His Uncollected
Seventeenth-Century
Printed Verse

ERNEST W. SULLIVAN, II

University of Missouri Press
COLUMBIA AND LONDON

University of Missouri Press, Columbia, Missouri 65201
Printed and bound in the United States of America
5 4 3 2 1   97 96 95 94 93

Library of Congress Cataloging-in-Publication Data

Sullivan, Ernest W.
    The influence of John Donne : his uncollected seventeenth-
century printed verse / Ernest W. Sullivan, II.
        p.   cm.
    Includes bibliographical references (p.) and index.
    ISBN 0-8262-0892-4 (alk. paper)
    1. Donne, John, 1572-1631—Bibliography.   2. Bibliography—
England—Early printed books—17th century.   I. Title.
Z8237.S85   1993
[PR2248]
016.821'3—dc20   93-20174
                                                                              CIP

⊗ This paper meets the requirements of the
American National Standard for Permanence of Paper
for Printed Library Materials, Z39.48, 1984.

Designer: Elizabeth Fett
Typesetter: The Composing Room of Michigan, Inc.
Printer and binder: Thomson-Shore, Inc.
Typeface: Palatino.

For Eleanor, Kahlua, and Cocoa

CONTENTS

ACKNOWLEDGMENTS

A Texas Tech University Faculty Development Leave, National Endowment for the Humanities Travel Grant and Summer Stipend, William Andrews Clark Memorial Library Summer Fellowship, and South Central Modern Language Association Huntington Library Fellowship supported the travel and research for this work.

For the services of their staff and allowing me to examine their books during extended stays, I am greatly indebted to the Bodleian Library, British Library, Cambridge University Library, Folger Shakespeare Library, Henry E. Huntington Library, and William Andrews Clark Memorial Library. I am also indebted for staff service and for the privilege of using the collections of Aberdeen University Library; Chetham's Library, Manchester; Duke University Library; Edinburgh University Library; Guildhall Library, London; Harvard University Library; John Rylands University Library, Manchester; King's College and Trinity College libraries, Cambridge; Magdalen College, Merton College, and Worcester College libraries, Oxford; Newberry Library; St. Paul's Cathedral Library; University of Illinois Library; University of Liverpool Library; University of London Library; University of Texas Library, Austin; Victoria and Albert Museum; and Yale University Library. Librarians who provided extensive bibliographical detail receive individual thanks in the text. I am greatly indebted to the Texas Tech University Library for purchasing innumerable microfilms.

I owe thanks to my colleagues Donald W. Rude, John T. Shawcross, Ed George, Paul Sellin, Bruce Cammack, Daniel Kinney and David Larmour for discovering new verse printings and for help with Renaissance Latin, Dutch, German, and Greek. Peter Beal, Tom Calhoun, Ted-Larry Pebworth, and Gary Stringer checked bibliographical details.

SHORT TITLES, VERSE

As the titles of Donne's verses have not been agreed upon by his editors, any listing of Donne verses by title requires an arbitrary choice of edition and the use of first lines to confirm the identity of the verse. Readers who do not find the title they are familiar with should utilize the Index of First Lines. The following short titles and first lines for Donne's verse are based on those in Herbert J. C. Grierson's *Poems of John Donne*; Donne verses not in Grierson's edition are preceded by an asterisk and identified by their earliest printed title or first line. The first lines are from Grierson or from the earliest printing for verses (including dubia) not in Grierson; their spelling and fonts have been modernized and regularized. Except in this listing and the Index of Verse, Translations, Adaptations, and Dubia, short titles for translations, adaptations, and dubia are prefixed by *T*, *A*, and *D*, respectively. In this listing, titles are alphabetized by initial word, with dubia listed separately.

"A Feaver": "Oh do not die, for I shall hate"
"A Funerall Elegie": "'Tis lost, to trust a tomb with such a guest"
"A Hymne to God the Father": "Wilt thou forgive that sin where I begun"
"A lame begger": "I am unable, yonder begger cries"
"A Lecture upon the Shadow": "Stand still, and I will read to thee"
"A licentious person": "Thy sins and hairs may no man equal call"
"A nocturnall upon S. Lucies day": "'Tis the year's midnight, and it is the day's"
"A Valediction: forbidding mourning": "As virtuous men pass mildly away"
"A Valediction: of weeping": "Let me pour forth"
"Amicissimo et Meritissimo Ben Jonson": "Quod arte ausus es hic tuâ, Poeta"
*"Annae Georgii More de Filiae": epitaph on Ann Donne
"Antiquary": "If in his study he hath so much care"
*"As a flower wet with last night's dew, and then": from *Ignatius His Conclaue*

"The Legacie": "When I died last, and, Dear, I die"
"The Progresse of the Soule": "I sing the progress of a deathless soul" [*Metempsychosis*]
"The Prohibition": "Take heed of loving me"
"The second Anniversarie": "Nothing could make me sooner to confess"
"The Storme": "Thou which art I, ('tis nothing to be so)"
"The Sunne Rising": "Busy old fool, unruly sun"
"The triple Foole": "I am two fools, I know"
"The Will": "Before I sigh my last gasp, let me breath"
"To Mr George Herbert, with one of my seals": "Qui prius assuetus serpentum fasce tabellas"
"To Mr R. W. If, as mine is": "If, as mine is, thy life a slumber be"
"To Mr T. W. All haile sweet Poët": "All hail sweet Poet, more full of strong fire"
"To Sr Edward Herbert. at Julyers": "Man is a lump, where all beasts kneaded be"
"To Sr Henry Wootton. Here's no more newes": "Here is no more news, than virtue, I may as well"
"To Sr Henry Wotton. Sir, more then kisses": "Sir, more than kisses, letters mingle souls"
"To Sir H. W. at his going Ambassador to Venice": "After those reverend papers, whose soul is"
"To the Countesse of Bedford. Honour is so": "Honor is so sublime perfection"
"To the Countesse of Bedford. Madame, You have refin'd": "Madame, You have refined me, and to worthiest things"
"To the Countesse of Bedford. T'have written then": "To have written then, when you wrote, seemed to me"
"To the Countesse of Huntingdon. Madame, Man to Gods image": "Man to God's image; *Eve*, to man's was made"
"To the Countesse of Salisbury. August. 1614": "Fair, great, and good, since seeing you, we see"
"To the Lady Magdalen Herbert: of St. Mary Magdalen": "Her of your name, whose fair inheritance"
"Twicknam garden": "Blasted with sighs, and surrounded with tears"
"Vpon Mr. Thomas Coryats Crudities": "Oh to what height will love of greatness drive"
"Witchcraft by a picture": "I fix mine eye on thine, and there"
*"With so great noise and horror": from *Ignatius His Conclaue*
"Womans constancy": "Now thou has loved me one whole day"

DUBIA

"A *Dutch* Captain of Foot": "I fighting die; how much more blest than they"

"Another. 'A cloud *Ixion* for a Goddess kist'": "A cloud *Ixion* for a goddess kissed"

"Another. 'An Hearb thou art'": "An herb thou art, but useless; for made fire"

"Another. '*Dukes-wood* where once thick bushes did appear'": "*Dukes-wood* where once thick bushes did appear"

"Another. '*Dutchman*! This Grove once hatcht'": "*Dutchman*! This grove once hatched the warlike spear"

"Another. 'Falne Okes the Axe doth into Timber hew'": "Fallen oaks the ax doth into timber hew"

"Another. 'Finn'd Soldiers here'": "Finned soldiers here in *Belgic* quarters jar"

"Another. 'Fishes now quarter where pavilions stood'": "Fish now quarter where pavilions stood"

"Another. 'From a Woods ruines'": "From a wood's ruins did these buildings rise"

"Another. 'Gudgeons, where soldiers lay'": "Gudgeons, where soldiers lay, lie trenched in sand"

"Another. 'Here Fishes dwell'": "Here fish dwell, till now not used to fields"

"Another. 'I die well paid'": "I die well paid, whilst my expiring breath"

"Another. 'I love thee not'": "I love thee not, nor thou me having tried"

"Another. 'Lothings, stincks, thirst'": "Loathings, stinks, thirst, rheums, aches, and catarrh"

"Another. 'Me the queld *Spaniard*'": "Me the quelled *Spaniard* to the next world sent"

"Another. 'Mere pleasant fields'": "Mere pleasant fields drowned by the wandering maze"

"Another. 'Niggards till dead are Niggards'": "Niggards till dead are niggards; so vile weed"

"Another. 'Say Painter, who's this'": "Say Painter, who is this whom thy hand hath made"

"Another. 'Shut thy purse-mouth, Old Trot'": "Shut thy purse-mouth, Old Trot, and let's appeal"

"Another. 'The drownd land'": "The drowned land here a crystal garment wears"

"Another. 'The ground whose head was once enricht'": "The ground whose head was once enriched with oaks"

"Another. 'The hungry Cow'": "The hungry cow here lately did mistake"

"Another. 'The place where once grew Ash'": "The place where once grew ash for warlike spears"

"Another. 'The tree her womb bred on the back'": "The tree her womb bred on the back now floats"

"Another. 'This naked Beam'": "This naked beam which bears up roofs from ground"

"Another. 'Thus conquering kild'": "Thus conquering killed, my ashes triumphs gain"

"Another. 'Thy senses faile thee'": "Thy senses fail thee, and pray God they may"

"Another. '*Venus*, when *Pygmalion* praid'": "*Venus*, when *Pygmalion* prayed"

"Another. 'We've conquer'd Boys'": "We have conquered boys; my wounds I highly rate"

"Another. 'When thy dry grissels'": "When thy dry gristles with my soft lips close"

"Another. 'Who's this, Painter'": "Who is this, Painter? Thy wife, Oh"

"Another. '*Wood* yeelds to *stone*'": "Wood yields to stone, boughs are made joists here"

"His Will": "Let heaven my soul, the foe my life, the grave"

"Idem *Anglicè* versum": "As wandering *Cinthia* all her nymphs excels"

"In Comædam celeberrimam *Cinthiam* dictam ad instantiam alterius fecit": "Sic vaga formosas superabat *Cinthia* nymphas"

"On a Bawdy-house": "Here *Mal*, providing for threescore"

"On an old Bawd": "Lo, I an old whore have to young resigned"

"On her unpleasing Kisses": "They can't be kisses called but toothless nips"

"On one particular passage of her action, when she was to be stript of her cloaths by *Fulvio*": "As *Fulvio Cinthia*'s glory would eclipse"

"On the same old Wife": "Thou art no woman, nor no woman's part"

"On the same. 'She, whose scarce yet quencht lust'": "She, whose scarce yet quenched lust to freeze begins"

"On the same. 'Though ramage grown'": "Though ramage grown, thou art still for carting fit"

SHORT FORMS OF REFERENCE, LIBRARIES

Short forms for American libraries are from the *National Union Catalog: Pre-1956 Imprints;* those for British libraries are from Donald Wing, ed., *Short-Title Catalogue of Books Printed in England, Scotland, Ireland, Wales, and British America and of English Books Printed in other Countries 1641–1700,* 2d ed. rev.; and those for other libraries are arbitrary.

AU   Aberdeen University, Aberdeen, Scotland
C   Cambridge University Library, Cambridge, England
CK   King's College, Cambridge, England
CLU-C   William Andrews Clark Memorial Library, Los Angeles, California
CSmH   Huntington Library, San Marino, California
CT   Trinity College, Cambridge, England
CtY   Yale University, New Haven, Connecticut
DFo   Folger Shakespeare Library, Washington, D.C.
E   Edinburgh University, Edinburgh, Scotland
ICN   Newberry Library, Chicago, Illinois
IU   University of Illinois, Urbana, Illinois
L   British Library, London, England
LG   Guildhall Library, London, England
LP   St. Paul's Cathedral Library, London, England
LU   University of London, London, England
LV   Victoria and Albert Museum, London, England
MC   Chetham's Library, Manchester, England
MH   Harvard University, Cambridge, Massachusetts
MR   John Rylands University, Manchester, England
NcD   Duke University, Durham, North Carolina
O   Bodleian Library, Oxford, England
OM   Magdalen College, Oxford, England
OME   Merton College, Oxford, England
OW   Worcester College, Oxford, England
TxU   University of Texas, Austin, Texas

THE INFLUENCE
OF
JOHN DONNE

INTRODUCTION

Editors of John Donne's poems and critics have paid the uncollected printings of his verse scant attention (except, of course, for the Anniversaries), concentrating instead on the seven seventeenth-century collected editions/issues of Donne's *Poems*. This focus on the collected editions to the virtual exclusion of the uncollected printings has produced a significantly incomplete understanding of the canon, chronology, texts, audience, uses, and thus the influence of Donne's printed verse in the seventeenth century.

The amount of verse by Donne contained in seventeenth-century uncollected printings suggests its potential importance for Donne textual, critical, and cultural studies. Wilhelm Bohm, E. K. Chambers, Charles Crawford, Rhodes Dunlap, Helen Gardner, M. Muriel Gray, Herbert J. C. Grierson, Geoffrey Keynes, Barbara Kiefer Lewalski, L. C. Martin, Wesley Milgate, John T. Shawcross, and A. J. Smith have identified 46 titles having 65 reported seventeenth-century editions and issues that contain 77 entire and 62 partial uncollected printings of Donne verse (a partial printing consists of at least one complete line or poem heading, counting each line or sequence of consecutive lines as a separate partial printing). In addition, they have identified 6 titles (including 2 that print no English verse) in 7 editions/issues printing 48 complete and 1 partial translation of Donne verse.[1] Credit for initial citation of the majority of items belongs to Keynes.

---

1. The authors and their relevant works: Bohm, *Englands Einfluss auf Georg Rudolf Weckherlin*; Chambers, ed., *Poems of John Donne*; Crawford, *Collectanea: Second Series* (Stratford-upon-Avon: Shakespeare Head Press, 1907); Dunlap, ed., *The Poems of Thomas Carew with His Masque Coelum Britannicum*; Gardner, ed., *John Donne: The Divine Poems* and *John Donne: The Elegies and The Songs and Sonnets*; Gray, "Drummond and Donne," *TLS*, April 8, 1920, p. 225; Grierson, ed., *The Poems of John Donne*; Keynes, *A Bibliography of Dr. John Donne*; Lewalski, *Donne's Anniversaries and the Poetry of Praise*; Martin, ed., *The Works of Henry Vaughan*; Milgate, ed., *John Donne: The Epithalamions Anniversaries and Epicedes* and *John Donne: The Satires, Epigrams and Verse Letters*; Shawcross, ed., *The Complete Poetry of John Donne*; and Smith, *John Donne: The Critical Heritage*.

The present census expands the number of titles to 83; the number of editions/issues to 239; and the number of uncollected printings of entire and partial poems to 207 and 653, as well as 7 titles (including 2 that print no English verse) in 12 editions/issues printing 59 entire and 24 partial translations.[2] As part of the overall effort to assess Donne's literary and cultural influence, the present work also lists 110 editions/issues of works printing 238 obvious adaptations and 3 titles in 4 editions printing 129 dubia presently considered possibly Donne's.[3]

The bibliography of Donne's uncollected seventeenth-century printed verse has far-reaching implications involving historical, literary, and cultural aspects of Donne's influence. (1) Substantially more Donne verse (including 6 Latin and 7 English verses not included in the Donne canon by his editors) was available in significantly greater quantity to a print audience earlier, later, and more consistently throughout the seventeenth century than has been previously thought. (2) Uncollected printings will have to play a far more important role in establishing the texts of Donne's verse and the facts of Donne's life (including his influence on seventeenth-century continental verse) than they have to date. (3) However much Donne may have thought of himself as a coterie poet, he was an extraordinarily popular poet not only among the intelligentsia, but also among the functionally illiterate. (4) Through acknowledged or unacknowledged intertextuality

---

2. I count as a single entire printing the version of "Insultus morbi primus" printed in twenty-three segments with each segment heading one of the Meditations in Donne's *Devotions vpon Emergent Occasions* because Donne intended the poem to appear in its segmented form. I do not include the partial printing of "The Storme" ("——*A hand, or eye, / By* Hilyard *drawne, is worth a history / By a worse Painter made*—" [ll. 3–5]) found in Miles Fletcher's "The Printer to the Understanders" prefacing the seventeenth-century collected editions of Donne's *Poems*.

3. This expansion of Donne's print presence in the seventeenth century roughly parallels the recent expansion of his manuscript presence. Grierson (1912), Gardner (*Divine*, 1978, and *Elegies*, 1965), and Milgate (*Epithalamions*, 1978, and *Satires*, 1967) collectively list forty-three Donne manuscripts; Shawcross (*Donne*, 1967) lists 157; Peter Beal (*Index of English Literary Manuscripts*, vol. 1, pt. 1, 1980) lists 219 manuscripts containing over 4,000 complete or partial texts of Donne's poems; and the textual editors of the variorum edition of Donne's poetry (Ted-Larry Pebworth, John T. Shawcross, and Ernest W. Sullivan, II) with the help of Peter Beal ("More Donne Manuscripts," *John Donne Journal* 6 [1987]: 213–18) have raised the number of manuscripts known to contain Donne verse to 240.

Donne's verse became part of the discourse of an entire society, from essayists, poets, translators, dramatists, musicians, biographers, historians, clergymen, and printers to schoolchildren, farmers, the tongue-tied lovelorn, aspiring Sir Fopling Flutters, and Lady Wouldbes. (5) Donne had influence because his verse had commercial, social, and personal value (based primarily on "wit" in all its manifestations) for a large and diverse audience over a long period. Each of these implications will be considered in turn in the five sections of this introduction.

CHRONOLOGY AND MAGNITUDE OF DONNE'S PRINT PRESENCE

The chronology of the seventeenth-century uncollected printings of Donne's verse undermines two truisms (based largely on analysis of the collected editions) about the chronology of Donne's print presence: (1) that during Donne's lifetime, very few of his poems saw print, so that his poetry was read almost exclusively in manuscript, and (2) that Donne's popularity diminished rapidly as the "School of Metaphysical Poetry" failed the social and aesthetic tests of the Restoration, particularly after the last seventeenth-century collected edition of Donne's *Poems* in 1669.

The first truism has been recently summarized and reiterated by Smith:

> The faith that Donne was a popular poet in his own day makes a good counter to romantic fairy tales of artists despised by their contemporaries, but hasn't much solid ground. Turning from myth to history we may wonder where the evidence of Donne's popularity is to be found in an age that doesn't seem to have had much to say even of the greatest of all its poets. . . . the peculiar circumstances in which he wrote and was read specifically exclude that possibility [that Donne "had a revolutionary impact while he was still writing"] for his poems were not, and could not have been, widely known in his own day. No more than five of them and some bits of another three were printed in his lifetime and no collected edition appeared until two years after his death, so that his contemporaries could have read most of his work only in manuscript. (p. 2)[4]

4. More recent statements of the truism are less complete. A typical anthology, the 1982 enlarged version of Alexander M. Witherspoon and Frank J. Warnke's *Seventeenth-Century Prose and Poetry*, 2d ed. (New York:

The uncollected printed verse undermines this idea that Donne had a very limited print audience during his lifetime in two ways: (1) it includes thirteen Latin and English verses published by Donne himself in his prose works during his lifetime but not included in Donne's canon by previous editors, and (2) it shows that more of Donne's poems were printed more frequently during his lifetime than has been previously noted.

The presence of verse material in the 1611 Latin edition of Donne's *Conclaue Ignati* published in England, as well as in Donne's 1611 English translation *Ignatius His Conclaue*, was first recognized in Appendix E of Chambers's 1896 edition of Donne's poetry. Chambers hypothesized that the verses might be Donne's: "In this [*Ignatius His Conclaue*] the scraps of Latin verse which appear in the other version are translated, and I therefore give the renderings here, with their originals. . . . I have been unable to identify any of the Latin passages, except the second, which is of course the first of the well-known lines attributed to the Emperor Hadrian. Possibly the rest, which do not always scan, are of Donne's own writing" (2:312–14). Five of the seven Latin "scraps" in the first Latin editions published in England and on the Continent are almost certainly Donne's. As noted above by Chambers, the second verse, "Animula, vagula blandula, / Comes hospesque corporis," originates with Hadrian, and T. S. Healy (*John Donne: Ignatius His Conclave*, p. 118) locates the verse line "Parsque minor tantum tota valet integra quantum" in Stephanus Quaranta's *Summa Bullarii* (Venice, 1609). Healy (p. 103) considers "Operoso tramite scandent" a verse adaptation by Donne of Albertus Magnus's *De Animalibus*, xxiii.5; however, Dennis Flynn, in "Donne's *Ignatius His Conclave* and Other Libels on Robert Cecil" (p. 182, n. 46), convincingly counters Healy's assessment by arguing that Donne's five lines of Latin verse and Albert's thirty words of Latin

---

Harcourt Brace Jovanovich, 1982), says, "Very little of Donne's poetry was published during his lifetime: the *First Anniversary* appeared in 1611 and the *Second Anniversary* in 1612, the 'Elegy upon the Death of Prince Henry' was published in Sylvester's collection entitled *Lachrymae Lachrymarum* in 1613, and a satiric poem of compliment by Donne preceded Thomas Coryat's *Crudities*, a travel book published in 1611" (p. 736). Arthur F. Marotti, in his *John Donne: Coterie Poet* (1986), states, "Except for the *Anniversaries*, the Prince Henry elegy, and the few lyrics that found their way into songbooks, Donne's poems did not appear in print during his lifetime" (p. x).

prose have only one word in common.[5] Flynn also notes that Donne's "Qualis hesterno madefacta rore" is a translation of lines 127–30 of Dante's *Inferno,* canto 2 ("*Ignatius,*" p. 182, n. 46); however, both the Latin translation and its subsequent English translation (as well as the other six English translations in *Ignatius His Conclaue*) are Donne's.

Even though not all the lines scan in all seven Latin "scraps," those in the verses original with Donne do: "Aversâ facie *Janum* referre" is hendecasyllabic; "Operoso tramite scandent," "Tanto fragore boatuque" (except for its last syllable), and "Aut plumam, aut paleam, quae fluminis innatat ori" are dactylic hexameter; and "Qualis hesterno madefacta rore" is Sapphic strophe. Furthermore, Donne's English translations of four of the five Latin verses consisting of more than one line and original with him are in couplets ("The lark by busy and laborious ways," "That the least piece which thence doth fall," "Feathers or straws swim on the water's face," and "As a flower wet with last night's dew, and then").

While the five Latin verses in *Ignatius His Conclaue* do not greatly expand Donne's previous canon of 194 poems, they and a sixth published by Donne during his lifetime—"Insultus morbi primus" (an introduction to the 1624 *Devotions vpon Emergent Occasions* first noted as verse by Chambers [Appendix F, 2:315–18] but not canonized in his or any subsequent edition)—nearly double his Latin verse canon. This expanded Latin canon strengthens Flynn's recent argument for Donne's possible authorship of "A sheaf of Miscellany Epigrams," 61 epigrams advertised as "Written in *Latin* by *J. D.*" and "*Translated by* J. Main *D.D.*" in their initial publication in Donne's *Paradoxes, Problems, Essayes, Characters.*[6]

Including these 13 new verses, 25 (rather than 5) different Donne poems were published in their entirety before his death in 1631: "A lame begger" (Thomas Deloney, *Strange Histories,* 1607);

---

5. Actually, two words are identical: the errata list (sig. E5v) corrects "Alanda" to "Alauda."

6. Flynn, in "Jasper Mayne's Translation of Donne's Latin Epigrams," reviews the lengthy controversy over the authorship of the epigrams and uses biographical and bibliographical evidence to argue that Donne could have written originals for all except numbers 53–57. Flynn does not specifically discuss epigram 59, *D*"In Comædam celeberrimam *Cinthiam* dictam ad instantiam alterius fecit," printed in Latin and thus possibly another original Latin poem by Donne.

"Amicissimo et Meritissimo Ben Jonson" (Ben Jonson, *Ben: Ionson his Volpone or the Foxe*, 1607); "The Expiration" (Alfonso Ferrabosco, *Ayres*, 1609);[7] "Vpon Mr. Thomas Coryats Crudities" and "In eundem Macaronicon" (Thomas Coryat, *Coryats Crudities*, 1611);[8] "The first Anniversary" and "A Funerall Elegie" (Donne, Anniversaries, 1611); "Aversâ facie *Janum* referre," "Operoso tramite scandent," "Tanto fragore boatuque," "Aut plumam, aut paleam, quae fluminis innatat ori," and "Qualis hesterno madefacta rore" (Donne, *Conclaue Ignati*, 1611); "Resemble *Janus* with a diverse face," "My little wandering sportful soul," "The lark by busy and laborious ways," "With so great noise and horror," "That the least piece which thence doth fall," "Feathers or straws swim on the water's face," and "As a flower wet with last night's dew, and then" (Donne, *Ignatius His Conclaue*, 1611); "Breake of day" (William Corkine, *The Second Booke of Ayres*, 1612); "The second Anniversarie" (Donne, Anniversaries, 1612); "Elegie upon the untimely death of the incomparable Prince Henry" (Josuah Sylvester, *Lachrymae Lachrymarum*, 1613); "A licentious person" (Henry Fitzgeffrey, *Satyres and Satyricall Epigram's*, 1617); and "Insultus morbi primus" (Donne, *Devotions vpon Emergent Occasions*, 1624).[9]

Additionally, 6 (rather than 3) Donne poems were published in part during his lifetime: lines 71–72 of "The Storme" (Thomas Dekker, *A Knights Coniuring*, 1607); lines 18–23 of "Satyre IIII" (Joseph Wybarne, *The New Age of Old Names*, 1609); line 1 of "The Baite" (William Corkine, *The Second Booke of Ayres*, 1612);[10] lines 3–4 of "Satyre V" (William Basse, *A Helpe to Discovrse*, 1629); and stanzas 1–2 of "The broken heart" and lines 1–4, 10–18 of "Song. 'Go, and catch a falling star'" (William Basse, *A Helpe to Memory and Discovrse*, 1630). The 21 titles containing Donne verse published prior to 1631 appear as 60 pre-1631 editions and issues containing 71 complete and 83 partial printings and reprintings of these 31 verses (including 5 of the Songs and Sonnets). In addition to works printing Donne verse, 8 titles comprising 17 edi-

---

7. Alfonso Ferrabosco's *Ayres* also prints line 1 of "The Expiration" separately.

8. Thomas Coryat's *The Odcombian Banqvet* (1611) also prints "Vpon Mr. Thomas Coryats Crudities" and "In eundem Macaronicon."

9. *Devotions vpon Emergent Occasions* prints "Insultus morbi primus" in its unified as well as in its segmented form.

10. Corkine's *The Second Booke of Ayres* prints line 1 of "The Baite" twice as well as line 1 of "Breake of day."

tions/issues print 71 obvious adaptations of Donne verse prior to his death (with 4 as early as 1613). Clearly, there was more of Donne's printed poetry with a larger circulation, a more general readership (as opposed to members of Donne's inner circle who had access to his manuscripts), and a greater potential influence during his lifetime than previously believed.

The second truism, the rapid disappearance of Donne's print presence in the final three decades of the seventeenth century, likewise needs revision in light of the existence of 30 titles (including 19 new ones) whose 69 editions/issues print 41 complete and 225 partial Donne verses after the last seventeenth-century collected edition in 1669. Again, Smith accurately summarizes the regnant perception of Donne's Restoration demise:

> The first signs we have of the turn against Donne appear quite suddenly in the late 1660s. . . . Walton added the "Valediction: forbidding Mourning" in the final version of his *Life of Donne*, 1675 . . . but his famous celebration of it then rings quite out of key with the times like a last valedictory flourish of the old order in the face of plain indifference or growing distaste. . . . It is plain that by the last three decades of the century Donne's poetry had become a mere curiosity which the amateur might indifferently patronise or discount. (p. 12)

The uncollected printings of Donne's verse do not support a precipitous or even a major decline in Donne's post-1670 presence in print and influence, though the statistics do suggest some decline. The 19 new titles after 1670 represent 23 percent of the 83 for the century. The 69 editions/issues are 29 percent of the 239 for the century. The 41 complete verses are 20 percent of the total of 207; the 225 partial verses, 34 percent of the total of 653. Even the 1690s saw the introduction of 4 new titles (though Dryden's *Works* and *Eleonora*, with their Donne verse in identical typesettings of *Eleonora*, are essentially duplicates). Only a drop in the number of obvious adaptations (39 of 239 for the century) suggests any major decline in Donne's influence, and even here the number of titles (10) and editions/issues (27) containing the 39 obvious adaptations is not inconsequential.

Nor would the uncollected printings of Donne's verse seem to support the perception of "amateurs" patronizing Donne after 1670. Such "amateurs" would include Izaak Walton, who uses Donne's verse not only to canonize Donne but also to elevate George Herbert and Henry Wotton through their association with

Donne; Andrew Marvell, whose use of Donne's verse is ambiguous (he used parts of "The Progresse of the Soule," itself a satire, to satirize the obscurity and metamorphoses of his opponents' arguments); William Winstanley, who praises Donne's "Ingenious expression" and includes Donne among the "most Famous English Poets"; S. N., the unidentified but patriotic compiler of *The Loyal Garland*; Nathaniel Lee, who uses Donne's verse to praise his patroness and who calls Donne "the best Writer of the Age"; the anonymous "Lords in the Tower," who incorporate Donne's verse into their lament for their impending deaths; Thomas Barlow, who reprints *Conclaue Ignati*; John Shirley, who includes Donne's verse among "the newest and choicest Songs, Poems, Epigrams, Satyrs"; Payne Fisher, who prints and translates "Ioannes Donne Sac: Theol: Profess"; the "several Gentlemen of the Universities," who include Donne's verse as their own; Henry Playford, who includes Pelham Humphryes's musical setting of "A Hymne to God the Father"; Thomas Pope Blount, who uses Donne to illustrate his argument; John Dryden, who incorporates and adapts Donne's verse for his elegy *Eleonora*; and Mary de la Riviere Manley, who uses line 51 of "The Will" to illustrate a point. Some of these printings certainly are the work of literary "amateurs," but Dryden is the only instance of "indifferent patronizing," and his "indifference" seems primarily a cover for his own unacknowledged borrowing. In a prefatory letter "To the Right Honourable the Earl of Abingdon," Dryden credits Donne's Anniversaries for the design of his poem *Eleonora* while "patronizing" Donne's poetry:

> *Doctor* Donn *the greatest Wit, though not the best Poet of our Nation, acknowledges, that he had never seen Mrs.* Drury, *whom he has made immortal in his admirable Anniversaries; I have had the same fortune; though I have not succeeded to the same Genius. However, I have follow'd his footsteps in the Design of his Panegyrick.*

Then Dryden silently writes lines 5–6 of "Obsequies to the Lord Harrington" and adapts lines 61–62 of "Elegie. Death" into *Eleonora* (ll. 340–58).[11]

In addition to providing a greater presence for Donne's poetry in print during his lifetime as well as during the Restoration, the uncollected printings depict a consistent presence in print for

11. Earl Miner identifies more parallels with Donne's verse in *Eleonora* (*Dryden's Poetry* [Bloomington: Indiana University Press, 1971], p. 342, nn. 1 and 6).

Donne's verse (and thus his influence) throughout the seventeenth century that differs somewhat from the pattern of Donne's presence and influence provided by the collected editions. The collected editions/issues suggest an immediate posthumous interest (1633, 1635, and 1639), another surge in interest around 1650 (1649, 1650, and 1654), and a lapse in interest after 1669—the next collected edition does not appear until 1719. Predictably, significant increases in the publication of works containing complete, partial, translated, or obviously adapted Donne verse immediately follow publication of the collected editions (after all, some of these works would have used the collected editions as sources for their Donne verse): 20 titles in 47 editions/issues printing 37 entire, 32 partial, 12 translated, and 23 obviously adapted verses between 1633 and 1641; 24 titles in 39 editions/issues printing 42 entire, 182 partial, 0 translated, and 22 obviously adapted verses between 1650 and 1656; and 15 titles in 20 editions/issues printing 8 entire, 50 partial, 20 translated, and 11 obviously adapted verses between 1669 and 1672. These peaks certainly exist (particularly that of 1650–1656); however, the uncollected printed verse suggests that Donne actually had a relatively consistent presence in print in the seventeenth century.

Indeed, consistency is the most remarkable characteristic of Donne's seventeenth-century verse print presence outside the collected editions. The following table illustrates Donne's verse presence during his lifetime, during the period of the collected editions, and during the period after the last collected edition. In all three cases, the proportion of printings during the period approximates the percentage of years represented by the period, with a slight peak in the 1632–1669 period and a slight decline in the 1670–1700 period.

	New Titles	Editions/ Issues	Entire Verses	Partial Verses
1607–1631	21	60	71	83
1632–1669	43	110	95	345
1670–1700	19	69	41	225

The publication frequency of the translations and obvious adaptations of Donne's verse does show a decline during the 1670–1700 period; however, reports of a precipitous decline in frequency (and thus influence) seem exaggerated. No translations of Donne verse appeared during his lifetime (except his translations of his own Latin verses from *Conclaue Ignati* into English in *Ignatius*

His Conclaue). The 1632–1669 period has 5 titles (including 2 in addition to the total above) in 6 editions/issues printing 38 entire and 19 partial translated verses; 1670–1700 has 3 titles in 6 editions/issues printing 21 entire and 5 partial translated verses. As for the obvious adaptations of Donne verse, in Donne's lifetime, 17 editions/issues printed 71; during 1632–1669, 66 printed 128; and during 1670–1700, 27 printed 39.

In fact, at least one volume containing uncollected Donne verse appeared nearly every year from 1607 to 1700; the exceptions are 1608, 1610, 1615, 1622, 1637, 1639, 1642, 1647, 1649, 1666, and 1699. And the 239 editions/issues containing uncollected Donne verse and translations are spread evenly throughout the century (see Chronology of Printings), with only 1640 (which has six issues of the first volume of *The Workes of Beniamin Jonson*) having more than ten. New works containing Donne's uncollected verse were introduced each year after 1607 except 1608, 1610, 1615, 1620, 1622, 1625–1631, 1634, 1636–1639, 1641–1644, 1646–1649, 1663, 1665–1667, 1671–1672, 1675, 1679, 1682, 1685–1686, 1689–1690, 1693–1695, and 1697–1700. The clustering in the 1650s of new titles (27) and of the works printing the most uncollected verse (*The Mirrour of Complements*, 1650; *Merlinvs Anonymvs*, 1653; and *The Harmony of the Muses*, 1654) does parallel the midcentury peak in Donne's influence suggested by the collected editions/issues appearing in 1649, 1650, and 1654.

The uncollected printings also affect our perception of Donne's possible influence as a Latin poet. Even if Jasper Mayne's fifty-six English translations in *A Sheaf of Miscellany Epigrams* are not from Latin originals by Donne and *D*"In Comædam celeberrimam *Cinthiam* dictam ad instantiam alterius fecit" is not a Donne Latin original, the early and frequent printing of the five additional Latin verses from Donne's *Conclaue Ignati*, of "Insultus morbi primus" from Donne's *Devotions vpon Emergent Occasions*, and of the epigraph ("Corporis haec animae sit syndon syndon Jesu") printed beneath Donne's portrait in *Deaths Dvell* (first recognized as verse by Gardner, *Divine*, pp. 112–13) gives Donne a much larger seventeenth-century Latin verse presence than hitherto suspected: the five verses appear in four editions of *Conclaue Ignati* and two editions of Thomas Barlow's *Papismus Regiae Potestatis Eversor*; "Insultus morbi primus," in complete and segmented form in seven editions/issues of *Devotions vpon Emergent Occasions*; and "Corporis haec animae sit syndon syndon Jesu," in four editions/issues of *Deaths Dvell*. If one adds Donne's Latin epitaphs on his wife ("Annae Georgii More de Filiae") and on himself ("Ioannes Donne Sac: Theol: Profess"),[12] the nine Latin verses appear

12. I have followed Milgate in including Donne's epitaph on himself ("Ioannes Donne Sac: Theol: Profess") carved in white marble above his monument in St. Paul's Cathedral and his epitaph on Ann Donne ("Annae Georgii More de Filiae") originally carved on a monument lost when St. Clement Danes was rebuilt. Milgate includes the epitaphs in a section entitled "Epitaphs and Inscriptions" (*Epithalamions*, pp. 80 and 78 respectively) and argues in his preface for their inclusion in the Donne verse canon: "these compositions occupy a position mid-way between prose and verse, and have relationships at some points with the poems" (p. v). Indeed, both epitaphs seem more verse than prose: their seventeenth-century printers set them off from their prose context by spacing and font, generally followed the verse convention of capitalizing the first word in each line, and sometimes treated the epitaphs as shaped verse. Henry Holland (*Ecclesia Sancti Pavli Illvstrata*, 1633) prints "Ioannes Donne Sac: Theol: Profess" as prose except the last three lines, set off in italics with the first word in each line capitalized. John Stow (*The Survey of London*, 1632) prints "Annae Georgii More de Filiae" (with only lines 10 and 18 not beginning with a capital letter) in the cruciform shape given it in Donne's holograph (DFo, shelfmark: Loseley ms.L.b.541, in which all lines begin with a capital letter) and "Ioannes Donne Sac: Theol: Profess" (only lines 4 and 5 do not begin with a capital), appropriately enough, in the shape of Donne's funeral monument of his body in its shroud, a shape the verse assumes when printed in centered units of sense. Izaak Walton, in the earliest printed state of his *Life and Death of Dr Donne*, reproduces "Ioannes Donne Sac: Theol: Profess" as a column with the first word in each line capitalized. In Walton's 1658 version, the epitaph is again a column, with only the first words in lines 2 and 7 not capitalized. In 1670 and 1675, it again has column form with the first word in all except overhanging lines capitalized. William Dugdale, in his *The History of S^t. Pauls Cathedral in London* (1658), prints "Ioannes Donne Sac: Theol: Profess" twice: first, attempting to reproduce the entire monument exactly, he prints the epitaph in all capitals and in a shape that roughly parallels the statue of Donne in his shroud; second, printing the epitaph with a title, four lines of prose, and four lines of poetry, he achieves a cruciform shape that also resembles the statue. Payne Fisher (*The Tombes, Monuments, and Sepulchral Inscriptions, Lately Visible in St. Pauls Cathedral*, 1684) prints "Ioannes Donne Sac: Theol: Profess" in column/human form, with all words beginning lines capitalized. The Donne variorum will include two additional epitaphs, on Elizabeth Drury ("Quo pergas, viator") and Robert Drury ("Roberti Druri / quo vix alter"), inscribed respectively on the south wall of the chancel and the monument to Robert Drury in the parish church in Hawstead, Suffolk; the inscription

fifty-four times during the century, with six of the poems appearing twenty times during Donne's lifetime.

Unfortunately the uncollected printings do not provide an earlier *terminus ad quem* than presently conjectured for the composition of any Donne poem; they do, however, bring some welcome certainty to the heretofore speculative dating of much of Donne's verse. Shawcross, who made the first comprehensive effort to date Donne's verse in his "Chronological Schedule of the Poems" (*Donne*, pp. 410–17), observes that "dating of the epigrams is particularly uncertain" and that "most of the songs and sonnets cannot be dated" (p. 416, nn. 1, 3). Attempting to arrange Donne's verse chronologically, John Carey observes, "Unfortunately not all of his writings can be dated exactly. Often a probable or approximate date can be offered, but for some works, notably most of the *Songs and Sonnets*, there are no clues to dating at all" (*John Donne*, p. xxxviii). Carey prints the Songs and Sonnets after a letter to George More dated February 2, 1602, and before "To Sir H. W. at his going Ambassador to Venice" (dated July 1604), though he does mention Alfonso Ferrabosco's *Ayres* (1609) and William Corkine's *The Second Booke of Ayres* (1612) to establish the *terminus ad quem* for composition of "The Expiration" and "Breake of day" respectively (p. 88). Using internal references, Carey assigns the Epigrams to 1596–1602. Shawcross (*Donne*) notes Joseph Wybarne's *The New Age of Old Names* (1609) for its publication of "Satyre IIII" and assigns composition to 1598, the second edition of William Basse's *A Helpe to Memorie and Discovrse* (1630) for "The broken heart" and "Song. 'Go, and catch a falling star'" and assigns them to 1593?–1601?, *Ayres* (1609) for "The Expiration" (1593?–1601?), and *The Second Booke of Ayres* (1612) for "Breake of day" and "The Baite" (1593?–1601?). Dates of the uncollected printings establish a *terminus ad quem* for the following 31 poems: "A lame begger," "The Storme," "Amicissimo et Meritissimo Ben Jonson" (1607); "The Expiration," "Satyre IIII" (1609); "Vpon Mr. Thomas Coryats Crudities," "In eundem Macaronicon," "The first Anniversary," "A Funerall Elegie," "Aversâ facie *Janum* referre," "Operoso tramite scandent," "Tanto fragore boatuque," "Aut plumam, aut paleam, quae fluminis innatat ori," "Qualis hesterno

---

("In propria venit") in the "Album Amicorum" of Michael Corvinus (C, shelfmark: Add.MS.8466); and an inscription in a bible ("In Bibliotheca Hospitii") at Lincoln's Inn. These verses were not published in the seventeenth century.

madefacta rore," "Resemble *Janus* with a diverse face," "My little wandering sportful soul," "The lark by busy and laborious ways," "With so great noise and horror," "That the least piece which thence doth fall," "Feathers or straws swim on the water's face," "As a flower wet with last night's dew, and then" (1611); "The Baite," "Breake of day," "The second Anniversarie" (1612); "Elegie upon the untimely death of the incomparable Prince Henry" (1613); "A licentious person" (1617); "Insultus morbi primus" (1624); "Satyre V" (1629); "The broken heart," "Song. 'Go, and catch a falling star'" (1630).

Other uncollected printings provide less certain but important evidence for dating. Donne's letter accompanying "To the Lady Magdalen Herbert: of St. Mary Magdalen," first printed in Izaak Walton's *The Life of Mr. George Herbert*, is dated *"July* 11. 1607"; and Henrik Rintjus's *Klioos Kraam* assigns a 1626 date to translations into Dutch by Constantin Huygens of "A Valediction: of weeping," "Breake of day" (already proved as early as 1612 by *The Second Booke of Ayres*), "The Legacie," "The triple Foole," "The Blossome," and "Song. 'Go, and catch a falling star.'"

Predictably, chronology affects the frequency of the printing of individual verses: the earlier a verse appears in print, the more frequently it appears in print. This phenomenon cannot be explained by arguing that the most popular poems would be the first into print (the relative number of manuscript copies of the particular poems does not support this argument) or by arguing that frequency in print may depend on the popularity of the work(s) in which the verse appears, a factor unrelated to the date of initial publication. Of the 14 poems that appear in at least 10 editions/issues, 10 are printed before 1633: "The Storme" (1607), "The first Anniversary" (1611), "The Baite" (1612), "Breake of day" (1612), "The second Anniversarie" (1612), "Elegie upon the untimely death of the incomparable Prince Henry" (1613), "Elegy: The Expostulation" (1616), "Satyre V" (1629), "Song. 'Go, and catch a falling star'" (1630), "Ioannes Donne Sac: Theol: Profess" (1633)—with "The first Anniversary" the runaway leader in 54 editions/issues.

TEXTUAL SIGNIFICANCE
OF THE UNCOLLECTED VERSE

Clearly, what is presently known about the 83 titles in 239 editions/issues with their 860 complete or partial Donne poems demonstrates that this enormous body of verse merits more attention in the study of Donne's texts than it has received. Uncollected printings account for 38 of the earliest appearances of Donne verses in print: the 25 complete and 6 partial printings of poems during Donne's lifetime discussed previously plus 6 additional entire printings—'Corporis haec animae sit syndon syndon Jesu" (Donne, *Deaths Dvell*, 1632); "Ioannes Donne Sac: Theol: Profess" (Henry Holland, *Ecclesia Sancti Pavli Illvstrata*, 1633); "Annae Georgii More de Filiae" (John Stow, *The Survey of London*, 1633); "Elegy: Going to Bed" and "Elegy: Loves Progress" (Robert Chamberlain, *The Harmony of the Muses*, 1654); and "To the Lady Magdalen Herbert: of St. Mary Magdalen" (Izaak Walton, *The Life of Mr. George Herbert*, 1670)—and 1 very significant partial printing—lines 29–46 of "Elegy: Loves Warr" (Chamberlain, *Harmony of the Muses*). These 38 earliest complete or partial printings descend immediately from holographs, manuscripts, or funeral monuments and have substantial textual authority. Sixteen of Donne's poems survived only in uncollected printings, and the first printings provide the most authoritative copy-text: "Corporis haec animae sit syndon syndon Jesu," "Aversâ facie *Janum* referre," "Feathers or straws swim on the water's face," "As a flower wet with last night's dew, and then," "The lark by busy and laborious ways," "With so great noise and horror," "Operoso tramite scandent," "That the least piece which thence doth fall," "Aut plumam, aut paleam, quae fluminis innatat ori," "Qualis hesterno madefacta rore," "Resemble *Janus* with a diverse face," "My little wandering sportful soul," "Tanto fragore boatuque," "In eundem Macaronicon," "To the Lady Magdalen Herbert: of St. Mary Magdalen," and "Insultus morbi primus." There are 9 poems for which modern editors generally have already used uncollected printings as copy-texts: "Amicissimo et Meritissimo Ben Jonson," "Vpon Mr. Thomas Coryats Crudities," "In eundem Macaronicon," "The first Anniversary," "A Funerall Elegie," "The second Anniversarie," "Elegie upon the untimely death of the incomparable Prince Henry," "Corporis haec animae sit syndon syndon Jesu," and "To the Lady Magdalen Herbert: of St. Mary Magdalen."[13]

Furthermore, even partial printings in volumes not immediately associated with Donne can have textual significance, as lines 29–46 of "Elegy: Loves Warr" in *The Harmony of the Muses*

---

13. Oddly, Grierson uses the first appearance in the collected editions as his copy-text for these eight poems.

demonstrate. The title page promises "transcendent Wit" in "severall excellent Poems" by "Dr. *Joh. Donn* Dr. *Hen. King* Dr. *W. Stroad* Sr. *Kenelm Digby* Mr. *Ben. Johnson*, Mr. *Fra. Beamont J. Cleveland T. Randolph T. Carew*. And others of the most refined Wits of those *TIMES. Never before Published*." The volume delivers four previously published Donne poems ("Elegy: The Autumnall," "A Valediction: forbidding mourning," "Loves diet," and "The Will"); two previously unpublished poems ("Elegy: Going to Bed" and "Elegy: Loves Progress"); and lines 29–46 of the previously unpublished "Elegy: Loves Warr." "Elegy: Going to Bed" and "Elegy: Loves Progress" eventually appear in the 1669 collected *Poems* (though their texts differ sufficiently from those in *The Harmony of the Muses* that the 1669 texts would seem to derive from a manuscript). No part of "Elegy: Loves Warr" appears in print elsewhere in the seventeenth century except for lines 29–32, 35–36, 39–40, and 43–46 in John Cotgrave's *Wits Interpreter* (1655); the elegy was not published in its entirety until Francis Godolphin Waldron's 1802 *The Shakespearean Miscellany* (London: Knight and Compton [pp. 1–5]) and *A Collection of Miscellaneous Poetry* (London: Knight and Compton [pp. 1–5]).

As Helen Gardner points out, a textual crux occurs in line 44 of "Elegy: Loves Warr": "The line is a foot short. Since no variants exist in the manuscripts to suggest emendation, it must be left" (*Elegies*, p. 130). Grierson and Shawcross (*Donne*), who use the New York Public Library's Westmoreland manuscript for copytext, print the relevant lines (43–46) essentially as does Gardner (who uses Cambridge University Library Add.MS.5778):

> Shall spring. Thousands we see which travaile not
> To warres, but stay, swords, armes and shot
> To make at home: And shall not I do then
> More glorious service, staying to make men?
> (Gardner, *Elegies*, p. 14)

The Harmony of the Muses prints:

> Shall spring; thousands we see which travell not
> To warres, but stay at home, swords, guns and shot
> Do make for others; Shall not I do then
> More glorious service, staying to make men.
> (p. 7)

The "at home" in line 44 of the version in *The Harmony of the Muses* not only makes perfect sense but also exactly restores the pentameter line; and its "for others" where previous editors have "at home" in line 45 also improves overall sense while preserving the pentameter line. "Do" in line 45 of *The Harmony of the Muses* where the other texts read "To" would seem an inferior reading; however, taking "home" in line 44 as the end of the unit of thought and having an understood "they" as the subject of "Do" would make sense of the text in *The Harmony of the Muses*. In any event, the "at home" (l. 44) and "for others" (l. 45) readings in *The Harmony of the Muses* produce better sense and metrics than do the readings of current texts. Unfortunately, the bibliographical authority of lines 29–46 of "Elegy: Loves Warr" in *The Harmony of the Muses* is uncertain because the copy manuscript remains unidentified (and may no longer exist); however, readings of *The Harmony of the Muses* surely represent the copy manuscript—the chance that a compositor would notice the missing foot in line 44, read down to line 45 to find the correct reading, go back to repair line 44, and appropriately insert "for others" on his own initiative in line 45 seems remote. Clearly, *The Harmony of the Muses* merits critical and textual study.

While the full value of the uncollected printings for unraveling the history of the transmission of Donne's texts and manuscripts awaits further study, it is already clear that some uncollected printings (particularly those that must derive directly from manuscripts) can assist study of the transmission of manuscripts containing Donne verse as well as the transmission of particular texts. *The Harmony of the Muses*, because it likely derives from a no-longer-extant manuscript, suggests the existence of another Donne manuscript in 1654—one with segments resembling Bodleian MSS. Ashmole 38 and 47 as well as Corpus Christi College, Oxford, MS. 328 (Ernest W. Sullivan, II, ed., *The Harmony of the Muses*, pp. xi–xii). The existence of yet another manuscript containing at least part of "Elegy: Loves Warr" is implied by John Cotgrave's 1655, 1662, and 1671 editions of *Wits Interpreter*, which print lines 29–32, 35–36, 39–40, and 43–46 of "Elegy: Loves Warr." The text in *Wits Interpreter* differs so from that in the only other possible print source, *The Harmony of the Muses* (which coincidentally prints lines 29–46), that there must have been two manuscripts extant in 1655 not described in Beal's *Index* having just this section of "Elegy: Loves Warr" (or else two copyists/compositors reproduced just this part of the poem—a remarkable coincidence).

One great advantage uncollected printings have over manuscripts for the study of the transmission of Donne's texts is the fact that they usually can be dated very specifically. Obviously, the readings of a version of a text in an uncollected printing cannot automatically be assigned the date of the printing, since the printed text may derive from a manuscript that preserves early readings; however, the printed texts can prove that a reading had entered the textual transmission by a particular date—information useful for sorting out the priority of various versions of Donne poems.

The texts and contexts of uncollected printings can even provide information about the history of Donne's manuscript circulation abroad, information with possible implications for Donne's biography and for cultural history. For example, the date as well as the sources of the translations of nineteen Donne poems into Dutch by Constantin Huygens, Donne's acquaintance and admirer, in his *Koren-Bloemen* (1658) are uncertain. The date and source(s) of these translations might allow us to date the meeting between Huygens and Donne, identify the owner of the manuscript(s) containing Donne verse circulating in the Netherlands, and better understand Anglo-Dutch cultural relations of the period:

> Huygens' translations play a crucial role in our understanding of the relation between the literary and political climates of England and Holland in the seventeenth century. They illuminate the Anglo-Dutch cultural relation. . . . Moreover, they provide a finely tuned insight into the differences between religious attitudes, both personal and universal, in an age when religious controversy and diversity was at its height.[14]

Henrik Rintjus's *Klioos Kraam* provides the first hard evidence that would date translation by Huygens of six of the nineteen poems as early as 1626. Koos Daley assigns Huygens's translations of "The Sunne Rising," "Elegy: The Anagram," "Elegy: Oh, let mee not," and "A Valediction: forbidding mourning" to the period between "August 8 and August 21, 1630" and those of the remaining fifteen poems to the period between "August 18 and October 17, 1633" (p. 165), with "Goodfriday, 1613. Riding Westward" ("August 31, 1633" [p. 110]) and "The triple Foole" ("October 7,

---

14. Koos Daley, *The Triple Fool: A Critical Evaluation of Constantijn Huygens' Translations of John Donne,* pp. 89–90.

1633" [p. 130]) dated very specifically.[15] After the text of Huygens's translations of "A Valediction: of weeping," "Breake of day," "The Legacie," "The triple Foole," "The Blossome," and "Song. 'Go, and catch a falling star,'" Rintjus subscribes the translations to "C. Huygens" and gives the date "1626."

The headings and English lines provided by Huygens in *Koren-Bloemen* as well as some features of his Dutch text in *Koren-Bloemen* and *Klioos Kraam* constitute important evidence for identifying the manuscript(s) used by Huygens for his translations. Daley points out the lack of hard evidence for identifying Huygens's copy manuscript(s) and suggests one possible contribution of *Koren-Bloemen* to the solution: "How and when Huygens obtained Donne's manuscripts remains an enigma. . . . It is interesting to note that only in a few of Donne's early manuscripts does this poem ["The Sunne Rising"] bear the title 'Ad Solem,' a clue perhaps to when and how these poems came into Huygens' possession" (p. 100).[16] Daley also speculates that "it is quite likely that by late 1633 Huygens possessed a copy of Donne's earliest volume of poetry. And when he readied his poems for the first edition of *Koren-bloemen*, in 1658, he checked his translations against the originals, adding the English titles and opening lines in the margins" (pp. 146–47).

What hard evidence can *Koren-Bloemen* and *Klioos Kraam* bring to bear on how and when Huygens obtained which Donne manuscripts? With each poem in *Koren-Bloemen*, Huygens prints the first line in English (except "Elegy: Oh, let mee not," for which he prints line 11, the first line of the translation); for three poems, he prints another heading in addition to his Dutch heading—"Elegy: The Anagram" ("The Anagram."), "Elegy: Oh, let mee not" ("Pars Eleg. vi."), and "The Extasie" ("*Ecstasis.*"). The headings for "Ele-

---

15. Daley also notes that Rosalie Colie (*Some Thankfullnesse to Constantine* [The Hague: Martinus Nijhoff, 1956], p. 58) suggests Donne might have had a manuscript of the poems since 1622 and that Leendert Strengholt ("Huygens' oudste Vertalingen naar Donne," *Tijdschrift voor NDL Taal-en Letterkunde* 102 [1986]: 190–201) argues for translation of the first four of the poems in 1630 (n. 5, p. 133).

16. The significance of the heading "Ad Solem" may be less than Daley suggests. She uses and translates Huygens's text from J. A. Worp, ed., *Gedichten*. Huygens heads the text of "The Sunne Rising" "De opgaende Son" in both the 1658 and 1672 *Koren-Bloemen*. Worp, who otherwise appears to print a modernized version of the *Koren-Bloemen* text, heads the poem "Aende Sonn."

gy: The Anagram" and "Elegy: Oh, let mee not" could derive from the collected editions of 1635, 1639, 1649, 1650, or 1654 (but not those of 1633 or 1669);[17] that for "The Extasie" would not seem to derive from a printed edition because the headings in the collected editions are in English ("The Extasie" or "Extasie"). On the other hand, the combination of English and Latin headings is more typical of the manuscripts, and the headings (generally rare in the manuscripts) and texts of the first lines likely will make it possible to identify at least the manuscript family (or families, since the texts in a single manuscript may come from different textual traditions) from which Huygens worked.

In addition to its 1626 date for the translations, *Klioos Kraam* contains textual clues about the manuscript source(s) and the composition process of Huygens's translations. *Klioos Kraam* contains only six of the nineteen translations and has them in a different order than does *Koren-Bloemen*; thus, Huygens might have used more than one manuscript and made the translations over a substantial period of time, and the manuscript(s) he used might not have had the poems in the *Koren-Bloemen* order. Although *Klioos Kraam* lacks the English lines present in *Koren-Bloemen*, its Dutch titles may be particularly helpful. In 1626, only "Breake of day" of the six poems had seen print (in *The Second Booke of Ayres* [1612], where it is untitled); thus, Huygens could not have translated the titles from Donne verse in print. The texts of *Koren-Bloemen* and *Klioos Kraam* differ in accidentals of spelling, and their translations of "The triple Foole" suggest that the compositor of *Klioos Kraam* had trouble reading the manuscript at line 8 (the missing second half of the line is marked by ellipsis) and that the copy manuscripts for *Koren-Bloemen* and *Klioos Kraam* for "The triple Foole" had a different word order in line 1 ("ICk ben tvvee Gecken: een, die daer van Minne sterv'" in *Koren-Bloemen*, and "TWe gekken ben ik een: een, die van minne sterv'" in *Klioos Kraam*). Indentation patterns are essentially identical in *Koren-Bloemen* and *Klioos Kraam*. The printed versions of the translations, then, are suffi-

---

17. Without a thorough analysis of Huygens's revisions on his manuscripts (available in the Royal Library of The Hague), one cannot determine if Huygens checked his translations against a copy of Donne's 1633 *Poems* as Daley speculates; however, it seems unlikely that Huygens, who titled his translation of "Elegy: Oh, let mee not" "Pars Eleg. vi.," added the English titles from a copy of the 1633 *Poems*, which titles the same elegy "*Elegie* VII." (p. 53).

ciently alike that they would seem to be from two manuscripts with a common source—perhaps *Koren-Bloemen* (with its added English lines and titles) derives from a slightly revised version of the copy manuscript for *Klioos Kraam*.

Identifying the owner(s) of this manuscript(s) might help resolve the controversy over the date and location of the first meeting between Donne and Huygens (Daley, pp. 83–85): if the manuscript(s) belonged to the Doncaster family (who did own at least three manuscripts containing Donne verse—O, MSS. Don.b.9, Don.c.54, and Don.d.58), then Paul Sellin's argument "that the young Constantijn met Donne in The Hague in late 1619, when Donne visited Holland as a member of the Doncaster mission" might gain ascendancy over the dominant view of a 1622 first meeting, as might Sellin's suggestion of an earlier and more extensive Donnean influence on seventeenth-century Dutch literature. If Huygens had met Donne as early as 1619, "one of the main objections to properly considering Donnean influence upon Huygens falls, and the possibility of English satirical and elegiac muses lurking in the shadows of 't Voorhout' or 't Costelick Mal' is by no means so readily excluded as scholarship tends to assume."[18] The uncollected printings, then, contain evidence that might solve or illuminate several textual, biographical, and historical problems—including the dates and nature of Donne's influence in the Netherlands.

Donne's Readers and Writers

Everyone is familiar with the solemn testimonials to Donne's intellect, recondite obscurity, and verbal pyrotechnics by England's greatest literary critics of the seventeenth, eighteenth, nineteenth, and twentieth centuries: Ben Jonson's prophecy "that Done himself for not being uñderstood would perish"; John Dryden's complaint that Donne "affects the Metaphysicks . . . and perplexes the Minds of the Fair Sex with nice Speculations of Philosophy"; Samuel Johnson's description of the metaphysical poets as learned and analytical in his life of Cowley; Samuel Taylor Coleridge's quatrain, "With Donne, whose muse on dromedary trots, / Wreathe iron pokers into true-love knots; / Rhyme's sturdy cripple, fancy's maze and clue, / Wit's forge and fire-blast, meaning's press and

18. Paul Sellin, "John Donne and the Huygens Family, 1619–1621," *Dutch Quarterly Review* 12 (1982–1983): 200.

screw"; and T. S. Eliot's explanation for our century's affinity for Donne: "poets in our civilization, as it exists at present, must be *difficult.*"[19] More recently, Arthur F. Marotti has characterized Donne as deliberately restricting his audience to a coterie of Inns of Court wits, prominent courtiers, and patrons of the arts and artists—all with access to Donne's manuscripts—and has described some of the plentiful evidence that Donne intended a restricted readership (p. xi). John Carey also sees Donne deliberately restricting his audience to an intellectual elite through the obscurity of his verse: "The frequent obscurity of the poems also enforces the rift between Donne and society. Obscurity protected his work from inferior minds, and flattered the intelligence of the chosen few he admitted to his confidence. . . . Having poems printed and published would have infringed his sense of lonely superiority" (pp. xxi–xxii).

The recent extraordinary increase in the number of manuscripts known to contain Donne verse begun by Shawcross (who increased to 157 the 43 listed by Grierson, Gardner, and Milgate) and continued by Peter Beal (to 219) and the textual editors of the Donne variorum (to 240) proves that once the poems began to circulate Donne lost all control over his manuscript readership. The evidence in Donne's own verse and letters confirms Marotti's and Carey's assessment that Donne wrote his poetry as a coterie poet; however, as Beal points out, Donne's own century made him a popular poet, even in manuscript: "probably more transcripts of Donne's poems were made than of the verse of any other British poet of the 16th and 17th centuries. The large number of extant transcripts (which must be only a fraction of the number once in existence) indicates the extraordinary popularity of Donne's verse in the 17th century" (1:245). A complete effort to identify Donne's seventeenth-century readers would incorporate this massive body of manuscript evidence, a task beyond my present one of describ-

19. Jonson, "Conversations with William Drummond of Hawthornden," in C. H. Herford and Percy Simpson, eds., *Ben Jonson*, 1:138; Dryden, "Discourse concerning the Original and Progress of SATIRE," in James Kinsley, ed., *The Poems of John Dryden* (Oxford: Clarendon Press, 1958), 2:604; Johnson, "Cowley" in *The Lives of the Most Eminent English Poets* (London, 1781), vol. 1; Coleridge, in Henry Nelson Coleridge, ed., *The Literary Remains of Samuel Taylor Coleridge* (London, 1836), 1:148; and Eliot, "The Metaphysical Poets," in *Selected Essays: New Edition* (New York: Harcourt, Brace & World, 1960), p. 248.

ing the contribution of the uncollected printed verse to specific identification of Donne's audience.

The expansion in Donne's known verse presence in manuscript is paralleled by the expansion in the number of known printings of Donne's uncollected poems. As noted above, seventeenth-century readers had access to much more Donne printed material than has been suspected. Furthermore, the chronological spread of the uncollected printings proves that Donne's audience extended beyond his manuscript readers sooner and that his presence lasted longer than previously thought.

But who composed this considerable and sustained audience? The uncollected printings offer specific evidence confirming the traditional identification of Donne's intellectually elite audience. Perhaps more interestingly, however, the uncollected printings also offer substantial inferential evidence for a large and previously unsuspected audience—the functionally illiterate. Specific identification of Donne's readership has been very hard to come by. Inferences from traditional critical and biographical/psychological assessments are insufficiently exact to satisfy literary or cultural historians, New Historicists, or even the mildly curious. Recent work on Donne manuscript materials has produced much valuable information about Donne's contemporary manuscript readership;[20] however, identifying the original owner(s) of many Donne manuscripts and proving that the owners as well as the copyists read the Donne verse generally remain problems—even the readers of the Verse Letters can be identified only when the addressee is known. In fact, Smith identifies only thirteen contemporary Donne readers on the basis of the manuscripts: "Indeed the brief list of known readers confirms that Donne kept his verse close for they are almost all associates or correspondents of his: Goodyer, Wotton, Rowland Woodward, Hoskins, Christopher and Samuel Brooke, Thomas and John Roe, Jonson, Mrs Herbert, the Earl of Dorset, Everard Guilpin, Joseph Hall" (p. 4). The many allusions to Donne in manuscript and print recorded by Smith offer a possible means of identifying more Donne readers; but the

20. See Robert A. Bryan, "John Donne's Poems in Seventeenth-Century Commonplace Books," *English Studies* 43 (1962): 170–74; Alan MacColl, "The Circulation of Donne's Poems in Manuscript," in A. J. Smith, ed., *John Donne: Essays in Celebration* (London: Methuen, 1972), pp. 28–46; Marotti (particularly pp. x and 292, n. 6); and, most important, Beal's introduction to his Donne manuscript listings (1.i:243–61).

allusions, like the manuscripts, frequently do not offer certain identification—how can one distinguish readers from name-droppers?

On the other hand, intertextual penetration by Donne's seventeenth-century uncollected printed verse into seventeenth-century print culture offers a limited but relatively certain and specific identification of Donne's contemporary readership. If a person has written a complete line of Donne verse or an obvious adaptation of Donne verse into his or her own prose or verse, or has translated Donne verse, then that person has read Donne verse. This criterion, while offering relative certainty, is limited. For example, George Herbert, who died in 1633, could not have read "Elegy: The Autumnall" and "To the Lady Magdalen Herbert: of St. Mary Magdalen" in Walton's "Life of Mr. *George Herbert*" in *The Temple* (1674), for which Herbert is the listed author; nor could Henry Wotton, who died in 1639, have read "To Sir H. W. at his going Ambassador to Venice" in *Reliquiae Wottonianae* (1654), for which he is the listed author. Even though evidence other than the uncollected printings establishes beyond any question that Herbert and Wotton read Donne poems, neither can appear on a list of readers derived from the information provided by those printings. Although not everyone included in the Index of Authors, Compilers, Contributors, and Translators (which includes authors of works containing dubia) qualifies as a relatively certain Donne reader, the Index provides a useful beginning point. By eliminating the listed authors who almost certainly could not have read the Donne verse and by identifying persons other than listed authors who provided the Donne verse in the work, one gets a list of relatively certain readers of Donne.

Dubia and death make some deletions (in addition to Herbert and Wotton) from the Index easy. Authors of, or contributors to, works containing Donne dubia (composers John Dowland, *A Pilgrimes Solace* [1612], and Orlando Gibbons, *Cantvs. The First Set of Madrigals and Mottets of 5. Parts* [1612], and translator Jasper Mayne, *Paradoxes, Problems, Essayes, Characters* [1652]) are not on the list of relatively certain readers (though they are considered in the discussion of the uses of Donne's uncollected verse). John Stow, who died in 1605, could not have known "Ioannes Donne Sac: Theol: Profess," the only Donne verse in *The Survey of London* (1633), a work begun by Stow but continued after his death to 1633 by the unidentified "*A.M. H.D.* and others." Nor could Sir William Scott (1175?–1234?), author of *Mensa Philosophica* (translated and enlarged into *The Philosophers Banqvet* [1614] by "*W: B. Esquire*"), have read Donne verse.

Instances of ambiguous authorship make inclusion and exclusion more difficult. William Basse and Edward Philips are only conjectural compilers of *A Helpe to Discovrse* and *A Helpe to Memorie and Discovrse*; however, Basse's probable work as translator and enlarger of *The Philosophers Banqvet* makes him a more likely reader than is Edward Philips; thus, I include Basse, but not Philips, in my list of relatively certain readers.[21] Thomas Jordan and John Mennes have each been conjectured as the compiler of *Wits Recreations*; however, Mennes makes the list because of his compilation of *Wit and Drollery*.

In some cases, the listed author is not responsible for assembling the work or for the part of the work containing the Donne verse. Charles Cotton and Robert Venables, authors of two of the works included in *The Universall Angler*, may not have read the third, Walton's *Compleat Angler*, which contains "The Baite." Jane Barker, listed as the author of *Poetical Recreations*, authored only the first part of this two-part work; the second part, wherein "The Will" appears, is described as having been authored by "several Gentlemen of the UNIVERSITIES, and Others." Francis Oscar Mann points out that Thomas Deloney did not author the section of *Strange Histories* that contains "A lame begger";[22] and because

21. William Basse is the conjectured compiler of *A Helpe to Discovrse* (the compiler is identified on the title page as "W. B.") and *A Helpe to Memorie and Discovrse* (probably because its contents resemble those of *A Helpe to Discovrse*). The preface to *The Philosophers Banqvet* identifies the translator and enlarger as "W: B. Esquire." The selection of Donne verse in *The Philosophers Banqvet*, the 1629 edition of *A Helpe to Discovrse*, and *A Helpe to Memorie and Discovrse* strongly suggests that "W. B." compiled all three works: *The Philosophers Banqvet* prints "The first Anniversary," ll. 127–30, 133–44, and 343–44; the 1629 edition of *A Helpe to Discovrse*, "The first Anniversary," ll. 127–28 and 133–34; and *A Helpe to Memorie and Discovrse*, "The first Anniversary," ll. 343–44.

22. Mann notes, "The edition of 1607 inserts *Salomon's Good Huswyfe* immediately after Canto I. and adds a number of miscellaneous poems after the prose *Speech betweene Certaine Ladies*. *Salomon's Good Huswyfe* is added to *The Table* of contents, but the other poems are unindexed as though they were added haphazard by the printer as an afterthought. Most of these are subscribed respectively with the initials T.R., A.C., and R. [as in "A lame begger"], and with the exception of *The Death of Faire Rosamond* it is quite evident that Deloney's authentic work does not extend beyond the prose which closes the 1602 edition" (*The Works of Thomas Deloney*, p. 585).

Deloney, who died in 1600, likely did not add the section containing "A lame begger" in 1609 to the 1602 edition, I exclude him.

Authors responsible for assembling multiple works (one or more of which contain Donne verse) into planned collections are included in the relatively certain reader list. Cyril Tourner, the listed author of *Three Elegies on the Most Lamented Death of Prince Henrie*, might not have read the adaptation of line 115 of "The first Anniversary" contained in John Webster's *A Monvmental Colvmne*, one of the three elegies; however, because Tourner was responsible for assembling the volume, I have included him. Likewise, Thomas Barlow, author of *Papismus Regiae Potestatis Eversor*, may not have read Donne's *Conclaue Ignati* published with it; but he, too, assembled the volume.

Sometimes one can identify the person other than the listed author responsible for the part of the work containing the Donne verse; thus, some names not included in the Index belong in the list of relatively certain readers. Pelham Humphryes, not Henry Playford (listed compiler of *Harmonia Sacra*), set "A Hymne to God the Father" to music; and John Playford, not John Wilson (the listed contributor of *Select Ayres and Dialogues for One, Two, and Three Voyces*), adapted "Song. 'Go, and catch a falling star.'" Humphrey Moseley, publisher of *The Last Remains of Sʳ John Svckling*, not John Suckling, placed the excerpt from "The Storme" in "To the Reader." The untitled poem in the anonymous *Horti Carolini* containing line 1 of "Elegie. Death" is subscribed to "Stephen Chase. Ch. Ch."

These considerations give us a list of fifty-nine relatively certain readers who fall into relatively predictable groupings, with writers predominating (authors may appear in more than one category depending on how they use the Donne verse):

Essayists: Thomas Barlow; Thomas Pope Blount; Thomas Coryat; Abraham Cowley; Thomas Dekker; William Drummond of Hawthornden; Lucius Cary, Viscount Falkland; Edmund Gayton; Johann Grindal; Mary de la Riviere Manley; Andrew Marvell; Samuel Sheppard; John Swan, Jr.; Izaak Walton; Richard Whitlock; William Winstanley; Joseph Wybarne

Poets: Daniel Baker, Francis Beaumont, Thomas Carew, Stephen Chase, Aston Cokayne, Abraham Cowley, John Dryden, Henry Fitzgeffrey, Thomas Forde, William Habington, Ben Jonson, Francis Quarles, Josuah Sylvester, Cyril Tourner, Henry Vaughan, John Webster

Compilers of verse miscellanies: William Basse, Robert Chamberlain, John Cotgrave, John Gough, John Mennes, Samuel Sheppard, John Shirley, Henry Stubbs, Abraham Wright

Translators: Payne Fisher, Johann Grindal,[23] Constantin Huygens, Henrik Rintjus, Henry Stubbs, Georg Rodolf Weckherlin

Composers: William Corkine, Alfonso Ferrabosco, Pelham Humphryes, William Lawes, John Playford

Dramatists: George Etherege; Thomas Killigrew; Nathaniel Lee; Margaret Cavendish, duchess of Newcastle; John Webster

Biographer/historians: William Dugdale, Payne Fisher, Henry Holland, Izaak Walton, William Winstanley

Educator: Joshua Poole

Minister: Daniel Price

Publisher: Humphrey Moseley

While the presence of Donne verse in the texts of the seventeenth-century intelligentsia hardly surprises, this presence (and demonstrable influence) in such a range of seventeenth-century cultural enterprises does, particularly in music and drama. Clearly, Donne had a more frequent and polyphonic voice in seventeenth-century discourse than we have heard heretofore.

Perhaps even more interesting than this somewhat unexpectedly diverse list of names and categories of readers among seventeenth-century intellectuals is another, totally unexpected, Donne readership and cultural influence implied by the nature of some works printing Donne's uncollected verse—the functionally illiterate. The evidence of the uncollected printings for this readership is less specific than it is for those who wrote Donne verse; however, categories of functionally illiterate readers can be identified: schoolchildren and adults in need of elementary education, "Strangers" to the language of polite conversation, farmers, women who aspired to fashion, would-be wits, artisans, and so forth. The title pages of several works containing uncollected Donne verse for the functionally illiterate act as advertisements for the books, carefully identifying their target audience much as illus-

---

23. One might not list Johann Grindal's *Aendachtige Bedenckingen*, a translation into Dutch of Donne's *Devotions vpon Emergent Occasions*, as a translation because it leaves Donne's "Insultus morbi primus" in the original Latin; however, I have listed Grindal as a translator because he translates the rest of the work.

trated covers and jacket copy would today. And the commercial success of these works, as measured by the number of their editions, at least implies the existence of the target audience and the value it placed on the contents of the works.

Joshua Poole's *The English Parnassus* proves that Donne's student readership extended beyond Oxford, Cambridge, and the Inns of Court. According to the heading of his dedicatory poem, Poole originally conceived the work to benefit "the hopeful young Gentlemen, his Scholars in that private School at *Hadley*, Kept in the house of Mr. *Francis Atkinson*" who needed help with writing poems for their classes. The dedicatory poem itself establishes that Poole's aspirants to the "School of Metaphysical Poetry" were very young indeed:

> For you (Ingenious spirits) thus I try
> To find a milky way to Poesie,
> That babes, as they the coral nipples lug,
> May find an Hippocrene within the dug;
> And the first milk that they shall feed upon,
> May be the sacred dew of Helicon,
> And when at first their steps the earth shall greet,
> At once may find their own and verses feet,
> After as they grow up, Pegasus may
> Be the first hobby-horse with which they play:
> And when to higher sports they come, may put
> An Homer's Illiads in their gamesome nut,
> And whilst they take their pastime in the sun,
> Together make their tops and verses run.
>
> (sig. A5)

Two issues of the first edition of *The English Parnassus* appeared in 1657 and a second edition in 1677, with a second issue in 1678.

Adults in need of the most basic of all education (how and what to eat and drink) could turn to the enlarged translation by "W: B. *Esquire*" of "THE PHILOSOPHERS BANQVET. NEWLY FUR-NISHED AND DECKED forth with much variety of many seuerall Dishes, that in the former Seruice were neglected. Where now not onely Meates and Drinks of *all Natures and Kindes are serued in, but the* Natures and Kindes of all disputed of. *As further*, Dilated by Table-conference, Alteration, and Changes of States, Diminution of the Stature of Man, Barrennesse of the Earth, with the effectes and causes thereof, Phisically and Philosophically" for tips on preparing food and drinking wine. Answers to such age-old questions as "Why Weedes prosper better then good Hearbs in the Earth" and "VVhether Bats be Birds or Mice" evidently had an audience: editions of *The Philosophers Banqvet* appeared in 1609, 1614, and 1633, with the 1609 edition lacking Donne verse.

For those "Strangers" to, or entry-level "Schollers" of, the language of polite conversation, John Gough advertised the requisite assistance: "THE ACADEMY OF Complements. Wherein *Ladies, Gentlewomen, Schollers,* and *Strangers* may accommodate their Courtly practice with gentile Ceremonies, Complementall amorous high expressions, and formes of speaking or writing of Letters most in fashion. A worke perused, exactly perfected, every where corrected and inriched, by the Author, with additions of witty Poems, and pleasant Songs. The sixt Edition, with two Tables, the one expounding the most hard English words, the other resolving the most delightfull fictions of the Heathen Poets." Taking the first three entries in these two tables as samples, one can see that the readers certainly did not possess a university education. The first, "A Table for the understanding of the hard ENGLISH words contained in this Book," glosses "ACute" as "Witty," "Amiable" as "Lovely," and "Apt" as "Fit"; the second, "A short Table of the delightfull fictions of Heathen Poets, with other usefull Collections out of ancient and moderne Historians," glosses "A*Pollo*" as the "God of Learning, and of the Muses," "*AEolus*" as "the blustring God of the Winds," and "*Bacchus*" as "the God of Wine, and good fellowes." Persons who hoped for initiation into the world of polite conversation purchased enough copies of *The Academy of Complements* to require fourteen editions and issues from 1639 to 1684, with the first four lacking any Donne verse.

Donne's verse also counseled countrymen in search of amusement as well as useful information about diet, exercise, compound interest, and the purchase of farmland via the seventeenth-century equivalent of *Reader's Digest* or the *Farmer's Almanac*, William Basse and Edward Philips's *A Helpe to Discovrse*: "Consisting of wittie, Philosophical and Astronomicall Questions *and Answers. As also, Of Epigrams, Epitaphs, Riddles, and Iests.* Together with the COVNTRYMANS Counsellour, next his yearely Oracle *or Prognostication to con-sult with.* Containing diuers necessary Rules and obseruations of much vse and consequence being knowne." Evidently countrymen liked what they read: *A Helpe to Discovrse* went through eighteen editions and issues between 1619 and 1682.

Seventeenth-century devotees of Trivial Pursuit in need of witty repartee like Ben Jonson's Sir Politic Wouldbe or George Etherege's Sir Fopling Flutter could forget their commonplace books if they had a copy of William Basse and Edward Philips's "*A HELPE TO MEMORIE AND DISCOVRSE. The two Syrens of the Eare, and ioynt Twins of Mans perfection.* Extracted from the sweating braines of *Physitians, Philosophers, Orators and Poets.* Distilled in their Assiduous, and witty *Collections.*" *A Helpe to Memorie and Discovrse* appeared in three editions from 1620 to 1630, with the first lacking any Donne verse.

Samuel Sheppard's *The Marrow of Complements* aimed at a wider audience "from the Noblemans Palace to the Artizans Shop"; however, the title page of this manual for letter writing and conversation most directly appealed to the tongue-tied lovelorn rather than to poet laureates: "A most Methodicall and accurate forme of Instructions for all Variety of Love-Letters, Amorous Discourses, and Complementall Entertainements. Fitted for the use of all sorts of persons from the Noblemans Palace to the Artisans Shop. *With many delightfull Songs, Sonnetts, Odes, Dialogues, &c.* Never before published." Perhaps by 1655 noblemen and artisans were better educated; *The Marrow of Complements* appears in only a single edition.

What did Donne's various audiences like to read? Variety was evidently the spice of seventeenth-century life: of the 216 known Donne verses, 97 appear in the complete or partial printings of his uncollected poems, with an additional 3 ("Antiquary," "The Flea," and "Niobe") among the translations and another ("The Dampe") among the adaptations. As discussed above, the poems earliest in print tend to appear most frequently: the publication of 4 editions of "The first Anniversary" and 3 of "The second Anniversarie" by 1625 has much to do with the 138 partial printings of "The first Anniversary" and 62 of "The second Anniversarie" during the seventeenth century. The keys to a large number of complete printings of a given poem seem to be appearances in frequently published works by other important poets ("Amicissimo et Meritissimo Ben Jonson" [9 complete printings] and "Elegy: The Expostulation" [8] in various states of Jonson's *Works*, "Elegie upon the untimely death of the incomparable Prince Henry" [10] in Sylvester's *Lachrymae*), in frequently published works by an indefatigable admirer like Walton ("To Sir H. W. at his going Ambassador to Venice" [5], "A Hymne to God the Father" [8, 7 in works by Walton], "To the Lady Magdalen Herbert: of St. Mary Magdalen" [7], and "The Baite" [9]), or in a frequently published verse miscellany like Gough's *The Academy of Complements* ("The Indifferent" [6]). Poems having double-figure appearances of partial printings ("The Progresse of the Soule" [57] gets a big boost from three printings of eleven segments quoted by Marvell) share only memorable expression (often in couplets) of common topics, the sort of material favored in commonplace books: "The Will" (35), "Breake of day" (29), "Elegy: The Autumnall" (29), "Satyre IIII" (29), "Satyre II" (22), "The Calme" (18), "The Storme" (18), "Satyre V" (14), "Elegy: Loves Warr" (13), "Song. 'Go, and catch a falling star'" (13), "Womans constancy" (13), "Obsequies to the Lord Harrington" (12), and "Elegie. Death" (10). In a century that loves bawdy poems, the absence of "The Flea" (except in translation in *Koren-Bloemen*) seems a bit of a mystery, at least for entire printings—the poem does not easily divide into quotable segments.

Except for a general lack of interest in the Divine Poems (only 8 of 36 appear, with 24 of the 29 total appearances being in the various printings of Walton's life of Donne) and an extraordinary interest in the Anniversaries, Epicedes, and Obsequies (6 of 12 printed 249 times), the seventeenth-century printings of Donne's uncollected poems (not including translations and adaptations) closely parallel twentieth-century critical interests. The Songs and Sonnets appear most frequently (27 of 57 Songs and Sonnets printed 178 times); 8 of 8 Satyres (including "Vpon Mr. Thomas Coryats Crudities," "In eundem Macaronicon," and "The Progresse of the Soule") appear 129 times; 10 of 18 Elegies (counting "Elegy: The Autumnall" and "Sapho to Philaenis" as elegies), 84 times; 14 of 37 Verse Letters, 82 times; 7 of 23 Epigrams, 16 times; and 1 of 3 Epithalamions, 2 times.

USES OF DONNE'S UNCOLLECTED VERSE

Clearly, an enormous and diverse body of uncollected Donne printed verse was available to a larger and more various audience sooner and over a longer period of time than has been realized. Furthermore, this uncollected verse tells us something very different about the attitudes toward and uses of Donne's verse in the seventeenth century than we have been deducing from the collected editions and manuscripts. While Donne's established literate audience used his verse in generally expected ways, the great range of his materials available to his functionally illiterate audience as well as the diversity of that audience led to a variety of less expected uses that suggest Donne's verse (and, by extension, verse in general) had unexpected values for a greater range of Renaissance social classes than Donne's traditional reputation as a poet of the cultured elite would lead anyone to suspect.

The most numerous of Donne's literate audience, the prose essayists, commonly incorporate Donne into their texts for intellectual ornamentation: they quote Donne to illustrate a point or to show off their own wit and taste. With the exception of Dekker (*A Knights Coniuring*), Drummond of Hawthornden (*A Midnights Trance* and *Flowres of Sion*), John Swan, Jr. (*Specvlvm Mundi*), and Samuel Sheppard (*Merlinvs Anonymvs*), these authors acknowledge Donne as the source of the verse quoted in their text. Interestingly, the essayist who makes the greatest use of Donne makes the most unusual use. Who could predict Samuel Sheppard's intertextual writing of Donne verse as the ravings of the demented astrologer Raphael Desmus in his parody of seventeenth-century almanacs (particularly those of Nicholas Culpepper), *Merlinus Anonymus. An Almanack, and no Almanack. A Kalendar, and no Kalendar. An Ephemeris (between jest, and earnest) for the year, 1653*. In the explanation of "The Parts of the Kalendar," Sheppard describes his fourth column (where he puts much of the Donne verse) as "a pune Chronicle, (quite different from *Spriggs* way) of some (you will say) remarkable passages, during the war, laugh, and be laxative" (sig. *A*4). Thus, for the month of January, the fourth column has the following entries: "The fall of a Chimney neer Saint *Peter Pauls Warfe*, 1643," "Mistresse *E: G.* carted, 1644," "Mr: *Newton* delivered his Dog over into the hands of Squire *Low*, 1645," "A cart of hay over thrown in Smithfeild, 1645," "*Nan Sharpe* (Rectresse of *Sodome*, and *Gubernatrix* of *Gomarah*) married to a Beadle, lash her Sirrah," and lines 15–16 of "The Calme," "The fighting place now / Seamens raggs supply, / And all the tackling is / a frippery" (sig. A5v). All told, Sheppard gives 224 lines from an amazingly diverse reading of Donne: "Vpon Mr. Thomas Coryats Crudities," "Satyre II," "Elegy: The Bracelet," "The Calme," "Satyre V," "To Sʳ Edward Herbert. at Julyers," "The first Anniversary," "Satyre IIII," "To the Countesse of Bedford. T'have written then," "To the Countesse of Bedford. Madame, You have refin'd," "To Sʳ Henry Wotton. Sir, more then kisses," "Satyre I," "To Sʳ Henry Wootton. Here's no more newes," "To the Countesse of Salisbury. August. 1614," "Elegy: On his Mistris," "To the Countesse of Huntingdon. Madame, Man to Gods image," "To Mʳ R. W. If, as mine is,"

"Epithalamion made at Lincolnes Inne," "Obsequies to the Lord Harrington," "To Mʳ T. W. All haile sweet Poët," and "To Sir H. W. at his going Ambassador to Venice." Donne's passages supported a second issue in 1653 and another *Almanack* in 1654, though this sequel has only lines 251–58 and 259–66 from "The first Anniversary."

By far the most common use of Donne's verse by his poet readers was unacknowledged intertextuality. John Dryden's theft of lines 5–6 of "Obsequies to the Lord Harrington" and unacknowledged adaptation of lines 61–62 of "Elegie. Death" for his *Eleonora* have been discussed above; unacknowledged Donne verse also appears in original or adapted form in the poetry of Daniel Baker, Francis Beaumont, Aston Cokayne, Thomas Carew, Henry Fitzgeffrey (who at least ascribes the poem to *"Incerti Authoris"*), William Habington, Ben Jonson, Francis Quarles, Henry Vaughan, and John Webster. Donne would not have approved:

> And they who write, because all write, have still
> That excuse for writing, and for writing ill;
> But hee is worst, who (beggarly) doth chaw
> Others wits fruits, and in his ravenous maw
> Rankly digested, doth those things out-spue,
> As his owne things; and they'are his owne, 'tis true,
> For if one eate my meate, though it be knowne
> The meat was mine, th'excrement is his owne.
> (Shawcross [*Donne*], "Satyre II," ll. 23–30)

Compilers of seventeenth-century verse miscellanies published far more Donne verse than did any other category of reader. While the compilers of these miscellanies would fall within Donne's literate readers, the miscellanies themselves were generally aimed at a functionally illiterate middle-class (and perhaps lower-class) audience; thus, miscellanies like *Parnassus Biceps, Recreation for Ingenious Head-peeces* (also known as *Wits Recreations*), *The Academy of Complements, The Loyal Garland, The Marrow of Complements, The Mirrour of Complements, Windsor=Drollery, Wit and Drollery,* and *Wits Interpreter* publish Donne's more risqué poems for their witty contribution to the general celebration of sex, alcohol, and tobacco.

Fortunately for those who would save Donne from the debauched masses, Robert Chamberlain compiled *The Harmony of the Muses*, as he says "To the Readers," to demonstrate the transcen-

dence of early seventeenth-century English verse over not only
the later verse of the century, but also the continental competition:

> *The* Genius *of those times produced many incomparable Witts, who
> being excellent in themselves, in a noble emulation, contended who
> should excell each other. From hence it is we have so many admirable*
> Pieces *of* Perfection *derived to us, every Subject, in every particular,
> being so choicely handled, that what room is left unto Posterity, is
> rather to admire and imitate, then to equall them. There were never in
> one Age so many contemporary Patterns of* Invention, *or ever* Witt
> *that wrought higher or cleerer. For though our homely Progenitors,
> with too vain admiration were accustomed to prosecute the Issues of*
> out-landish Witts, *and believed nothing to be exquisite, but what
> came from* France *or* Italy; *yet this Age by Experience hath found,
> that without the least Imitation, we have given them Examples of our
> own, and excelled them as much in soundness as in Beauty.* (sig.
> A3r–v)

To prove the excellence of Renaissance English poetry, Chamberlain primarily used Donne and Carew: one partial and seven complete poems by Donne and eight by Thomas Carew. Even though
Chamberlain's choice of authors (including William Strode, Ben
Jonson, Henry King, and Francis Beaumont) and his purported
purpose would appeal to a sophisticated audience, it is difficult to
tell if he is being apologetic or a good marketer when he
warns/alerts the reader to potential bawdiness in the verse: "*If any
shall object, that here and ther the* Fancy *seems some time too loose for
such Reverend* Names, *let him impute it to the lightness of the Subject*"
(sig. A3v).

Given Donne's complexity and vocabulary, translation would
seem an unlikely use of his poetry; but Donne's uncollected verse
includes translations into English, German, Dutch, Greek, and
Latin. Donne translated five of his own Latin verses as well as one
each of the emperor Hadrian and Stephanus Quarantus from his
Latin *Conclaue Ignati* into English in his *Ignatius His Conclaue*. Walton included an anonymous translation into English of lines 3–24
of "To Mr George Herbert, with one of my seals" in the 1658, 1670,
and 1675 versions of his life of Donne (the complete poem and its
translation first appeared in Donne's 1650 collected *Poems*); and
Payne Fisher translated "Ioannes Donne Sac: Theol: Profess" into
English in *The Tombes, Monuments, and Sepulchral Inscriptions, Lately
Visible in St. Pauls Cathedral*. Recently, Flynn has reopened the

debate over the authenticity of the sixty-one Latin originals translated by Jasper Mayne into English as *"A sheaf of Miscellany EPI-*
GRAMS. Written in *Latin* by *J. D. Translated by* J. Main *D.D.*" in
Donne's *Paradoxes, Problems, Essayes, Characters*. Flynn argues that
Donne could have written originals for all except numbers 53–57
("Epigrams," pp. 121–30).[24] In 1641, Georg Rodolf Weckherlin
(1584–1653), German poet and man of letters, published German
translations of Donne's "Niobe," "Hero and Leander," "A licentious person," "Antiquary," and "Phryne" in *Gaistliche und*
Weltliche Gedichte. His 1648 second edition reprinted these transla-
tions plus a German adaptation of "A lame begger." A 1615 date
beside the first of Weckherlin's epigrams (p. 177) suggests that his
translations could date from much earlier than 1641 and could be
based on a manuscript. As noted above, Henrik Rintjus's *Klioos*
Kraam published Constantin Huygens's 1626 translation into
Dutch of Donne's "A Valediction: of weeping," "Breake of day,"
"The Legacie," "The triple Foole," "The Blossome," and "Song.
'Go, and catch a falling star.'" In his 1658 first and 1672 second
editions of *Koren-Bloemen*, Huygens translated into Dutch eighteen
entire and one partial Donne verse and printed each with its En-
glish first line (except "Elegy: Oh, let mee not," which begins with
line 11): "The Flea," "The Apparition," "Witchcraft by a picture,"
"Twicknam garden," "Song. 'Go, and catch a falling star,'" "The
triple Foole," "A Valediction: of weeping," "The Dreame," "Elegy:
The Anagram," "Elegy: Oh, let mee not," "The Extasie," "The
Blossome," "Womans constancy," "A Valediction: forbidding
mourning," "The Sunne Rising," "Breake of day," "Loves Deitie,"
"The Legacie," and "Goodfriday, 1613. Riding Westward." In *Deli-*
ciae Poetarum Anglicanorum in Graecvm Versae, Henry Stubbs pro-
vided facing printings of "A Valediction: forbidding mourning,"
"Hero and Leander," and "A licentious person" in English and
Greek, with the titles of "A Valediction: forbidding mourning" and
"A licentious person" in Latin.

After the assault on Donne's meter by critics like Ben Jonson
("that Done for not keeping of accent deserved hanging" [Herford
and Simpson, 1:133]) and Samuel Johnson ("The metaphysical poets . . . instead of writing poetry . . . only wrote verses, and very
often such verses as stood the trial of the finger better than of the
ear; for the modulation was so imperfect, that they were only

24. I omit numbers 53–57 and treat the remainder as dubia.

found to be verses by counting the syllables" [1:27–28]), who would expect to find composers among Donne's reader/writers.[25] Yet composers are among the earliest and latest users of Donne. Alfonso Ferrabosco's *Ayres* (1609) contains the earliest printing of, and a musical score for, "The Expiration." William Corkine's *The Second Booke of Ayres* (1612) contains the earliest printing of, and a musical score for, "Breake of day" and the earliest printing of line 1, as well as a musical score, for "The Baite." John Dowland (*A Pilgrimes Solace*) and Orlando Gibbons (*Cantvs. The First Set of Madrigals and Mottets of 5. Parts*) publish settings and texts of lines printed as the first stanza of "Breake of day" in the 1669 edition of Donne's collected *Poems* and treated as dubia in the present work. John Wilson's *Select Ayres and Dialogues for One, Two, and Three Voyces* contains John Playford's setting and text of Francis Beaumont's "Womans Mutability" (an adaptation of "Song. 'Go, and catch a falling star'") and a setting by Henry Lawes of Thomas Carew's "Secresie protested" (an adaptation of "The Dampe"). Later, Henry Playford's *Harmonia Sacra* (1688) includes the text (ascribed to "*Dr.* Dunn") of "A Hymne to God the Father" with a score by Pelham Humphryes.

Among the dramatists, Webster, Killigrew, and Etherege—as had most of the poets—simply incorporated Donne's verse into their plays as dialogue with no acknowledgment. Margaret Cavendish, the duchess of Newcastle, the only dramatist who did acknowledge Donne's contribution to the dialogue, did so to establish the character of her heroine and, in so doing, illustrated Donne's continuing reign as the "universall Monarchy of wit" in the mid-seventeenth century while ridiculing medicine and the traditional literary canon. In scene 9 of act 1 of *The Second Part of the Lady Contemplation* (1662), Nurse Careful fears for the sanity of the witty young heroine, Lady Ward:

> *Nurse Careful.* O my Child, I am told that on a sudden you turned mad!
> *Lady Ward.* Surely Nurse your fear; or what else it may be, you seem to me to be more mad than I can find in my self to be.
> *Nurse Caref.* That shews you are mad. . . .

---

25. In his "Appendix B," Smith lists nine "Poems by Donne which are known to have been set to music down to the nineteenth century" (p. 495).

Lady Ward. Prethee Nurse, lest thou shouldst become mad, goe sleep to settle thy thoughts, and quiet thy mind, for I remember a witty Poet, one Doctor *Don*, saith,
>   *Sleep is pains easie salve, and doth fulfil*
>   *All Offices, unless it be to kill.*
>   (pp. 218–19)

Lady Ward's recitation of lines 35–36 of "The Storme" leads to medical malpractice and to an early assault on the traditional literary canon:

> *Nurse* Careful *cries out, as in a great fright.*
> *Nurse Caref.* O Heavens, what shall I do, what shall I do!
>   *Enter Doctor* Practice.
> *Doctor Pract.* What is the matter Nurse, what is the matter you shreek out so?
> *Nurse Caref.* O Doctor, my Child is mad, my Child is mad; for she repeats Verses.
> *Doctor Pract.* That's an ill signe indeed.
> *Lady Ward.* Doctor, did you never repeat Latine Sentences when you have read Lectures, nor Latine Verses, when you did Dispute in Schools?
> *Doctor Pract.* Yes, Sweet Lady, a hundred times.
> *Lady Ward.* Lord, Doctor, have you been mad a hundred times, and recovered so often!
> *Nurse Caref.* Those were Latine Verses, those were Latine Verses Child. . . .
> *Doctor Pract.* Nurse, she is not well, she must be put to a diet.
> *Lady Ward.* But why, Doctor, should you think me mad? I have done no outragious action; and if all those that speak extravagantly should be put to a diet, as being thought mad, many a fat waste would shrink in the doublet, and many a Poetical vein would be dryed up, and the flame quench'd out for want of radical oyl to prolong it; Thus Wit would be starved, for want of vapour to feed it; The truth is, a spare diet may make room in a Scholars head for old dead Authors to lie in; for the emptyer their heads are of wit, the fuller they may be filld with learning; for I do not imagine, old dead, Authors lie in a Scholars head, as they say souls do, none knows where, for a million of souls to lie in as small a compass as the point of a needle. (p. 219)

Doctor Practice then prescribes the usual male remedies for "hotly distemper'd" women—bed, medicine, and rules: "Her brain is hotly distemper'd, and moves with an extraordinary quick motion, as may be perceiv'd by her strange fancy: wherefore Nurse you had best get her to bed, if you can, and I will prescribe some medicine and rules for her" (p. 219). Lady Ward's quick wit, sense of irony, logical skills, and "strange fancy" make her an appropriate voice for Jack Donne.

Biographers and historians used Donne's verse selectively to characterize the saintly Dean and to enhance the lives of their other subjects. Editions of Izaak Walton's life of Donne initially print just "A Hymne to God the Father," the heading of "Hymne to God my God, in my sicknesse," and "Ioannes Donne Sac: Theol: Profess" (1640) but swell to include also "A Valediction: forbidding mourning," a partial printing and partial translation of "To Mr George Herbert, with one of my seals," and lines 1–8 and 26–30 of "Hymne to God my God, in my sicknesse." William Winstanley, who got much of the material for his biographical sketches of Donne in *England's Worthies* (1660) and *The Lives of the Most Famous English Poets* (1687) from Walton, prints "A Hymne to God the Father." Walton's and Winstanley's inclusion of Donne's Divine Poems is atypical: the only other printings of Donne's Divine Poems in the seventeenth century outside the collected editions and various editions of Walton's life of George Herbert (which contains "To the Lady Magdalen Herbert: of St. Mary Magdalen") are one line and a translation of "Goodfriday, 1613. Riding Westward" in Huygens's *Koren-Bloemen* and "As due by many titles I resign" and "Thou hast made me, and shall thy work decay" in the anonymous *The Mirrour of Complements* (1650). Historians of St. Paul's Cathedral like William Dugdale, Payne Fisher, and Henry Holland, or of London ("*A.M. H. D.* and others") print "Ioannes Donne Sac: Theol: Profess." Walton also includes appropriate Donne verse in his hagiographies of Wotton and Herbert, possibly to enhance the subjects through their association with the saintly Dean: "To Sir H. W. at his going Ambassador to Venice," three pieces of "Elegy: The Autumnall," and "To the Lady Magdalen Herbert: of St. Mary Magdalen."

With the exception of Donne's biographers, the seventeenth century (including the clergy) virtually ignored Donne's religious verse and rarely adapted the secular verse for theological use. Without acknowledgment, Daniel Price adapted three segments

from "The second Anniversarie" for one sermon on the death of
Prince Henry (*Prince Henry His First Anniversary*, 1613) and six
segments from "The second Anniversarie" as well as the refrain
"Shee, shee is dead; shee's dead" from "The first Anniversary" for
two more sermons in *Spiritvall Odovrs to the Memory of Prince Henry*
(1613).

Printers used Donne's verse for marketing and promotion.
Humphrey Moseley (publisher of Donne's *Paradoxes, Problems, Essayes, Characters* and the second issue of his *Biathanatos*) quotes the
same parts of lines 3–5 of "The Storme" to praise John Suckling in
his "To the Reader" of Suckling's *Mortimer* (1659) as Miles Fletcher
(or Flesher) had used to praise Donne in "The Printer to the Understanders" of Donne's 1633 *Poems*:

> Now, as it is to have
> been wish'd that this Tragedy had
> come whole and compleat to publick
> View, so is it some happiness that
> there is so much of it preserved; It
> being true of our *Author*, what
> Dr *Donne* said of a famous Artist of
> his time,
> ——*A hand or eye*
> By HILLIARD *drawn, is worth a History*
> By a worse Painter made.——
>
> (sig. a3r–v)

Compilers of works intended for a functionally illiterate audience use Donne's verse in ways that at first seem very different
from those of authors writing for the fully literate. Such compilers
use Donne's verse in overtly pragmatic ways—they generally
make at least some pretense of an educational function for the
work (and hence for the verse), and (in a very major difference
from all authors, except the composers, writing for a sophisticated
audience) they expect the readers to use the material (and frequently the verse) in the work as some form of self-help. These
works occupied the same place in the Renaissance bookstore that
"how-to" books occupy in our bookstores. In an increasingly sophisticated society with a dramatic increase in access to books, but
with very limited access to higher education, people turned to self-
education to acquire the literacy (or at least its appearance) newly
necessary for a better life. Interestingly, these compilers, unlike

the essayists writing for Donne's literate audience, rarely identify the source of their quotes; the material has value for its own sake, not from the prestige of its author. In these works and in the applications made of them by their audience, Donne's verse transcends the boundaries of print intertextuality to become public discourse, the literal voice of his readers.

Poole's *The English Parnassus* illustrates most overtly the educational intent of works for the functionally illiterate as well as the expected use of the material in the work to enhance the literacy of the audience. In an effort to improve the writing of poetry among schoolchildren (and any other would-be poets), Poole collected and published rhyming monosyllables, "choicest Epithets," and "some General Forms" (quotations of one or more entire lines) from authors he considered England's greatest writers—such as Chaucer, Shakespeare, and Donne. The title page of *The English Parnassus* accurately describes the work as a seventeenth-century verse erector set: "*A COLLECTION* Of all Rhyming Monosyllables, The choicest Epithets, and Phrases: With some General Forms upon all Occasions, Subjects, and Theams, Alphabetically digested." The volume provides anonymous verse (a list of authors consulted does appear as a preface), arranged by topic, which "his Scholars in that private School at *Hadley*, Kept in the house of Mr. *Francis Atkinson*" could assemble into poems for their classes. Two samples of the twenty-three fragments of Donne verse show that Poole understood the interest of male children in violence and large animals: lines 435–39 of "The first Anniversary" appear under the topic "Forms of breaking off" ("But as in cutting up a man that's dead, / The body will not last out to have read / On every part, and therefore men direct / Their speech to parts that are of most effect" [sig. 2S7]) and lines 381–83 of "The Progresse of the Soule" appear under "Elephant" ("The stiff-kneed carry castle. Natures great Master-piece. The only harmlesse great thing. Giant of beasts." [sig. Y1]). Ascertaining the extent to which students (or other aspiring poets) actually used *The English Parnassus* for its intended purpose is probably impossible: one suspects that a relatively low percentage of readers published any line of Donne verse. Even so, the readers were expected to write Donne verse, and the fact that *The English Parnassus* came out in a second issue in 1657 as well as in a second edition in 1677 with yet another issue in 1678 suggests that the work may very well have produced some writing of Donne's verse.

Renaissance compilers of self-help books for adults were sophisticated marketers and could be quite specific about the potential usefulness of their books. As previously noted, the title page was the primary marketing device, but a preface could sink the hook once the bait was taken. The title page of the second edition of *W. B.* Esquire's translated and enlarged version of Sir Michael Scott's *The Philosophers Banqvet* offers instruction to those seeking help with food and drink as well as those in need of something to say about typical Renaissance topics of conversation: *"THE* PHILOSOPHERS BANQVET. NEWLY *FVRNISHED AND DECKED* forth with much variety of many seuerall Dishes, that in the former Seruice were neglected. Where now not onely Meates and Drinks of *all Natures and Kindes are serued in, but the* Natures and Kindes of all disputed of. *As further*, Dilated by Table-conference, Alteration, and Changes of States, Diminution of the Stature of Man, Barrennesse of the Earth, with the effectes and causes thereof, Phisically and Philosophically." Evidently realizing that a browsing functional illiterate might not be attracted by a diet of pure edification and might not recognize the usefulness and value of his book, "W. B." provides a preface ("To the Iuditious Reader, and him that would buy this Booke, thus further in the commendation and *vse thereof*") that promises to delight as well as teach:

> The vse of this Booke is, to make a mã able to Iudge of the disposition and state of his owne body, of the effects, natures, and dispositions of those things we daily feede our bodies with. The next is, to giue vs a generall insight and briefe knowledge of Emperors and Kings, or men of greatest place and eminencie that are most notified to yᵉ world for vertue or vice. Lastly, wee haue heere certaine Epigrams and Iestes to exhillerate and solace our bodies and mindes at our tables, all these interlaced, with excellent positions, witty questions and answeres vpon diuers and sundry arguments, the perfect vse and insight whereof doth accomplish a man for discourse, behauiour and argument at the Table of our superiors. . . . (sig. A4v)

Donne's verse becomes "discourse" as it provides "answeres" to the "witty questions" and gives voice to the illiterate. Lines 127–30 and 133–44 of "The first Anniversary" help explain why contemporary heroes are not up to those of old; lines 343–44 of "The first Anniversary," the "Excellencie, vertue, and nature" of turquoise. Another edition in 1633 adds lines 121–22 and 143–44 of "The first Anniversary" on the problem of why men are no longer as large as they used to be and lines 221–23 and 181–82 of "The second Anniversarie" on "What is the Soule?"

The pragmatic attitude of the compilers shows in their ability to change their selection of Donne verse as the times change. In simple times, a rustic in search of amusement or information about compound interest, land purchase, diet, and exercise could turn to Basse and Philips's *A Helpe to Discovrse*. Thus, lines 203–4 and 117–20 of "The first Anniversary" explain "Why did men liue longer before the floud then since?" in the "Covntry-mans Covnsellor":

And now the springes and Sommers
which we see,
Like sonnes of Women after fiftie
bee.

Lastly, they be more continent in their liues, more satisfied in their desires, which since, *Gluttonie* and her *new Cookerie*, haue kil'd more then the *sword, famine,* or *pestilence.*

Their knowledge in all Arts was more enlarged, the influences of the Planets better known, and how they worke vpon humane bodies, as the same Author to the same purpose wittily followeth it.

Then if a slow pac'd star had stolne away,
Frō the Obseruers marking, he might stay
Two or three hundred years to see it again
And so make vp his obseruation plaine.
                                        (sigs. M4v–5v)

These answers were also good enough for the editions of 1620, 1621, and 1623; however, with the addition of lines 133–34 and 127–28 from "The first Anniversary" in 1627, Donne's verse entered the discourse of social protest over enclosure:

Leases say they, are but of base account, the Lessee many times hauing his Lease taken ouer his head, when free Inheritance cannot be shaken, and to purchase for life wee know is but a slender hold at the best, and yet lately more vncertaine then euer, as hath been by the suddaine fall of many thousands experienced, of the breuity whereof these Verses seeme to complaine:
So short's our life, that euery Peasant striues,
In a torne house or field to haue three liues:

What man is hee that liues vnto the age,
Fit to become Mathusalem *his Page.*
                    (sig. M2)

Farmers continued to complain about leases through the edition of
1628 and added politicians to their protests in 1629 with the earliest printing of any part of Donne's "Satyre V" (ll. 3–4):

> Q. *What was a great man of this kingdome vsed to compare Court-*
> *iers vnto?*
> A. To Ember weekes or Fasting Eues, the hungriest and lean-
> est of themselues, yet bordering still vpon great ones. As like-
> wise hee vsed to call promising, the vigill of giuing. And con-
> cerning a Book called, Rules for a Courtier, he would
> sometimes say,
> *Those Rules well practis'd, rightly vnderstood,*
> *Might make good Courtiers, yet few Courti-*
> *ers, good.*
>   (p. 116)

Old age, leases, and politicians remained under siege through the
dozen editions from 1630 to 1682.

Compilers kept a watchful eye on any shifts in their potential
audiences as well. A popular genre of self-help books borrowing
verse from the "universall Monarchy of wit" in the seventeenth
century is the "how to pick up significant others" manual. Not
surprisingly, the title pages of these works suggest the semiliterate
nature of the expected audience; however, their implications that
this audience would first read and then speak/write Donne verse
provide some insight into the social and economic power of verse
at lower levels of seventeenth-century society, and the evolution of
these title pages through their several editions illustrates an important evolution in the seventeenth-century reading audience
and in Donne's influence.

Consider the level of verbal skills and education of the expected audience implied by the title page quoted above from John
Gough's 1645 *The Academy of Complements.* Recognizing that he had
an audience in search of a user's manual, Gough provided a
lengthy and explicit instruction in the proper use of his work in
"The Authors Preface to the Reader." This preface is worth quoting
at length to show exactly how Gough conceived of the educational
and social level of his audience and how he expected them to
adapt his materials for their own use:

THere is no question but eloquence is a principall part in a well-qualified man . . . and adornes a man as usefull in all occasions . . . it is Eloquence which adornes our Discourse, gives a grace and life to our actions, opens us the gates and doors to the best company, and puts us in such esteeme, as well borne spirits ought to arrive to: without this we resemble walking Rocks . . . our words without effect, our conceits without fruits, and our lives disgusted with those, with whom wee ordinarily associate our selves: to this purpose in this little volume, feast thy fancy with variety of most eloquent expressions, and formes of delivering thy minde to all, from the King, to persons of the most inferiour ranke and quality; for in this last Edition . . . thou hast choise and select Complements set thee down in a form, which upon an occasion offered, thou mayest immitate, or with a little alteration make use of: thou hast in the next place variety of Subjects, with expression to the height of eloquence penn'd to quicken thy minde upon the like objects presented to thy view or fancy, thou hast witty disputes, amorous discourses, with an addition of most excellent Love Poems, Songs, complementall and most sweetly harmonious, fitted to the tastes of *Cupids* Guests: Thou hast exquisite Letters . . . then thou hast Dedications, Superscriptions fitted to thy own desires for thy use, upon any sudden occasion . . . in summe, both Eloquence and Love, with their secrets and mysteries, are made naked, and manifestly revealed to the weakest judgement. (sigs. A5–6)

The changes in the title pages' appeal to the audience and in the selection of Donne verse for the ten editions/issues of *The Academy of Complements* containing Donne verse suggest the sensitivity of the compilers to the possible uses of Donne's verse. The only fragment of Donne verse in this first edition—lines 1–2, 4–3, and 5–6 of "Breake of day"—is emended slightly and inserted as the second stanza in "A *Song*" (p. 166). The 1646 edition contains "an Addition of a new Schoole of Love, and a Present of excellent Similitudes, Comparisons Fancies, and Devices." The "new Schoole of Love" retains the previous excerpt from "Breake of day" and adds another, lines 15–18, under the topic "No businesse like that of Love" (p. 136). Evidently finding success with Donne, the editor retained the previous borrowings and added "The Indifferent" in its entirety for the editions of 1650, 1654, 1658, 1663, and 1670. By 1684, however, the anticipated audience of *The Academy of Complements* had changed from predominately male to exclusively fashion-conscious, refined females, as shown by the completely new title page: "THE Academy OF COMPLEMENTS WITH Many New Additions OF Songs and Catches *A-la-mode*. STORED With Variety of Complemental and Elegant Expressions, of LOVE and COURTSHIP. Also Witty and Ingenious Dialogues and Discourses, *Amorous and Jovial*. With Significant LETTERS upon Several Occasions. Composed for the use of *Ladies* and *Gentlewomen. By the most refined* Wits *of this Age*." The "Expressions" are now "Elegant"; the "Wits," "refined." Thus, the suggestive first stanza of "Breake of day" and the risqué "The Indifferent" disappear. On the other hand, the admonishing words of the female speaker of lines 15–18 of "Breake of day" remain under the topic heading "No business like that of Love": "The fair, the false love can / Admit all but the busie man: / He that hath business, and makes love, does do / Such wrong as if a married man should woo" (p. 94). Even though the audience will now consist of cosmopolitan females, the anticipated use of *The Academy of Complements* as a guide to writing remains ("With Significant LETTERS upon Several Occasions. Composed for the use of *Ladies* and *Gentlewomen*"); and Donne's verse, voiced as it is by the female speaker of "Breake of day," could easily and appropriately be inserted in such letters. Life had indeed imitated art: Donne had become the literal voice of a generation of real-life Lady Wards.

Indeed, Samuel Sheppard's *The Marrow of Complements* shows exactly how Donne verse might be used to write a prose letter. Again, the title page, as quoted above, appeals to the functionally illiterate lovelorn. A twentieth-century reader might expect Donne verses in the "Songs" or "Sonnetts"; however, Sheppard gives us a prose adaptation of "Elegy: The Expostulation" in the form of a model letter for an affair gone sour (as well as a highly original interpretation of the dramatic setting of the poem):

> *The Lover finding himself abus'd by her who promis'd him Marriage (she deserting him and electing another) may thus vent himselfe.*
> *Mistresse,*
> TO make the doubt clear that no Woman can be constant, was it my fate to prove it fully in you? did I think there was but one woman that breathed pure ayre, and must she needs be as perfidious, as she is beautious? is it the mark of your youth, or splendor, or your perfection, to bid defiance to realitie? or think you Heaven is deaf, or cannot see, or having eyes winks at

your perjur'd instabilitie? are vows so cheap with women? or is the matter so liquid whereof they are made, being written in water and blown away with every wind? who would have thought so many sweet accents, tun'd to our so many sighes, should meet blown from our hearts, sprinkled with so many oaths and tears with the divine impression of stoll'n kisses, that sealed all, should now prove but emptie nothings? did you draw bonds (Mistresse) with a mental reservation, having a full intent to forfeit? did you sign to breake, or must we take all truths that we receive from you, by the contrarie to that you speak, and find the truth out the wrong way? I sooner should have thought the Sun would have ceased to chear the earth with his beams, that Rivers would runne backward, or the *Thames* frozen o're in *June*. May he be curst that thus hath murthered our Love, let misery in plaguing him use her utmost Art, let all eyes shunne him, and he shunne all Society, till his body become as noysome as his infamy. But my passion too much transports me, it is you (Mistresse) whom I rather ought to rail on, which (though you deserve it) because I will not do, I here conclude, committing you as a convict to the horrour of your owne conscience.

R. L.

(pp. 41–42)

Compare lines 1–11, 13–21, 27–30, 39, and 42–44 of "Elegy: The Expostulation":

> To make the doubt cleare, that no woman's true,
>   Was it my fate to prove it strong in you?
> Thought I, but one had breathed purest aire,
>   And must she needs be false because she's faire?
> Is it your beauties marke, or of your youth,
>   Or your perfection, not to study truth?
> Or thinke you heaven is deafe, or hath no eyes?
>   Or those it hath, smile at your perjuries?
> Are vowes so cheape with women, or the matter
>   Whereof they're made, that they are writ in water,
> And blowne away with winde? . . .
>   Who could have thought so many accents sweet
> Form'd into words, so many sighs should meete
>   As from our hearts, so many oathes, and teares

Sprinkled among, (all sweeter by our feares
  And the divine impression of stolne kisses,
That seal'd the rest) should now prove empty blisses?
  Did you draw bonds to forfet? signe to breake?
Or must we reade you quite from what you speake,
  And finde the truth out the wrong way? . . .
Sooner I'll thinke the Sunne will cease to cheare
  The teeming earth, and *that* forget to beare,
Sooner that rivers will runne back, or Thames
  With ribs of Ice in June would bind his streames . . .
Curst may hee be, that so our love hath slaine . . .
  In plaguing him, let misery be witty;
Let all eyes shunne him, and hee shunne each eye,
  Till he be noysome as his infamie . . .
                              (Shawcross [*Donne*], pp. 71–72)

Sheppard has simply done for his reader what Gough suggested his reader might do for himself: "upon an occasion offered, thou mayest immitate, or with a little alteration make use of" the material in the compilation. Donne's personae were to become the voices of real persons.

Compilers of these self-help books used Donne's verse as an educational and entertainment commodity, a product with commercial value to its functionally illiterate consumers. The readers of these self-help books, relatively uneducated adults who needed assistance in getting ahead in daily life, used the books as a source for witty conversation, amusement, and advice on wining and dining, purchasing farmland, calculating compound interest, and improving their love life. Authors writing for the functionally illiterate rarely identified Donne as their source, suggesting that these readers (and speaker/writers, too, if the works achieved their purpose) found value in Donne's verse as it became part of their discourse. Highly literate authors writing for a literate audience also treated Donne verse as a commodity; however, for many of them and for their audience the prestige of Donne's name was part of the value of the commodity, and they generally capitalized on that prestige by identifying Donne as their source. Ironically, some of England's greatest writers (John Webster, Henry Vaughan, George Etherege, and John Dryden) made exactly the same use of Donne as had the most illiterate consumer of the self-help books: they helped themselves to his verse, and Donne became their voice as well.

NATURE OF DONNE'S INFLUENCE

On the basis of sensitive readings by critics and literary historians, the thirty-seven manuscripts identified by Grierson, the seven collected edition/issues, and the uncollected verses known to Keynes and others, Donne has been appointed the Dean of the "School of Metaphysical Poetry" and one of the authors most significant for developments in the literature of the seventeenth century. Now additional hard evidence exists to support, expand, and clarify this traditional view of Donne's place in literary history: 240 manuscripts containing texts of Donne's poems identified by Beal and others plus the uncollected printed verse identified in the present work. While it is beyond the scope of the present work to assess the influence of Donne's manuscripts and collected editions, the uncollected printings cataloged here suggest some significant revisions in the present understanding of the possible influence of Donne's printed verse. The presence of the printings both establishes influence (if Donne had no influence, his verse would not have seen print) and increases possible influence (the printings may have influenced additional readers).

Using Donne's uncollected printed verse to determine specific influence by Donne on any person or group of persons requires some caveats. Even when such verse can identify a Donne reader with certainty, the nature of the influence may be ambiguous. For example, *Koren-Bloemen* proves that Constantin Huygens translated nineteen Donne poems into Dutch; and, as Daley points out, "Huygens' translations of Donne have elicited and continue to elicit speculations concerning any direct influence of Donne's difficult metaphysical style on Huygens' own poetry and on Dutch poetry in general in the seventeenth century" (p. 85). The ambiguous nature of any influence shows in Daley's disclaimer of direct influence on Huygens, a disclaimer that nonetheless suggests the existence of some influence, however subtle:

> Although this book is concerned with the quality of the translations and the development of the translation process, some notes on this so-called influence are necessary at this point. I tend to disclaim any direct influence of Donne on Huygens' work. Donne's poetry may have sharpened Huygens' already sharp pen; moreover, the Donnean echoes we hear at times in Huygens' poetry are more likely to be an articulate tribute to Donne than a slavish borrowing of obscure images and a perversion of Huygens' "lucid" style. (pp. 85–86)

Furthermore, publication of Donne's poems may not correlate directly to interest in Donne's poetry—many uncollected printings of Donne's poems undoubtedly owe more to the popularity of the work in which they appear (works by Ben Jonson, Abraham Cowley, and John Dryden) than they do to the popularity or influence of Donne.

Even with these caveats, however, the uncollected verse printings do provide significant evidence of the extent and chronology of Donne's influence as well as of its literary and social elements. The continued presence of Donne verse surely reflects a judgment that such verse would enhance the volumes in which it was published whether through the prestige of his name or through the value to the reader of the verse itself. And the continued presence of Donne verse in many of the works in multiple editions reflects conscious decision rather than simple reprinting: in works like *A Helpe to Discovrse* and *The Academy of Complements*, the selections of Donne verse change from edition to edition, apparently because the compilers perceived changing interests in the potential readership or even a change in the readership itself. The picture of Donne that emerges from the printings and uses of his uncollected verse is of an individual talent very much a part of an entire culture, a truly "popular" poet.

The uncollected printings significantly enlarge Donne's early, late, and total print presence (and thus his influence) in the seventeenth century in England and on the Continent. As detailed above, Donne himself published thirteen more verses than editors have included in his canon and had a much larger and more consistent print presence during his lifetime and throughout the remainder of the seventeenth century than has previously been realized. Uncollected printings were particularly important to Donne's early print presence and possible influence because they introduced 38 of his poems to a print audience, an audience very different from the coterie with access to his manuscripts. Printings of uncollected verse also prove that Donne's influence in seventeenth-century Germany and the Netherlands was also both earlier and more extensive than hitherto thought. Donne's uncollected verse first appeared in Germany with the publication of the 1611 continental edition of Donne's Latin *Conclaue Ignati* in Hanau (Paul Sellin, *So Doth, So Is Religion: John Donne and Diplomatic Contexts in the Reformed Netherlands, 1619–1620*, p. 22). Weckherlin's translations (possibly made as early as 1615) into German of five Donne epigrams in his *Gaistliche und Weltliche Gedichte* were published in 1641, with a German adaptation of "A lame begger" added in the 1648 second edition. Even if Daley's caveats about Donne's direct influence on Dutch poetry are true, the uncollected printings strongly suggest an early and significant Donne influence in the Netherlands. Weckherlin published both editions of his *Gaistliche und Weltliche Gedichte* in Amsterdam. In 1655, Johann Grindal's *Aendachtige Bedenckengen* translated Donne's *Devotions vpon Emergent Occasions* for a Dutch audience, though Grindal did not translate "Insultus morbi primus" from the original Latin. The *Klioos Kraam* compiled by Rintjus printed translations of six Donne poems (likely done before 1626) into Dutch by Huygens, and the 1658 and 1672 editions of Huygens's *Koren-Bloemen* print eighteen complete and one partial Donne verse in Dutch.

Donne's extensive presence in uncollected printed verse suggests that he could have influenced not only a larger but also a more diverse audience in England than it has been possible to identify previously. The fifty-nine relatively certain Donne readers identified above are, predictably, the seventeenth-century cultural elite, the very persons Donne has always been thought to have influenced; however, even this elite audience has an unpredicted diversity. Of the essayists, poets, and dramatists who dominate this audience, only one (Henry Vaughan) of the fifteen poets would now be considered "Metaphysical," and four of the five dramatists wrote during the Restoration. The near absence of the clergy and the presence of so many compilers of verse miscellanies, translators, composers, and biographers also surprise. The biggest surprise, however, comes from enormously popular (in all senses of the word) uncollected printings that extend Donne's poetic influence beyond the "Metaphysical School," Oxford, Cambridge, and the Inns of Court to schoolboys who studied handbooks on the writing of poetry like Poole's *The English Parnassus* and to functionally illiterate farmers, "Would-be" ladies, Fopling Flutters, artisans, and so forth who turned to compilations of verse and prose offering them self-education for the betterment of their lives and a discourse for their thoughts and feelings—works like *A Helpe to Discovrse, Wits Recreations, The Academy of Complements, The Marrow of Complements, The Mirrour of Complements, The Philosophers Banqvet, Wit and Drollery,* and *Wits Interpreter*. The popularity of these self-help works implies that Donne's verse (and verse in general) had value for, and therefore influence on, a much greater range of Renaissance culture and society than one would expect from Donne's traditional elitist literary reputation. It may seem odd to think of Donne's verse as a model for schoolboys and the functionally illiterate lovelorn, but only an extraordinarily influential and popular poet could have generated Donne's monumental presence in manuscript and print.

How did Donne acquire this influence and what is its nature? Both Donne's literate and functionally illiterate audience, though they read Donne's verse in very different ways, valued it for the same quality—wit. Donne's uncollected verse suggests that his greatest influence upon seventeenth-century language, literature, and culture is his promulgation of the love of verbal wit, a joy in the combined capabilities of the mind and the English language. In "An Elegie upon the death of the Deane of Pauls, D^r. Iohn Donne," Thomas Carew crowned Donne *"The universall Monarchy of wit,"* a crown grudgingly restored by John Dryden in his prefatory letter to the earl of Abingdon (*"Doctor Donn the greatest Wit, though not the best Poet of our Nation"*) and lovingly polished by the great English literary critics of the succeeding centuries. When a seventeenth-century essayist needed a witty point, phrase, or image, he or she could turn to Donne. When a poet needed a witty line or stanza, he or she could turn to Donne. When a Restoration dramatist needed witty dialogue, he or she could turn to Donne. A compiler of verse miscellanies in search of "transcendent Wit" in the best English poets could turn to Donne. And for the very same things, so could a schoolboy, a farmer, an artisan, or a lovelorn adolescent. In fact, the contexts for many of the uncollected verses call attention to their wit: seventeen works printing Donne's uncollected verse have some form of the word "wit" on their title page,[26] and Chamberlain used Donne's "transcendent Wit" to argue the superiority of English poetry over that produced in Italy and France (Sullivan, sig. A3r–v).

The uncollected verse printings ultimately suggest that both Donne's fully literate and functionally illiterate audiences were influenced in the same way by Donne's verse. The wit in the verse had commercial, social, and personal value for both audiences:

26. The seventeen are: *The Odcombian Banqvet; Satyres: and Satyricall Epigram's; Certain Elegies, Done by Svndrie Excellent Wits; A Helpe to Discovrse; A Helpe to Memorie and Discovrse; Wits Recreations; Recreation for Ingenious Head-peeces; The Academy of Complements; The Mirrour of Complements;* the 1654 edition of *Merlinvs Anonymvs; The Harmony of the Muses; Wits Interpreter; Wit and Drollery; Parnassus Biceps; A Chain of Golden Poems . . . by Sr Aston Cokayn; A Theatre of Wits;* and *Virtus Rediviva.*

Donne's verse was like so many used bricks to be selected, cleaned, and rearranged for new purposes. Some of the fully literate audience valued the bricks more if enough of their original markings remained to identify their original use; others (who wanted the bricks mistaken for new) carefully eliminated such markings. The functionally illiterate doubtlessly discovered that they had easier access to Donne's verse than to the education that would have empowered them to make their own (though the educational nature of the works printed for this audience demonstrates that these readers very much wanted to make their own verse; and, if they used the materials as the compilers intended, they very well may have spoken or written Donne verse). The uncollected verses, then, establish that Donne had influence because his verse had value and a greater diversity of value for a greater diversity of users over a longer period than analysis of the manuscripts and collected editions would suggest. Ascertaining whether Donne's verse created a love of verbal wit that permeated language at every level of Renaissance society (as Gough's "Preface" to *The Academy of Complements* illustrates) or simply satisfied an already present demand may be impossible; however, Donne's seventeenth-century uncollected printed verse shows that Donne's influence on English Renaissance language, literature, society, and culture was larger than even the very great influence with which he is presently credited. Donne very nearly correctly placed his individual talent within the tradition when he wrote "I ame / The Trumpet, at whose voice the people came" ("The second Anniversarie," ll. 527–28); the uncollected printed verse shows that he was the voice of the people as well.

DONNE'S UNCOLLECTED SEVENTEENTH-CENTURY PRINTED VERSE

ENTRY FORMAT

Because the chief concern of the present study is to locate and analyze uncollected printings of Donne verse, the bibliographical descriptions of the items containing that verse are not as full as those in a critical edition or complete primary bibliography, though multiple copies of originals of all but unique works have been examined and attention has been given to distinguishing various states of the works.

Siglum. The siglum for each entry in the sequence of items containing verse by John Donne consists of the following: the date of publication from the title page or elsewhere within the volume, a number giving the item a position within the works published that year (arranged alphabetically by author), and a letter identifying the priority of the state of the work (capital letters identify states printed on large paper). Entries in this sequence may, in addition to Donne verse, contain translations and adaptations as well as dubia. Sigla for entries in the sequence of works containing translations but no Donne verse have a *T* preceding the date; sigla for entries containing adaptations but no Donne verse, an *A*; and sigla for entries containing dubia but no Donne verse, a *D*.

Author(s). The name(s) of the author(s), compiler(s), contributor(s), or translator(s) under which the work is usually cataloged are given.

Title. The title page of the specific copy described of the earliest printing of the work is transcribed diplomatically, with material printed in red placed within pointed brackets, < >.

Collation. The format, collation, and collational variants are given for the original leaves (many copies have had leaves added during rebinding) of the copy described. I have speculated about missing blank leaves (listed in the collational variants and followed by a question mark). The variants in the collation are listed less cryptically than is usual in critical editions.

STC or Wing. When possible, items in the entries are identified by their number in A. W. Pollard and G. R. Redgrave, eds., *A Short-Title Catalogue of Books Printed in England, Scotland, & Ireland and of English Books Printed Abroad 1475–1640*, or in Wing. When items in the entries have been described and assigned sigla in a standard bibliography, these sigla are also listed.

Copy. The location and shelfmark of the specific copy of the work chosen to serve as the exemplar for the bibliographical information and text are provided.

Separate title(s). Since many of the works cataloged were published in modular form so that parts could be (and frequently were) published separately, diplomatic transcriptions are provided of title pages appearing between the initial title page and the Donne verse.

Verse. The short title of the Donne verse, translation (short title begins with *T*), adaptation (short title begins with *A*), or dubium (short title begins with *D*) as well as the relevant line numbers for partial printings are provided.

Text. In the case of the fifteen verses not previously included in the Donne canon by his editors (the five Latin verses in *Conclaue Ignati*, seven English translations of verse in *Ignatius His Conclaue*, "Insultus morbi primus" in *Devotions vpon Emergent Occasions*, "Annae Georgii More de Filiae," and "Ioannes Donne Sac: Theol: Profess"), I provide the text and context of the verses in their original format from the described copy.

Additional seventeenth-century editions/issues. Each entry has a siglum; date (from title page if possible); STC, Wing, and standard bibliography sigla (if available); and page numbers (or signatures) of the text of the Donne verse. Items in additional entries receive a complete description when their priority and that of the item in the initial entry are uncertain and the items all represent possible first printings of the work. Later items also receive complete descriptions when the selection or source of the Donne verse, translation, adaptation, or dubium changes. When their priority is uncertain, items in additional entries that are not possible first printings of the work receive a diplomatic transcription of their title pages and any additional bibliographical detail necessary to distinguish the entries. When their STC, Wing, or standard bibliography sigla are ambiguous, items in additional entries have the library location and shelfmark of the copy examined.

Optional computer disks. A floppy disk (3.5 inch, double-sided, double-density, MS.DOS, ASCII) available by request from the author provides the immediate context (unless the Donne verse is a separate verse in a series of poems) and text of the Donne verse, translation, adaptation, or dubium quoted in the original format from the copy described or, for additional entries, the listed copy when the selection or possible source of the Donne verse changes. The original lineation, even of prose, has been preserved to provide a sense of how the authors integrated the Donne verse into their own material.

Works Containing Donne Verse

1607:1a

> Author: Thomas Dekker
> Title: A | KNIGHTS | Coniuring. | Done in earneſt: | Diſcouered in Ieſt. | By *Thomas Dekker*. | [printer's device] | LONDON, | Printed by *T. C.* for *VVilliam Barley*, and | *are to be ſolde at his Shop in* | Gratious ſtreete, | 1607.
> Collation: 4°. A–K⁴ L² ($3: A1, blank?, wanting; A2, title, un-signed; A4, signed; C4, signed; G3, missigned H3; I2, missigned H2; L2, wanting)
> STC: 6508
> Copy: CSmH 60147
> Verse:[1] "The Storme" (ll. 71–72), sig. B2

1. Earliest printing of any part of "The Storme."

1607:2a

> Author: Thomas Deloney
> Title: [ornament] | Strange Hiſtories, | OR | Songes and Sonets, of Kings, Princes, | Dukes, Lordes, Ladyes, Knights, | and Gentle-men. | Very pleaſant either to be read or ſonge: | and a moſt excel-lent warning | for all eſtates. | ornament | Imprinted at London for *W. Barley*, and | are to be ſold at his Shop in Gratious | ſtreete againſt S. Peters Church, | 1607.
> Collation: 8°. A–E⁸ ($4: A1, title, unsigned)[1]
> STC: 6567
> Copy: CSmH 60173
> Verse:[2] "A lame begger": sig. E6

1. Sheet B of the described copy was turned end for end during printing. The signatures run B1, B4, B3, B2; the leaves are in the following order: B1, B3v, B4, B2v, B3, B1v, B2, B4v, B5, B7v, B8, B6v, B7, B5v, B6, B8v.

2. Earliest printing of "A lame begger." No Donne verse occurs in the 1st and 3d eds. of 1602 (STC: 6566) and 1612 (STC: 6568). Mann notes that Deloney did not author the section of poems containing "A lame begger": "The edition of 1607 inserts *Salomon's Good Huswyfe* immediately after Canto I. and adds a number of miscellaneous poems after the prose *Speech betweene Certaine Ladyes. Salomon's Good Huswyfe* is added to *The Table* of contents, but the other poems are unindexed as though they were added haphazard by the printer as an afterthought. Most of these are

subscribed respectively with the initials T.R., A.C., and R., and with the exception of *The Death of Faire Rosamond* it is quite evident that Deloney's authentic work does not extend beyond the prose which closes the 1602 edition" (p. 585).

1607:3a

Author: Ben Jonson

Title: BEN: IONSON | his | VOLPONE | Or | THE FOXE. |—*Simul & iucunda, & idonea dicere vitæ.* | Printed for *Thomas Thorppe.* | 1607.

Collation: 4⁰. π¹ ¶⁴ A–N⁴ O² ($3: π1, title; A3, unsigned; K3, unsigned; 02, wanting, blank)

STC: 14783; Keynes: 69

Copy: CSmH 61886

Verse:[1] "Amicissimo et Meritissimo Ben Jonson," sig. A1

---

1. Earliest printing of "Amicissimo et Meritissimo Ben Jonson."

1609:1a

Author: Alfonso Ferrabosco

Title [within ornament]: AYRES: | BY | *Alfonſo Ferraboſco.* [swash *A*] | [ornament] | LONDON: | Printed by T. SNODHAM, for IOHN BROVVNE, | and are to be ſould at his ſhoppe in S. | Dunſtones Church-yard | in Fleetſtreet. | 1609.

Collation: 2⁰. *A*² B–I² K¹ χ² ($2: *A*1, title; χ1, blank; χ2, blank)

STC: 10827; Keynes: 69a

Copy: CSmH 59751

Verse:[1] "The Expiration," sig. C2v; "The Expiration" (l. 1), sig. K1v

---

1. Earliest printing of "The Expiration." For musical setting, see plate 1.

1609:2a

Author: Joseph Wybarne

Title [within single rules top and bottom, double rules along margins]: THE | NEW AGE | OF | OLD NAMES. | [rule] | By *Ioſ. Wib.* Maſter of Artes of Trinitie Colledge | in Cambridge. | [rule] | Ἱππον Ἀλέξανδρος προτίθεις κενταύριον ἴοις, | Ἀνερα δ᾿Ἱπποκράτης, οὐνομά τεσσι μαχή. | [rule] | [ornament] | [rule] |

VII.

O, fo, leaue off, this laft lamen- ting kiffe, which fucks two foules and vapours

both a- way, Turne thou ghoft that way, And let me turne this, and let our felues be-night our happy

day, we aske none leaue to loue, nor will we owe any fo cheape a death as

faying goe. We aske none leaue to loue, nor wil we owe a- ny fo cheape a death as faying goe.

Goe, goe, and if that word haue not quite kild thee,
Eafe me with death by bidding me goe to :
O, if it haue let my word worke on me,
And a iuft office on a murderer doe.
Except it be too late to kill me fo,
Being double dead, going and bidding goe.

PLATE 1. Musical setting of "The Expiration" (1609:1a). Reproduced by permission of The Huntington Library, San Marino, California.

LONDON | Printed for *William Barret*, and *Henry Fetherſtone*. | 1609.
Collation: 4°. A–S^4 ($3: A1, title, unsigned; S4, blank)
STC: 26055
Copy: CSmH 79887
Verse:[1] "Satyre IIII" (ll. 18–23), pp. 112–13

1. Earliest printing of any part of "Satyre IIII."

1611:1a

Author: Thomas Coryat

Title [engraved]: CORYATS | Crudities | *Hastily gobled vp in five | Moneths trauells in France, | Sauoy, Italy, Rhetia comonly | called the Grisons country, Hel= | uetia aliàs Switzerland, some | parts of high Germany, and the | Netherlands; | Newly digested in the hungry aire | of ODCOMBE in the County of | Somerset, & now dispersed to the | nourishment of the trauelling Mem= | bers of this Kingdome. | Quadrigis, pedibus benè viuere, nauibus atq | Gallia. Ger= mania. Italia.*

Second title [typeset, within single rules top and bottom, double rules in margins]: *THREE* [swash *R*] | CRVDE VEINES | ARE PRESENTED IN | This BOOKE following (beſides the fore- | ſaid CRVDITIES) no leſſe flowing in the | body of the BOOKE, then the CRVDITIES | *themſelues, two of* Rhetoricke and one | of POESIE. | That is to ſay, a moſt elegant Oration, firſt written | in the Latine tongue by HERMANNVS KIRCHNERVS, a | *Ciuill Lawyer, Oratour, Cæſarean Poet, and profeſſor of Elo-* | quence and Antiquities in the famous Vniuerſitie | of MARPVRG in the Langrauiat of Haſsia, in | praiſe of Trauell in generall. | Now diſtilled into Engliſh Spirit through the ODCOMBIAN | Limbecke. *This precedeth the CRVDITIES. Another alſo com-* | poſed by the Author of the former, in praiſe of Trauell of Germanie | *in particular, ſublimed and brought ouer the Helme in* | *the Stillitorie* of the ſaid Trauelling THOMAS: | This about the *Center* or *Nauell* of the | *CRVDITIES.* | Then in the Poſterne of them looke, and thou ſhalt find the | *Poſthume Poems of the Authors Father, comming as neere* | Kinſemen to the worke, being next of blood to the | Booke, and yonger brothers to the | Author himſelfe. | [rule] | LONDON, | *Printed by* VV.S. *Anno Domini* [swash *P, D*] | 1611.

Collation: 8°. π^2 a–b^8 ^{2}b^4 c–g^8 ($4: π1, engraved title; π2, typeset title, printed as 3E1; unsigned leaf printed as 3E2 between a3 and a4; ^{2}b3, unsigned; ^{2}b4, unsigned; f3, missigned F3) h–l^4 ($3: l3, unsigned) B–C^8 ($4) D^1 D^3 D–3C^8 ($4: D1, wanting; leaf with illustration between Z4 and Z5; leaf with illustration between 2L7

and 2L8; leaf with illustration between 2N8 and 2O1; 2X4, unsigned) 3D⁴ ($3) 3E² (3E1, missigned 3E3; 3E2, missigned 3E4)
    STC: 5808; Keynes: 70
    Copy: CLU-C *PR2237 C61
    Verse:[1] "Vpon Mr. Thomas Coryats Crudities," sigs. d3–4; "In eundem Macaronicon," sig. d4

---

    1. Earliest printing of "Vpon Mr. Thomas Coryats Crudities" and "In eundem Macaronicon."

1611:2a

    Author: Thomas Coryat
    Title: THE | ODCOMBIAN | BANQVET: | Diſhed foorth | BY | *THOMAS* THE *CORIAT*, [swash *C, R, A*] | AND | *Serued in by a number of Noble Wits* [swash *N*] | in prayſe of his | CRVDITIES *and* CRAMBE *too.* | ASINVS | PORTANS | MYSTERIA. | [ornament] | Imprinted for *Thomas Thorp.* | 1611.
    Collation: 4º. A–P⁴ ($3: A1, blank?, wanting; A2, title, unsigned; C4, signed)
    STC: 5810; Keynes: 70a
    Copy: CLU-C *PR2237 C62
    Verse: "Vpon Mr. Thomas Coryats Crudities," sigs. E2v–3v; "In eundem Macaronicon," sig. E4

1611:3a

    Author: John Donne
    Title [within ornament]: *AN* | ANATOMY | of the World. | WHEREIN, | BY OCCASION OF | the vntimely death of Miſtris | ELIZABETH DRVRY | the frailty and the decay | of this whole world | is repreſented. | [rule] | LONDON, | Printed for *Samuel Macham.* [swash *M*] | and are to be ſolde at his ſhop in | Paules Church-yard, at the | ſigne of the Bul-head. | AN. DOM. | 1611.
    Collation: 8º. A–B⁸ ($4: A1, wanting; A2, title, unsigned)
    STC: 7022; Keynes: 74
    Copy: CSmH 60189
    Verse:[1] "The first Anniversary," sigs. A5-B6; "A Funerall Elegie," sigs. B7–8v

Additional seventeenth-century editions:

1611:3b 1612

Title [within double rules]: *The First Anniuerſarie.* | AN | ANAT-OMIE | of the World. | *Wherein,* | BY OCCASION OF | *the vntimely death of Miſtris* | ELIZABETH DRVRY, | the frailtie and the decay of | this whole World is | repreſented. | [ornament] | LONDON, | Printed by *M. Bradwood* for *S. Macham,* and are | to be ſold at his ſhop in Pauls Church-yard at the | ſigne of the Bull-head. 1612.

Collation: 8°. A–H⁸ ($4: A1, title, unsigned; D8, blank; E1, separate title, unsigned; H6–8, wanting)

STC: 7023; Keynes: 75

Copy: CSmH 60180

Verse: "The first Anniversary," sigs. A5-D2v; "A Funerall Elegie," sigs. D3–7v

Separate title [within double rules]: *The Second Anniuerſarie.* | OF | THE PROGRES | of the Soule. | *Wherein:* | BY OCCASION OF THE | Religious Death of Miſtris | ELIZABETH DRVRY, | the incommodities of the Soule | *in this life and her exaltation in* | the next, are Contem- | *plated.* | [rule] | LONDON, | Printed by *M. Bradwood* for *S. Macham,* and are | to be ſould at his ſhop in Pauls Church-yard at | the ſigne of the Bull-head. | 1612.

Verse:² "The second Anniversarie," sigs. E5-H5

1611:3c 1621 (STC: 7024; Keynes: 76): sigs. A6-D3v, D4–8v, E5-H5

1611:3d 1625 (STC: 7025; Keynes: 77): sigs. A7-D4v, D5-E1v, E6-H6

---

1. Earliest printing of "The first Anniversary" and "A Funerall Elegie."
2. Earliest printing of "The second Anniversarie."

1611:4a

Author: John Donne

Title: [rule] | *Conclaue Ignati:* [swash *C, I*] | [rule] | Siue | EIVS IN NV- | PERIS INFERNI | COMITIIS | *Inthroniſatio.* [swash *I*] | Vbi varia | *De Ieſuitarum Indole,* | *De nouo inferno creando,* | *De Eccleſia Lunatica inſtituenda,* | per Satyram congeſta ſunt. | *Acceſsit & Apologia* [swash first *A, a*] | *pro Ieſuitis.* | Omnia | *Duobus Angelis Aduerſariis,* [swash *D*] | *qui Conſiſtorio Papali, & Col-* | legio Sorbonæ præſi- | dent, dedicata.

Collation: 12°. A–D¹² E⁶ ($5: A1, title, unsigned; A1v, blank; D5, unsigned; E5, unsigned; E6, blank)

STC: 7026;[1] Keynes: 2
Copy: CT C.11.161
Verse:[2] "Aversâ facie *Janum* referre"
Text:

> ANGELIS
> TVTELARIBVS,
> Consistorio Papali,
>   & Collegio Sorbonæ
>   *Præsidentibus.*
>
> N*Obilissimum par Ange-*
> *lorum,* ne nunquam vos
> conuenisse diceretur,
> semper autem vos mu-
> tuo abhorrere, & semper
>   *Auersâ facie Ianum referre,*
> his saltem in cartulis meis vos vni-
> re tentaui, non vt lites vestras com-
> ponam, nec enim à vobis in me
> compromissum est; sed vt de com-
> muni vobis inimico caueatis, quæ
> vidi referam.
>
>   (p. 1)

Verse:[3] "Operoso tramite scandent"
Text:

>   Supera cùm perlustras-
> sem omnia, tum sicuti
>   - *operoso tramite scandent*
> *Aethereum montem, tangens vicinia*
>   *solis,*
> *Hymnus ad Phœbi plectrum modula-*
>   *tur Alanda:*
> *Compressis velis, tandem vt reme-*
>   *aret, alarum,*
> *Tam subitò recidit, vt saxum segnius*
>   *ijsset.*
>
>   (pp. 2–3)

Verse: "Tanto fragore boatuque"
Text:

> Clamauit
> autem, intonuitque *Ignatius*
> > *Tanto fragore boatuque,*
> *Vt nec sulphureus puluis, quo tota*
> > *Britanna*
> *Insula, per nimbos Lunam volitasset*
> > *ad imam,*
> *Si cum substratus Cameræ, concepe-*
> > *rat ignem,*
> *Æquando fremeret nostro fragore*
> > *boatuque.*
> > > (p. 27)

Verse:[4] "Aut plumam, aut paleam, quae fluminis innatat ori"
Text:

> Vt autem
> aliquando videram
> *Aut plumam, aut paleam, quæ flumi-*
> > *nis innatat ori,*
> *Cùm ventum ad pontem fuerit, qua*
> > *fornice transit*
> *Angusto flumen, reijci tumide quere-*
> > *pelli;*
> *Duxerat at postquam choreas, atque*
> > *orbibus vndæ*
> *Luserat, à liquidis laqueis, & fauci-*
> > *bus hausta,*
> *Fluminis in gremium tandem cedit,*
> > *reditumque*
> *Desperat spectator scænæ;*
> Ita *Machiauellus* sæpe se erigens,
> sæpe repulsus, tandem euanuit Ego
> autem in facie vultuque *Luciferi*
> hærebam.
> > (pp. 60–61)

Verse:[5] "Qualis hesterno madefacta rore"
Text:

Ego autem ad corpus re-
deo, quod
Qualis hesterno madefacta rore,
Et nouo tandem tepefacta sole,
Excutit somnū, Tremulam Coronam
Erigit Herba,
Quæ prius languēs, recidens, recurua,
Osculum terræ dederat, Iubarque
Denegatum tamdiu, nunc refulgens
Solis anhelat.
(pp. 93–94)

Additional seventeenth-century edition:

1611:4b 1611?[6]

Title: CONCLAVE IGNATI: | Siue | EIVS IN NVPERIS | INFER-
NI COMITIIS | INTHRONISATIO. | *Vbi varia* [swash *v*] | De
Iefuitarum Indole, | De nouo inferno creando, | De Ecclefia Luna-
tica inftituēda, | *per Satyram congefta funt.* | ACCESSIT ET APOLO-
GIA | PRO IESVITIS. | Omnia | *Duobus Angelis Aduerfariis, qui Con-*
fiftorio Papali, & Collegio [swash 1st *A*] | *Sorbonæ præfident, dedicata.* |
[ornament]

Collation: 4°. A–D⁴ E² ($3: A1, title, unsigned; A1v, blank; E2,
unsigned)

STC: none; Keynes: 3

Copy: L C.110.f.46

Verse: "Aversâ facie *Janum* referre," p. 5; "Operoso tramite
scandent,"[7] p. 5; "Tanto fragore boatuque," p. 13; "Aut plumam,
aut paleam, quae fluminis innatat ori," p. 23; "Qualis hesterno
madefacta rore," p. 34

---

1. STC microfilm 7026 (reel 728) is actually the described copy of
1611:4b.

2. Earliest printing of "Aversâ facie *Janum* referre," "Operoso tramite
scandent," "Tanto fragore boatuque," "Aut plumam, aut paleam, quae
fluminis innatat ori," and "Qualis hesterno madefacta rore." Chambers
first recognized the verses in 1611:4a and 1611:5a and hypothesized that
they might be Donne's: "In this [1611:5a] the scraps of Latin verse which

appear in the other version [1611:4a] are translated, and I therefore give the renderings here, with their originals. . . . I have been unable to identify any of the Latin passages, except the second, which is of course the first of the well-known lines attributed to the Emperor Hadrian. Possibly the rest, which do not always scan, are of Donne's own writing" (2:312–14). Two Latin verses in *Conclaue Ignati* are not original with Donne: as noted by Chambers (2:314), "*Animula, vagula blandula, / Comes hospesque corporis*" (*Conclaue Ignati*, p. 1) is Emperor Hadrian's famous farewell to his soul; and Healy (p. 118) locates the verse line "*Parsque minor tantum tota valet integra quantum*" (*Conclaue Ignati*, p. 30) in Quaranta's *Summa Bullarii*.

3. Healy considers "Operoso tramite scandent" a verse adaptation by Donne: "Donne here puts into verse the description of the lark which Albertus Magnus gives in his *De Animalibus*, xxiii. 5: 'Alauda . . . cantat ascendendo per circulum volans, et cum descendit, primo quidem paulatim descendit, et tandem alas ad se convertens in modum lapidis subito decidit et in illo casu cantum dimittit'" (p. 103). Flynn argues that "Comparison of Donne's twenty-seven Latin words in five lines of verse to Albert's thirty words of Latin prose shows that they have only one word in common (i.e., "subito"), suggesting that Donne was not merely versifying Albert the Great" ("*Ignatius*," p. 182, n. 46). Actually, two words are identical: the errata list (sig. E5v) corrects "Hymnus" and "Alanda" to "Hymnos" and "Alauda."

4. Healy (p. 137) regards "Aut plumam, aut paleam, quae fluminis innatat ori" as Donne's and finds parallels with "Elegy: Oh, let mee not" (ll. 15–17) and "Satyre III" (ll. 103–8).

5. As Flynn ("*Ignatius*," n. 46) observes, "Qualis hesterno madefacta rore" is a translation of ll. 127–30 of Dante's *Inferno*, canto 2.

6. 1611:4b was printed at Hanau (Sellin, p. 22), but its publication date is unknown. Sellin identifies the printer as Thomas de Villiers and traces the route of the possible copy manuscript (pp. 21–23). Healy argues for the priority of 1611:4a (pp. xliii–xlv) but does not date 1611:4b. The format of the 1611:4b errata list (p. 35) strongly suggests that 1611:4a served as copy-text for 1611:4b.

7. The errata list (p. 35) corrects "Hymnus" and "Alanda" to "Hymnos" and "Alauda" in "Operoso tramite scandent."

1611:5a

Author: John Donne

Title [within single rules]: *Ignatius his Conclaue:* [swash *I, C*] | OR | His Inthroniſation in a late | Election in Hell: | Wherein many things are min- | *gled by way of Satyr;* | Concerning | *The Diſpoſition of Ieſuits,* [swash *D*] | *The Creation of a new Hell, (Moone.* | *The eſtabliſhing of a Church in the* [swash *C*] | There is alſo added an

Apology | *for Iefuites.* | All dedicated to the two Aduerfary | Angels, which are Protectors of the | Papall Confiftory, and of the | Colledge of Sorbon. | *Tranflated out ofLatine.* | *LONDON,* [swash D] | Printed by *N.O.* for *Richard More,* [swash M] | and are to be fold at his fhop in | S. Dunftones Church- | yard. 1611.

Collation: 12⁰. A–G¹² ($5: A1, blank, unsigned; A2, title, unsigned; D5, unsigned; G9r–v, blank; G10r–v, blank; G11r–v, blank; G12, second title; G12v, blank)

STC: 7027; Keynes: 4

Copy: L C.111.a.12

Verse:[1] "Resemble *Janus* with a diverse face," "My little wandering sportful soul"

Text:

TO THE TWO
Tutelar Angels, prote-
ctors of the Popes Consisto-
ry, and of the Colledge
of Sorbon.

MOST noble couple
of *Angels,* least it
should be sayd that
you did neuer a-
gree, and neuer
meet, but that you did euer ab-
horre one another, and euer
Resemble Ianus *with a diuerse face,*
I attempted to bring and ioyne
you together once in these papers; not that I might compose
your differences, for you haue
not chosen me for *Arbitrator;*
but, that you might beware of
an enemy cōmon to you both,
I will relate what I saw. I was
in an *Extasie,* and
My little wandring sportful Soule,
Ghest, and Companion of my body
had liberty to wander through
all places, and to suruey and
reckon all the roomes, and all

the volumes of the heauens, and
to comprehend the situation,
the dimensions, the nature, the
people, and the policy, both of
the swimming Ilands, the *Planets,* and of all those which are
fixed in the firmament.

(pp. 1–2)

Verse:[2] "The lark by busy and laborious ways"
Text:

When I had surueid al the Hea-
uens, then as
*The Larke by busie and laborious
     wayes,*
*Hauing climb'd vp th'eternall hill,
     doth raise*
His Hymnes to Phœbus *Harpe,
     And striking then*
*His sailes, his wings, doth fall downe
     backe agen*
So suddenly, that one may safely say
*A stone came lazily, that came that
     way,*
In the twinckling of an eye, I
saw all the roomes in Hell open
to my sight.

(pp. 3–4)

Verse: "With so great noise and horror"
Text:

Here *Ignatius* cried,
and thundred out,
*With so great noise and
     horror,*
*That had that powder taken fire, by
     which*
*All the Isle of Britaine had flowne
     to the Moone,*
*It had not equalled this noise and
     horror.*

(pp. 40–41)

Verse:[3] "That the least piece which thence doth fall"
Text:

> It had beene
> "reason, that they should first
> "haue exercised their force
> "vpon those verses, and so
> "haue purged and deliuered
> "them, if not from Heresie,
> "yet from Barbarousnesse, and
> "*solæcismes*; that Heretiques
> "might not iustly say, there
> "was no truth in any of them,
> "but onely the last; which
> "is,
> "*That the least peece which thēce*
>   *doth fall,*
> "*Will doe one as much good as all.*
>   (p. 46)

Verse: "Feathers or straws swim on the water's face"
Text:

> But as I had sometimes
> obserued
> *Feathers or strawes swimme on the*
>   *waters face,*
> *Brought to the bridge, where*
>   *through a narrow place*
> *The water passes, throwne backe,*
>   *and delai'd;*
> *And hauing daunc'd a while, and*
>   *nimbly plai'd*
> *Vpon the watry circles, Then haue*
>   *bin*
> *By the streames liquid snares, and*
>   *iawes, suck'd in*
> *And suncke into the wombe of that*
>   *swolne bourne,*
> *Leaue the beholder desperate of*
>   *returne:*

So I saw *Machiauel* often put
forward, and often thrust back,
and at last vanish.

(p. 91)

Verse:[4] "As a flower wet with last night's dew, and then"
Text:

And I returned to my
body; which
As a flower wet with last nights
  dew, and then
Warm'd with the new Sunne, doth
  shake of agen
All drowsinesse, and raise his trem-
  bling Crowne,
Which crookedly did languish, and
  stoope downe
To kisse the earth, and panted now
  to finde
Those beames return'd, which had
  not long time shin'd,
was with this returne of my
soule sufficiently refreshed.

(pp. 142–43)

The L copy (shelfmark: C.111.a.12) has an additional, earlier
title page (Keynes: 5) on sig. G12. This earlier title page contains
many errors and seems never to have been used in a published
copy:

Title [within decorative border]: *Ignatius his Conclaue:* [swash *I*,
C] | OR | His Inthroniſation in a late | Election in Hell: | Wherein
many things are min- | *gled by way of Satyr;* | Concerning | *The
Diſpoſition of ſuits,* [swash *D*] | *The Creation of a new Hell, (Moone.* |
The eſtabliſhing of a Church in the [swash *C*] | There is alſo added an
Apology | *for Ieſuites.* | All dedicated to the two Aduer- | ſary
Angels, which are Protectors | of the Papall Conſiſtory, and of | the
Colledge of Sorbon. | [rule] | *LONDON,* [swash *D*] | Printed by
N.O. for *Richard More,* | and are to be ſold at his ſhop | in
S. Dunſtones Church- | yard. 1611.

The CSmH copy (shelfmark: 60176) has a loose, laid-in, photo-
graphic copy of the modern title page created for the W. A. White
copy (formerly Keynes: 6) of 1611:5a now at Harvard.

Additional seventeenth-century editions:

1611:5b 1626 (STC: 7028; Keynes: 7): pp. 1–2, 3–4, 40–41, 46, 91, 142–43

1611:5c 1634 (STC: 7029; Keynes: 8): pp. 1–2, 3, 38, 43–44, 86–87, 134–35

1611:5d 1635 (STC: 7030; Keynes: 9): pp. 1–2, 3, 38, 43–44, 86–87, 134–35

---

1. Earliest printing of "Resemble *Janus* with a diverse face," "My little wandering sportful soul," "The lark by busy and laborious ways," "With so great noise and horror," "That the least piece which thence doth fall," "Feathers or straws swim on the water's face," and "As a flower wet with last night's dew, and then." "*Resemble . . . face*" is Donne's translation of "Aversâ facie *Janum* referre"; "*My . . . body*" is Donne's translation of Emperor Hadrian's verse farewell to his soul: "*Animula, vagula blandula, / Comes hospesque corporis*" (1611:4a, p. 1).

2. For discussion of whether Donne's Latin was original, see 1611:4a, n. 3. The errata list (sig. G8) corrects "eternall" to "etheriall."

3. Donne's verse translates a Latin verse from Quaranta (see 1611:4a, n. 2).

4. "As a flower wet with last night's dew, and then" ultimately derives from Dante's *Inferno;* see 1611:4a, n. 5.

1612:1a

Author: William Corkine

Title [within ornament]: THE | SECOND BOOKE | OF | AYRES, | Some, to Sing and Play to the | Baſe-Violl alone: | Others, to be ſung to the Lute and | Baſe Violl. | VVith new Corantoes, Pauins, Almaines; | as alſo diuers new Deſcants vpon old Grounds, | ſet to the Lyra-Violl. | By *William Corkine.* [swash C, k] | *LONDON:* [swash N, N] | Printed for *M. L. I. B.* and *T. S.* | Aſſigned by *W. Barley.* | 1612.

Collation: 2°. A–I² ($2: A1, title, unsigned; C2, unsigned)

STC: 5769; Keynes: 71

Copy: CSmH 13571

Verse:[1] "Breake of day," sig. B1v; "The Baite" (l. 1), sig. G2v; "Breake of day" (l. 1), sig. I2v; "The Baite" (l. 1), sig. I2v

---

1. Earliest printing of "Breake of day" (musical setting, plate 2) and any part of "The Baite" (musical setting, plate 3).

PLATE 2. Musical setting of "Breake of day" (1612:1a). Reproduced by permission of The Huntington Library, San Marino, California.

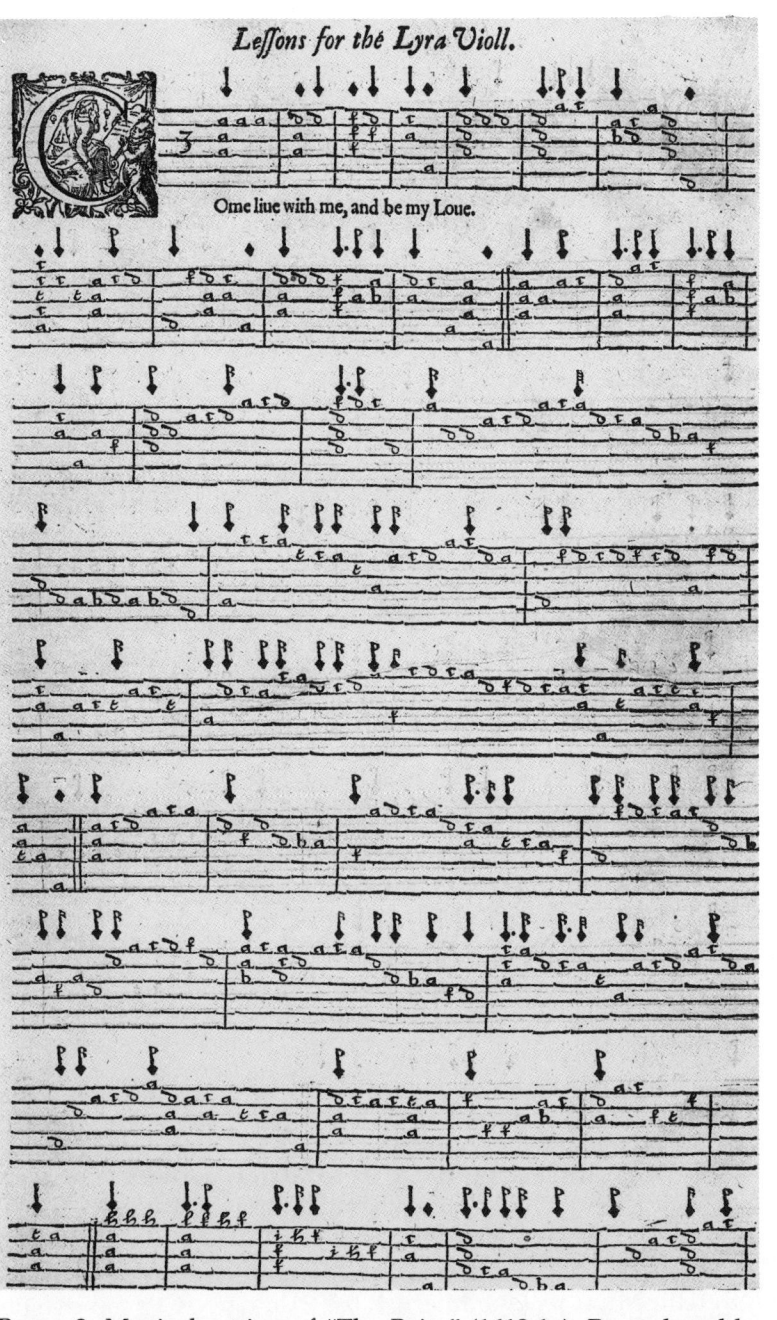

PLATE 3. Musical setting of "The Baite" (1612:1a). Reproduced by permission of The Huntington Library, San Marino, California.

1613:1a
Author: Josuah Sylvester
Title [within double rules, xylographic]:[1] [crest of Prince of Wales] | Lachrymæ Lachrymarū. | or | *The Spirit of Teares*, [swash *f*] | Distilled | *for the vn-tymely Death* [swash *D*] | *of* | The incomparable Prince, | *PANARETVS.* [swash [*P*] | *by Iosuah Syluester.* | The third Edition, | *with Addition of His Owne.* | [double rule] | *and* | other Elegies.
Collation: 4°. A–C⁴ C–D⁴ D–I⁴ ($2: A1, title, unsigned; C2, unsigned; C-D2, unsigned; D1, separate title, unsigned; D3, signed; F2, unsigned; F3, signed; G3, signed; H1, separate title, unsigned; H3, signed)
STC: 23578; Keynes: 72; Case:[2] 41(c)
Copy: LU [D.-L.L.] (XVII) Bc [Sylvester] S.R.
Separate title: SIX | FUNERAL | ELEGIES, | *ON THE VNTIMELY* [swash *N, T, N, T, E, Y*] | Death of the moſt ex- | cellent PRINCE, | HENRY, | *Late,* PRINCE *of* WALES. | Compoſed by ſeuerall | AVTHORS. | [rule] | [ornament] | [rule] | 1613. | [rule]
Cancel separate title: SVNDRY | FVNERAL | ELEGIES, | *ON THE VNTIMELY* [swash *N, T, N, T, Y*] | Death of the moſt ex- | cellent PRINCE, | HENRY; | *Late,* PRINCE *of* VVALES. | Compoſed by ſeuerall | AVTHORS. | [rule] | [ornament] | [rule] | 1613.
Verse:[3] "Elegie upon the untimely death of the incomparable Prince Henry," sigs. E1–2v
Examination of multiple copies of the 1613 second edition shows that it went through at least the following states (though not necessarily in the order listed here): (1) the initial conception of the edition as comprising Sylvester's elegy "Lachrimæ Lachrimarvm" from the 1612 first editions plus six additional elegies on Prince Henry; (2) sheet B was reset; (3) sheet C was reset; (4) the original "Six" elegies title page (sig. D1) was canceled and sheet C-D with a "Svndry" elegies title page (sig. C-D3) was inserted after original sheet C (the described LU copy has both the original and the cancel title page); (5) sig. C-D4v was reset to reflect the cancel of the original separate title on sig. D1; (6) the outer forme of sheet G was reset; and (7) sheets H and I, containing a separate title page dated 1613 for an additional elegy by Sylvester on the death of Sir William Sidney, were added. Sheet E, containing "Elegie upon the untimely death of the incomparable Prince Henry," has not been reset in any of the examined copies, though the MR copy (shelfmark: R37802) and two CtY copies (shelfmarks: Ig Sy57 612Lc and Ig Sy57 612Ld) have sheet E3 signed

whereas the other examined copies do not; however, the typesetting of the MR and CtY copies is identical to that in all other examined copies—perhaps the unnecessary signing was removed in a stop-press correction or happily fell out.

STC distinguishes by number only two of the above states: 23577.5 has the "earlier" state of sheet B or C or both; 23578 has the "later" sheet of both. The priority of the settings of sheet B is uncertain; however, the correction of "happies" to "harpies" (sig. B3, l. 7) and "aud" to "and" (sig. B, l. 9) in the version with "oftentymes" (rather than "oftentimes") in the last line of sig. B3 would seem to be the resetting, contrary to the priority assigned by the STC. Even so, STC numbers assigned to any copies below are on the basis of the STC criteria of the readings in sheets B and C.

The examined copies are composites of the evolutionary states described above. I have selected the LU copy as the described copy primarily because it is perhaps the only extant copy with the canceled separate title leaf, D1, that embodies Sylvester's original conception of six additional elegies.[4] I have selected other copies as examples of the various states when they possessed the dominant characteristic of that state even though they, too, are composites; and, when the chronological order of the states cannot be determined, I have ordered the states in the order of the revised sheets. For all states and issues, the typesetting and text of the Donne verse are identical to that in 1613:1a.

Additional seventeenth-century states/issues:

1613:1b 1613 (STC: 23578. DFo, shelfmark: STC 23578.2): sigs. E1–2v

This copy has the uncorrected state of the title page (corrected by a stop-press correction in all other examined copies) characterized by omission of the comma after "Prince" (l. 6) and "*Ow.*" for "*Owne.*" (l. 10) and lacks sheets H and I.

1613:1c 1613 (STC: 23578. ICN, shelfmark: Case Y 185.S 9993): sigs. E1–2v

This state has the probably earlier setting of sheet B characterized by sig. B3 last line "oftentimes."

1613:1d 1613 (STC: 23577.5. CtY, shelfmark: Ig Sy57 612Ld): sigs. E1–2v

This state has the probable resetting of sheet B characterized by sig. B3 last line "oftentymes."

1613:1e 1613 (STC: 23577.5. MC, shelfmark: J.1.39): sigs. E1–2v
This state has the earlier setting of sheet C characterized by sig.
C1 catchword "Weepe."

1613:1f 1613 (STC: 23578. CtY, shelfmark: Ig Sy57 612Lc): sigs.
E1–2v
This state has the resetting of sheet C characterized by sig. C1
catchword "Weep."

1613:1g 1613 (STC: 23578. DFo, shelfmark: STC 23578 copy 4): sigs.
E1–2v
This state lacks leaf D1, replacing it with sheet C-D and a new
separate title page on sig. C-D3 reading "SVNDRY FVNERAL ELE-
GIES," and has the earlier setting of sheet C-D characterized by
the omission of a catchword on sig. C-D4v and the uncorrected
reading "*Should I not not my Treasure* tell" in l. 5 of "An Epitaph" (sig.
C-D4v).

1613:1h 1613 (STC: 23578. DFo, shelfmark: STC 23578 copy 1): sigs.
E1–2v
This state lacks leaf D1, replacing it with sheet C-D and a new
separate title page on sig. C-D3 reading "SVNDRY FVNERAL ELE-
GIES," but has the resetting of sheet C-D characterized by the
catchword "I. *ELEGIE*" on sig. C-D4v (added to accommodate the
cancellation of D1) and the corrected reading "*Should I not my
Treasure* tell" in l. 5 of "An Epitaph" (sig. C-D4v).

1613:1i 1613 (STC: 23577.5. MH, shelfmark: STC 21652
[14455.35.17*]): sigs. E1–2v
This copy has the earlier setting of sheet G characterized by G1
and G3 missigned F1 and F3 as well as by the last line of sig. G3
beginning "In whom all Grace."

1613:1j 1613 (STC: 23577.5. MR, shelfmark: R37802): sigs. E1–2v
This copy has the resetting of sheet G characterized by correct
signing and the last line of sig. G3 beginning "In whom thou
mightst."

---

1. The examined copies of *Lachrymæ Lachrymarū* have lost text to trim-
ming either at the right edge or bottom of their title pages; the present
description is a composite of copies having the corrected state of the title
page (for the uncorrected state, see 1613:1b).

2. Arthur E. Case, *A Bibliography of English Poetical Miscellanies, 1521–1750.*

3. Earliest printing of "Elegie upon the untimely death of the incomparable Prince Henry." The colophon reads "LONDON | Printed by *Humfrey Lownes.* | 1613." (sig. I4). No Donne verse occurs in the 1st and 2d eds. of 1612 (STC: 23576, 23577).

4. According to John Philip Edmond, "Elegies and Other Tracts Issued on the Death of Henry, Prince of Wales, 1612," in *Papers of the Edinburgh Bibliographical Society, 1901–1904* (Edinburgh, 1906), the original separate title leaf D1 also occurs in "A copy formerly in the libraries of Mr Thos. Gaisford and Mr John Scott, and now in the possession of Mr George P. Johnston" (p. 156).

1614:1a

Author:[1] Michael Scott

Title: *THE* | PHILOSOPHERS | BANQVET. | [rule] | NEWLY | *FVRNISHED AND DECKED* | forth with much variety of many ſeuerall | Diſhes, that in the former Seruice | were neglected. | [rule] | Where now not onely Meates and Drinks of | *all Natures and Kindes are ſerued in, but the* | Natures and Kindes of all diſputed of. | [rule] | *As further,* | Dilated by Table-conference, Alteration, and | Changes of States, Diminution of the Sta- | ture of Man, Barren- | neſſe of the Earth, with the ef- | fectes and cauſes thereof, Phi- | ſically and | Philoſophically. | [rule] | *The ſecond Edition,* | Newly | corrected and inlarged, to almoſt as | much more. By *W. B.* Eſquire. | [rule] | *LONDON,* | Printed by *T. C.* for LEONARD BECKET, | and are to bee ſolde at his ſhoppe in the | Temple, neere the Church. | 1614.

Collation: 8°. A⁸ *⁴ B–R⁸ S⁴ ($4: A1, title, unsigned; C5, signed; D5, signed; E5, signed; F5, signed; G5, signed; H5, signed; Q5, blank; S4, unsigned)

STC:[2] 22062

Copy: CSmH 59403

Verse: "The first Anniversary" (ll. 127–30, 133–44), pp. 124–25; "The first Anniversary" (ll. 343–44), p. 204

Additional seventeenth-century edition:

1614:1b 1633

Title: THE | PHILOSOPHERS | BANQVET. | Newly | *Furniſhed and decked forth* [swash *k*] | with much variety of many ſe- | verall Diſhes, that in the former | Service were neglected. | Where now not only Meats and | Drinks of all Natures and Kinds are | ſerued

in, but the Natures and Kinds | *of all difputed of.* | *As further,* |
Dilated by Table-conference, alteration | and Changes of States,
Diminution of the | Stature of Man, Barrenneffe of the Earth, | *with*
the effects and caufes thereof, | Phifically and Philofophically. | *The*
third Edition. | Newly corrected and inlarged, to almoft as | much
more. By W.B. Efquire. | [double rule] | LONDON: | Printed for
Nicholas Vavafour, and are to [swash N] | bee fold at his fhop in the
Temple, | neere the Church. 1633.

Collation: 12°. A–Q¹² R⁶ ($5: A1, title, unsigned; K3, unsigned;
R4, unsigned; R5, unsigned)

STC: 22063

Copy: CLU-C *RM215 M54E 1633

Verse: "The first Anniversary" (ll. 127–30, 133–44), pp. 138–39;
"The first Anniversary" (ll. 343–44), pp. 223–24; "The first Anniversary" (ll. 121–22, 143–44), p. 340; "The second Anniversarie"
(ll. 221–23, 181–82), pp. 345–46

---

1. 1614:1a is a translation into English and enlargement by "W: B.
Esquire" (probably William Basse; see Introduction, above, n. 21) of Michael Scott's Latin *Mensa Philosophica.*

2. The 1609 1st ed. (STC: 22061.5) lacks Donne verse.

1616:1A

Author: Ben Jonson

Title [engraved]: THE | WORKES | OF | *Beniamin Jonson.* |
—*neque, me vt miretur turba,* | *laboro:* | *Contentus paucis lectoribus.* |
Imprinted at | *London by* | *Will Stansby* | *Anᵒ D. 1616.*

Collation: 2°. ¶⁶ A–4P⁶ 4Q⁴ ($3: ¶1, title, unsigned; ¶2, portrait,
unsigned; A1, separate title, unsigned; G1, separate title, unsigned; 3E1, separate title, unsigned; 3E3, missigned 2E3; 3L3,
missigned 3K3; 4B1, separate title, unsigned; 4D3, separate title,
unsigned; 4F2, separate title, unsigned)¹

STC: 14751

Copy: CSmH 62101

Verse: "Amicissimo et Meritissimo Ben Jonson," sig. ¶6

Large-paper (324 × 214 mm) issue of vol. 1, 1st ed.

Additional seventeenth-century editions/issues:

1616:1a 1616 (STC: 14751. CSmH, shelfmark: 62104): sig. ¶6

Small-paper (273 × 178 mm) issue. The title pages of 1616:1A
and 1616:1a are identical; however, the case on sig. ¶6 has been

loosened on the right margin to allow the insertion of "*Vpon Seian-nus.*", "*In Vulponem.*", and "*In Vulponem.*" in the right margin alongside the appropriate commendatory poem. The setting of the text of "Amicissimo et Meritissimo Ben Jonson" was undisturbed. "*In Vulponem,*" thus, is not properly part of the heading of "Amicissimo et Meritissimo Ben Jonson": the four other congratulatory poems on sigs. ¶6r–v related to specific plays that do not identify the relevant play in their headings have been similarly tagged in the margin of this copy. The CSmH (shelfmark: 62101) and L (shelfmark: G.11630) copies of 1616:1A lack the marginalia on sig. ¶6.

1616:1b 1616 (STC: 14751. TxU, shelfmark: Ah J738 +B616a): sig. ¶6

Title [engraved]: THE | WORKES | OF | *Beniamin Jonson.* | _neque, me vt miretur turba,_ | *laboro:* | *Contentus paucis lectoribus.* | LONDON | *Printed by* | *William* | *Stanfby.* | *An° D. 1616.*

Collation: 2°. ¶⁶ A–4P⁶ 4Q⁴ ($3: ¶1, blank, unsigned; ¶2, title, unsigned; A1, separate title, unsigned; G1, separate title, unsigned; 3E1, separate title, unsigned; 3E3, missigned 2E3; 3L3, missigned 3K3; 4B1, separate title, unsigned; 4D3, separate title, unsigned; 4F2, separate title, unsigned)

Small-paper (286 × 183 mm) issue of vol. 1, 1st ed., 2d issue. The text of "Amicissimo et Meritissimo Ben Jonson" is identical to that in 1616:1A.

1616:1C 1616 (STC: 14752. TxU, shelfmark: Ah J738 +B616ab): sig. ¶6

Title [engraved]: THE | WORKES | OF | *Beniamin Jonson.* | _neque, me vt miretur turba,_ | *laboro:* | *Contentus paucis lectoribus.* | LONDON | *printed by W:* | *Stansby, and are* | *to be fould by* | *Rich: Meighen.* | *An° D. 1616.*

Large-paper (330 × 200 mm) issue of vol. 1, 1st ed., 3d issue. The text of "Amicissimo et Meritissimo Ben Jonson" is identical to that in 1616:1A.

1616:1c 1616 (STC: 14752. CSmH, shelfmark: 62100): sig. ¶6

Small-paper (284 × 177 mm) issue of vol. 1, 1st ed., 3d issue. This copy lacks the marginalia on sig. ¶6, and the text of "Amicissimo et Meritissimo Ben Jonson" is identical to that in 1616:1A.

The priority of 1616:1A, 1616:1a, 1616:1b, 1616:1C, and 1616:1c is uncertain: W. W. Greg, in *A Bibliography of the English Printed*

Drama to the Restoration, discusses the variant issues of vol. 1, 1st ed., and conjectures their order (3:1071–73).

1616:1D 1640 (STC: 14753. C, shelfmark: Syn.2.64.1): sig. A5v
Large-paper (345 × 225 mm) issue of vol. 1, 2d ed.

1616:1d 1640 (STC: 14753. O, shelfmark: Don.d.65): sig. A5v
Small-paper (284 × 180 mm) issue of vol. 1, 2d ed. The text of "Amicissimo et Meritissimo Ben Jonson" is identical to that in 1616:1D.

1616:1e 1640
Title [within double rules]: BARTHOLMEW | FAYRE: | A COM-EDIE, | ACTED IN THE | YEARE, 1614. | By the Lady *ELIZABETHS* [swash *B*] | Servants. | And then dedicated to King IAMES, of | *moſt Bleſſed Memorie;* [swash *B, M, third e*] | [rule] | By the Author, Beniamin Iohnson. | [rule] | *Si foret in terris, rideret* Democritus: *nam* | *Spectaret populum ludis attentiùs ipſis,* | *Vt ſibi præbentem, mimo ſpectacula plura.* | *Scriptores autem narrare putaret aſſello* | *Fabellam ſurdo.* Hor. lib. 2. Epiſt. 1. | [ornament] | [rule] | *LONDON,* [swash *N, D, N*] | Printed by *I.B.* for Robert Allot, and are [swash *B*] | to be ſold at the ſigne of the *Beare,* in *Pauls* | Church-yard. 1631.

Collation: 2°. A⁶ B–Y⁴ 2A–2H⁴ 2I⁶ ($3: A1, blank; A2, title, unsigned; D3, unsigned; N1, separate title, unsigned; X3, unsigned; 2C3, missigned C3; 2D–2H, missigned D1, D2, D3, E1, etc.; 2I1–3, missigned I1–3; 2I4, missigned I4) *A–K⁴ L² M–R⁴ A–P⁴ Q² R–V⁴ B–Q⁴ R² S–X⁴ Y² Z–2O⁴ 2P² 2Q⁴* ($2: *A*1, separate title, unsigned; *C*2, missigned C2; *C*3, signed; *G*2, missigned G2; *M*1, separate title, unsigned; *N*1, missigned N1; *R*1, missigned R1; *R*2, missigned R2; *A*1, separate title, unsigned; *I*1, separate title, unsigned; *Q*2, unsigned; *R*1, separate title, unsigned; ²*B*3, signed; ²*C*1, separate title, unsigned; ²*R*2, unsigned; *Y*2, unsigned; *Z*1, separate title, unsigned; 2*B*2, missigned B2; 2*P*2, unsigned; 2*Q*2, separate title, unsigned)
STC: 14754
Copy: O Gibson 518
Separate title: [double rule] | UNDER-WOODS. | CONSISTING OF | DIVERS | *POEMS.* [swash *P*] | [rule] | *By* [swash *B*] | Ben. Iohnson. | [rule] | Martial—*Cineri, gloria ſera venit.* | [rule] | LON-DON. | [rule] | Printed M. DC. XL. | [rule]
Verse:² "Elegy: The Expostulation," pp. 204–6
Small-paper (287 × 187 mm) issue with initial blank in place of general title of combined 1st ed. of vols. 2 and 3.³

Sorting out the publication history of the "second" and "third" volumes of Jonson's *Works* is currently impossible: as Greg notes, "The various forms in which appear what are here called the second and third volumes of Jonson's works, those namely that were first printed between 1631 and 1641, are so complicated that no formal treatment can be altogether satisfactory" (3:1074). I follow the overall classification of these forms discussed by Greg (3:1074–82). The true 1st ed. of vol. 2 contains only *Bartholomew Fayre*, *The Staple of Newes*, and *The Divell is an Asse*—all with title pages dated 1631. Vol. 3, 1st ed., consists of *The Magnetick Lady*, *A Tale of a Tub*, *The Sad Shepherd*, several masques, "Vnder-woods" (containing "Elegy: The Expostulation"), entertainments, "Horace, his Art of Poetrie," "The English Grammar," and "Timber: or, Discoveries." Vol. 2, 1st ed., can occur independently (as in the O copy [shelfmark: Gibson 519][4] and four TxU copies [shelfmarks: Ah J738 +B641 copies 2, 3, 4, and 5]) or even bound up with vol. 1, 1st ed. (as in the TxU large-paper copy [shelfmark: Ah J738 +B616ab]). Vol. 3, 1st ed., also appears independently (see 1616:1I and 1616:1i below). As Greg observes, however, "No doubt the second and third are usually found bound together, and most bibliographers have treated them as one" (3:1075); thus, I have assigned entries (as does Greg) to bibliographically significant combinations of vols. 2 and 3, 1616:1e through 1616:1h.

1616:1F 1640 (STC: 14754. CSmH, shelfmark: 62101, vol. 2): pp. 204–6
Title [within double rules]: THE | VVORKES | OF | *BENJAMIN JONSON*. [swash *B, N, J, N, J, N, N*] | [rule] | The *ſecond Volume*. | [rule] | CONTAINING | THESE PLAYES, | *Viz.* [swash *z*] | 1 Bartholomew Fayre. | 2 The Staple of Newes. | 3 The Divell is an Aſſe. | [rule] | [ornament] | [rule] | *LONDON*, [swash *N, D, N*] | Printed for RICHARD MEIGHEN. | 1640.
Collation: 2°. A⁶ B–Y⁴ 2A–2C⁴ ²D–²H⁴ ²I⁶ ($3: A1, general title, unsigned; A2, separate title, unsigned; D3, unsigned; N1, separate title, unsigned; X3, unsigned; 2C3, missigned C3; ²I4, signed) A–P⁴ Q² R–V⁴ ²B–²Q⁴ ²R² ²S–²X⁴ ²Y² ²Z–²²O⁴ ²²P² ²²Q⁴ A–K⁴ L² M–R⁴ ($2: A1, separate title, unsigned; I1, separate title, unsigned; Q2, unsigned; R1, separate title, unsigned; ²B3, signed; ²C1, separate title, unsigned; ²R2, unsigned; ²Y2, unsigned; ²Z1, separate title, unsigned; ²2B2, missigned ²B2; ²2P2, unsigned; ²2Q2, separate title, unsigned; A1, separate title, unsigned; C2, missigned C2; C3, missigned G2; M1, separate title, unsigned; N1, missigned N1)

Large-paper (324 × 214 mm) issue of the combined vols. 2–3, 1st ed., with general title page. The text of "Elegy: The Expostulation" is identical to that in 1616:1e.

1616:1f 1640 (STC: 14754. TxU, shelfmark: Ah J738 +B641): pp. 204–6
Small-paper (284 × 183 mm) issue of the combined vols. 2–3, 1st ed., with general title page. The text of "Elegy: The Expostulation" is identical to that in 1616:1e.

1616:1g 1640/1641 (STC: 14754. LG, shelfmark: Bay H.7.5 n. 23): pp. 204–6
Small-paper (281 × 185 mm) reissue of 1616:1e. This issue lacks a general title page and has the 1631 title pages for *Bartholomew Fayre* and *The Staple of Newes* but a 1641 title page for *The Divell is an Asse*. The text of "Elegy: The Expostulation" is identical to that in 1616:1e.

1616:1h 1641 (STC: 14754a. TxU, shelfmark: Ah B738 +B641 cop. 9): pp. 204–6
Title: THE DIVELL | IS | AN ASSE. | [rule] | A COMEDIE | ACTED IN THE | YEARE, 1616. | *BY HIS MAJESTIES* [swash *B, Y, M, J*] | Servants. | [rule] | The Author Ben: Iohnson. | [rule] | Hor. de Art. Poet. | *Fucta voluptatis Cauſa, ſint proxima veris.* [swash *v, C, v*] | [ornament] | [rule] | Imprinted at London, 1641.
Small-paper (288 × 188 mm) issue without a general title page and consisting of the 1641 *The Divell is an Asse* (without *Bartholomew Fayre* and *The Staple of Newes*) and vol. 3.[5] The text of "Elegy: The Expostulation" is identical to that in 1616:1e.

1616:1I 1641 (CK, shelfmark: Keynes collection, C.S.14): pp. 204–6
Large-paper (321 × 218 mm) copy of vol. 3 by itself with no general title page and in a contemporary binding. Vol. 3 is not distinguished by Wing. The text of "Elegy: The Expostulation" is identical to that in 1616:1e. The title page, collation, and contents are given below as relevant to Greg's conjecture that a general title page and unknown additional materials might have been intended for vol. 3 (3:1079 and n. 2, p. 1080).[6]
Title: THE | MAGNETICK | LADY: | *OR,* [swash *R*] | HVMORS | RECONCIL'D. | [rule] | A COMEDY compoſed | *By* [swash *B*] | Ben: Iohnson. | *Iam lapides ſuus ardor agit ferrumq; tenetur,* | *Illecebris.*——Claud. de Magnet. | [rule] | LONDON, | [rule] | Printed M. CD. XL. | [rule]

Collation: 2°. A–P⁴ Q² R–V⁴ ²B–²Q⁴ ²R² ²S–²X⁴ ²Y² ²Z⁴ 2A–2O⁴ 2P² 2Q⁴ A–K⁴ L² M–R⁴ ($2: A1, title, unsigned; I1, separate title, unsigned; Q2, unsigned; R1, separate title, unsigned; ²B3, signed; ²C1, separate title, unsigned; ²R2, unsigned; ²Y2, unsigned; ²Z1, separate title, unsigned; 2B2, missigned B2; 2P2, unsigned; 2Q2, separate title, unsigned; A1, separate title, unsigned; C2, missigned C2; C3, signed; G2, missigned G2; M1, separate title, unsigned; N1, missigned N1; R1, missigned R1; R2, missigned R2)

Contents: (1) *THE MAGNETICK LADY*, A1 (2) *A TALE OF A TUB*, I1 (3) *THE SAD SHEPHERD*, R1 (4) *CHRISTMAS HIS MASQUE*, ²B1 (5) *A Masque PRESENTED IN THE HOUSE OF THE RIGHT HONORABLE THE Lord Haye*, ²C1 (6) *THE VISION OF DELIGHT*, ²C4v (7) *PLESURE RECONCILED TO VERTUE*, ²D3v (8) *FOR THE HONOUR OF WALES*, ²E3v (9) *NEWES FROM THE NEVV VVORLD*, ²F4 (10) *A MASQUE OF THE METAPORPHOS'D GYPSIES*, ²G4 (11) *THE MASQUE OF AUGURES*, ²M1 (12) *TIME VINDICATED*, ²N2v (13) *NEPTUNES TRIUMPH*, ²P1 (14) *PANS ANNIVERSARIE*, ²Q3v (15) *THE MASQUE OF OWLES*, ²S1 (16) *THE FORTUNATE ISLES*, ²S3 (17) *LOVES TRIUMPH THROUGH CALLIPOLIS*, ²V2v (18) *CHLORIDA*, ²X2 (19) *UNDER-WOODS*, ²Z1 (20) *MORTIMER HIS FALL*, 2Q2 (21) *HORACE HIS ART OF POET-RIE*, A1 (22) *THE ENGLISH GRAMMAR*, D4 (23) *TIMBER; OR, DISCOVERIES*, M1

1616:1i 1641 (TxU, shelfmark: Ah J738 +B641 cop. 7): pp. 204–6

Small-paper (283 × 183 mm) issue of vol. 3 by itself with no general title page. The text of "Elegy: The Expostulation" is identical to that in 1616:1e. The title page, collation, and contents of the present and the DFo copy (shelfmark: 14754 copy 4 Pt. 2–4) are identical to those in 1616:1I.

1616:1j 1692 (Wing: J1006): sigs. A4v, 4Cr–v

---

1. The normal arrangement of the first two leaves in sheet ¶ is: ¶1, blank; ¶1v, portrait; and ¶2, title.

2. For a summary of the extensive debate over whether Donne or Jonson authored "Elegy: The Expostulation," see D. Heywood Brock's "Jonson and Donne: Structural Fingerprinting and the Attribution of Elegies XXXVIII–XLI," *Papers of the Bibliographical Society of America* 72 (1978): 519–27. My *The First and Second Dalhousie Manuscripts: Poems and Prose by John Donne and Others* (Columbia: University of Missouri Press, 1988), p. 11, and Beal have strengthened the manuscript evidence used by Evelyn Simpson ("Jonson and Donne: A Problem in Authorship," *Review of English Studies* 15 [1939]: 274–82) to assign the poem to Donne.

3. This copy has the following note in pencil on sig. A1v: "This volume contains both the 'Second Volume,' containing three plays of 1631, and the 'Third Volume,' consisting of the additions of 1640–1. In the present copy A1 (the leaf on which this is written), conjugate with A6 of the 1631 *Bartholmew Fair* (as could be clearly seen before this copy was repaired) is blank. The sheet was later passed through the press a second time, and a general title to the 'Second Volume,' dated 1640, printed on the recto of A1. This title, however, is rare, and apparently only a few copies were issued with it. Possibly it was intended to print a joint title-page to the 'Second' and 'Third Volumes': if so the intention was abandoned, perhaps owing to disputes over the copy right.

"The present copy wants the whole of *The Sad Shepherd* which appears to have been accidentally omitted when the book was issued, since it appears to be in a contemporary binding. I have laid in the missing sheets from another copy.

"W. W. G. [Walter Wilson Greg]"

Greg laid in a copy of *The Sad Shepherd* with a 1641 title page and pages that measure 262 × 183 mm.

4. This copy of the 1st ed. of the true vol. 2 (consisting of only the plays) with the general title page has the following bibliographical note signed by Greg on the verso of its flyleaf: "This is the true 'Second Volume' of Ben Jonson's Works containing the three plays of 1631 with the general title-page of 1640, but without the additions which constitute the 'Third Volume.' Copies of the three plays sometimes occur, like the present one, by themselves in early bindings, and no doubt a certain number of copies were put on the market in 1640 without the additions. Neither separate copies of the 'Second Volume' nor copies of the 1640 title-page are, however, common.

"The 1640 title-page is printed on the original A1, conjugate with A6 of the 1631 *Bartholmew Fair*, the sheet having been passed through the press a second time. Before the present copy was repaired the two leaves could be clearly seen to form a single sheet."

5. A manuscript note on the blank preliminary leaf of the L copy (shelfmark: 1482.d.15) reads: "This volume contains the 'Third Volume' of Ben Jonson's Works, 1640–1, to which is prefixed a reprint, dated 1641, of *The Devil is an Ass*. Evidently this was made to take the place of the 'Second Volume' after the stock of the original plays of 1631 was exhausted. W. W. G. [Walter Wilson Greg]." Greg (3:1078–79) locates at Welbeck Abbey and describes a 1669 reissue of 1616:1h with a cancel title page ("Imprinted at London, and are to be sold in Fleetstreet, and Westminster-Hall. 1669") replacing the original A1 of 1641. According to Greg, this "only copy recorded is found in a volume that also contains the 1640 general title, the other two 1631 plays (preceding *The Devil is an Ass*), and the third volume of the works" (3:1078). Since Henry Herringman had just acquired the rights to the "Third Volume" (*Stationers' Register*: 19 Aug. 1667), he might have been responsible for the cancel; as Greg points

out, "He is, however, not otherwise reported at the addresses mentioned" (3:1079). Much of the Welbeck Abbey collection passed to the University of Nottingham Library, but I am unable to trace this possible 1669 copy.

6. The O copy of the small-paper issue (shelfmark: Gibson 520) has the following bibliographical note by Greg on the verso of the flyleaf: "This is a separate copy of the additions of 1640–1, which were known as the 'Third Volume' of Ben Jonson's Works. copies occasionally occur, like the present, in contemporary bindings, showing that the volume was issued separately as well as appended to the slim 'Second Volume.' The rights in the present volume were acquired in 1658 by Humphrey Moseley, who records that it was edited by Sir Kenelm Digby (preface to *The Last Remains of Sir J: Suckling*, 1659)." Such an independently published copy in a contemporary binding supports the possible existence of a copy with its own title page.

1617:1a

Author: Henry Fitzgeffrey

Title: *SATYRES:* [swash *R*] | AND | SATYRICALL | EPIGRAM'S: | With | Certaine Obſeruations at *Black-Fryers*? | By H: F: Of LIN-COLNES- | INNE Gent: | [rule] | Horat: Serm: Lib. I. |— — — — — — —*Nil mî officit vnquam* | *Ditior hic aut eſt quia Doctior: eſt Locus vni-* | *cuiq̨ ſuus:*— - — - — - — - — - | It neuer vexeth me a whit | That this man hath more welth or wit: | Euery one hath where he may ſit. | [rule] | [printer's device] | [rule] | LONDON | Printed by *Edw: All-de*, for *Miles Patrich*, and [swash *A*] | are to be ſold at his ſhop neare St. *Dnnſtons-* | Church in Fleet-ſtreet. 1617.

Collation: 8°. A–G⁸ ($4: A1, blank, unsigned; A2, title, unsigned; A4, unsigned; C2, unsigned; E3, unsigned; G8, wanting)

STC: 10945

Copy: L C.57.aa.35.(3)

Verse:[1] "A licentious person," sig. D7v

---

1. Earliest printing of "A licentious person."

1618:1a

Author: Henry Fitzgeffrey

Title: CERTAIN | ELEGIES, | *DONE* | BY SVNDRIE | Excellent Wits. | *WITH* | *Satyres and Epigrames.* | [rule] | [ornament] | [rule] | LONDON, | Printed by *B: A:* for *Miles Partriche*, and are | to be ſolde at his ſhoppe neare Saint | *Dunſtons* Church in Fleet- | ſtreete. 1618.

Collation: 8º. A⁸ ($4: A1, title, unsigned) A–G⁸ ($4: A1, want-ing; A2, wanting; A4, unsigned; C2, unsigned; E3, unsigned; G7, blank; G8, wanting)
STC: 10945.3
Copy: L C.39.b.42
Verse: "A licentious person," sig. D7v

Additional seventeenth-century edition:[1]

1618:1b 1620 (STC: 10945.6): sig. D7v

---

1. According to an endnote in an 1843 reprinting by G. E. Palmer for Edward V. Utterson of the 1620 *Certain Elegies, Done by Sundrie Excellent Wits. With Satyrs and Epigrams*, an undated edition also exists: "Of these Elegies, &c. there were four editions: the first in 1617, the second in 1618, another in 1620, and the last without date." The 1617 edition referred to is 1617:1a; I have not located a copy of the undated edition.

1619:1a

Compilers: W. B. and E. P. [William Basse and E. Philips?]
Title [within single rules]: A | HELPE TO | DISCOVRSE. | OR | *A Miscelany of Merriment.* | Confisting of wittie, Philofophical | and Aftronomicall Queftions | *and Anfwers.* | As alfo, | *Of Epigrams, Epitaphs, Riddles,* | *and Iefts.* | Together with the | COVNTRYMANS | Counfellour, next his yearely Oracle | *or Prognoftication to con-* | *fult with.* | Containing diuers neceffary Rules | and obferuations of much vfe and | confequence being knowne. | By W.B. & E.P. | *Dauus es? huc venias & eris mox Oedipus alter.* | LONDON, | Printed by *Bernard Alfop* for *Leonard* | *Becket,* and are to be fold at his fhop in the [swash *k*] | Temple neere the Church, 1619.
Collation: 12º. A–N¹² ($5: A1, blank, unsigned; A2, blank, un-signed; A3, title, unsigned; A12, blank; C3, missigned B3; D2, wanting; D6, wanting; D7, wanting; G3, unsigned; L5, separate title, unsigned; M3, unsigned)
STC: 1547
Copy: O D.49.(1)Th.
Separate title: THE | COVNTRY-MANS | COVNSELLOR. | OR | Neceffary addition to his yearely | *oracle or Prognoftication.* | Calcu-lated by Art as a Tutor for | *their helpe, that otherwife buy* | *more than they vnderstand.* | Beginning with this yeare of our Lord | God 1619. And fo continuing | forward as the Benefite and | Vfe fhall incou-rage. | *With many other neceffary Rules and* | *Obferuations of much*

profit and | *vſe being knowne.* [swash *k*] | By E.P. Philomathem. | [rule] | Loɴᴅoɴ. | Printed by Bern. Alſop for Leonard Becket, | and are to bee ſold at his ſhop in the | Temple neere the Church. | 1619.

Verse: "The first Anniversary" (ll. 203–4), sig. M5; "The first Anniversary" (ll. 117–20), sig. M5v

Additional seventeenth-century editions/issues:

1619:1b 1620 (STC: 1548): sigs. M5, M5v

1619:1c 1621 (STC: 1549): pp. 259, 260

1619:1d 1623 (STC: 1549.5): pp. 195, 196

1619:1e 1627
Title [within double rules]: A HELPE | TO DISCOVRSE. | Oʀ | *A Miſſelany of Seriouſneſſe with* [swash *A, M*] | *Merriment.* | Conſiſting of witty Philoſophicall, | Gramaticall, and Aſtronomicall | Qᴠᴇꜱ-ᴛɪoɴꜱ *and* Aɴꜱᴠᴠᴇʀꜱ. | AS ALSO, | Of *Epigrams, Epitaphs, Riddles, and Ieſts.* | Together with | *The Countrey-mans Counſellour,* next his | yearely Oracle or Prognoſtication | *to conſult with.* | Contayning diuers neceſſary Rules and | Obſeruations, of much vſe and conſ-equence | *beeing knowne.* [swash *k*] | Now the ſixt time publiſhed, and much | *inlarged by the former Authors,* [swash *A*] | W.B. and E.P. | *Davus es? huc venias & eris mox Oedipus alter.* | [rule] | LONDON. | Printed by *B.A.* and *T. Fawcet,* for *Leo-* | *nard Becket,* and are to be ſold at his Shop in the [swash *k*] | *Temple,* neere the Church. 1627.

Collation: 12°. A⁶ B–P¹² Q⁶ ($5: A1, title, unsigned; I5, unsigned; K1, separate title, unsigned; K5, unsigned; M5, unsigned)

STC: 1550

Copy: L C.95.a.32

Separate title: THE | COVNTRY-MANS | COVNSELLOR: | OR | Neceſſary addition to his yearely | *Oracle* or *Prognoſtication.* [swash 2d *n*] | Calculated by Art as a Tutor for | their helpe, that otherwiſe buy more | *then they vnderſtand.* | Beginning with this yeare of our Lord | God, 1627. And ſo continuing for- | ward as the Benefit and Vſe | ſhall incourage. | [rule] | With many other neceſſary Rules and | Obſeruations, of much profit and | vſe being knowne. [swash *k*] | *By E.P. Philomathem.* [swash *B, P*] | [rule] | *LONDON,* [swash *D, N*] | Printed by *B.A.* and *T. Fawcet,* for *Leonard* | *Becket,* and are to bee ſold at his ſhop in | the Temple neere the Church, | 1627.

Verse: "The first Anniversary" (ll. 203–4), sig. K10; "The first

Anniversary" (ll. 117–20), sig. K10v; "The first Anniversary" (ll. 133–34, 127–28), sig. M2

1619:1f 1628 (STC: 1551): pp. 217, 218, 249

1619:1g 1629
Title [within double-ruled, ornamental border]: A HELPE | TO DISCOVRSE. | OR, | *A Miſſelany of Seriouſneſſe with* [swash *A, M*] | *Merriment.* | Conſiſting of witty Philoſophicall, | Grammaticall, and Aſtronomicall | *Queſtions* and *Anſwers.* [swash *Q, A*] | AS ALSO, | Of *Epigrams, Epitaphs, Riddles,* and *Ieſts.* [swash *R*] | Together with | *The Countrey mans Counſellour,* next his | yearely Oracle or Prog-noſtication | to conſult with. | Containing diuers neceſſary Rules and Ob- | ſeruations, of much vſe and conſequence | being knowne. | Now the ſeuenth time publiſhed, and much | inlarged by the former Authors, | W.B. and E.P. | *Davus es? huc venias & eris mox Oedipus alter.* | [rule] | LONDON, | Printed by *Miles Fleſher,* for *Leonard Becket,* [swash *k*] | and are to be ſold at his Shop in the *Temple,* | neere the Church, 1629.
Collation: 12°. A–Q¹² ($5: A1, title, unsigned; K3, unsigned; K4v, missigned K3; M3, separate title, unsigned; Q12, blank)
STC: 1551.3
Copy: DFo STC 1551.2
Verse:[1] "Satyre V" (ll. 3–4), p. 116
Separate title: THE | COVNTRY-MANS | COVNSELLOR: | OR | Neceſſary addition to this yearely | Oracle, or Prognoſtication. | Calculated by Art as a Tutor for | their helpe, that otherwiſe buy more | *then they vnderſtand.* | Beginning with this yeare of our Lord | God, 1628. And ſo continuing for- | ward as the Benefit and Vſe | ſhall encourage. | [rule] | With many other neceſſary Rules | and Obſeruations, of much profit and | vſe being knowne. | [rule] | *By* E. P. Philomathem. | [rule] | LONDON, [swash *D*] | Printed by *M. Fleſher,* for *Leonard* [swash *M*] | *Becket,* and are to be ſold at his ſhop in [swash *k*] | the Temple neere the Church, | 1628.
Verse: "The first Anniversary" (ll. 203–4), p. 217; "The first Anniversary" (ll. 117–20), p. 218; "The first Anniversary" (ll. 133–34, 127–28), p. 249

1619:1h 1630 (STC: 1551.5): pp. 116, 217, 281[18], 249

1619:1i 1631 (STC: 1551.7): pp. 116, 217, 218, 249

1619:1j 1635 (STC: 1552): pp. 117, 230, 231, 265

1619:1k 1636 (STC: 1553): pp. 124[114], 220, 221, 253

1619:1l 1638 (STC: 1554): pp. 114, 220, 221, 253

1619:1m 1640 (STC: 1554.5): pp. 114, 220, 221, 253
    Stop-press corrections produced two states of the 1640 title page. DFo (shelfmark: STC 1554.2 copy 1) has the uncorrected state (l. 11, "*&c. readded*"; l. 20, "*alter*"; and l. 23, "*aoe*"); DFo (shelfmark: STC 1554.2 copy 2) has the corrected (l. 11, "*&c re-added*"; l. 20, "*alter.*"; and l. 23, "*are*"). Their texts of "Satyre V" (ll. 3–4) and "The first Anniversary" (ll. 203–4, 117–20, and 133–34, 127–28) are in the same typesetting.

1619:1n 1648 (Wing: E23): pp. 109, 214, 214, 246

1619:1o 1654 (Wing: E24): pp. 109, 214, 214, 246
    The O (shelfmark: Douce D 28) and L (shelfmark: 1506.417) copies of 1619:1o have a second, earlier title page at sig. Q12 and sig. Q11 respectively. This earlier, less complete title page (second description below) seems not to have been used in a separate published volume.
    Title [within double rules]: A HELP TO | DISCOVRSE: | OR, | *More Merriment mixt with* | *ſerious Matters.* | Conſiſting of witty Philoſophicall, | Grammaticall, Phyſical, Aſtronomicall | *Queſtions* and *Anſwers.* | As alſo, | *Epigrams, Epitaphs, Riddles, Jeſts,* | *Poeſies, Love-toyes, &c.* re-added, [swash P] | *and plentifully diſperſed.* | Togeth-er with | The *Country-mans Counſellor,* and his [swash 1st C] | yearly Oracle, and Prognoſtication, with ad- | ditions, or a Help to pre-ſerve his Health, | never before Printed. | Alſo the Art of Cookery, and ſundry Experi- | ments and their Extractions of Oyl, | Waters, &c. | [rule] | *The fourteenth Edition.* | *Davus es? huc venias, & eris mox Oedipus alter.* | [rule] | LONDON, | Printed by *E.T.* for *Andrew Crooke,* at the [swash A, k] | Signe of the green Dragon in *Pauls* | Church-yard. 1654.
    Title [within single rules]: A HELP TO | DISCOVRSE: | OR, |

More Merriment mixt with | *ferious Matters.* | Confifting of witty Philofophicall, | Grammaticall, Phyficall, Aftronomicall | *Queftions* and *Anfwers.* | As alfo, | *Epigrams, Epitaphs, Riddles, Jefts,* | *Poefies, Love-toyes, &c. re-added,* [swash P] | *and plentifully difperfed.* | Together with | The *Country-mans Counfellor,* and his [swash 1st C] | yearly Oracle, and Prognoftication, with ad- | ditions, or a Help to pre-ferve his Health, | never before Printed. | [rule] | *The fourteenth Edition.* | *Davus es? huc venias, & eris mox Oedipus alter.* | [rule] | LONDON, | Printed by *E.T.* for *Andrew Crooke,* at the [swash A, k] | Signe of the green Dragon in *Pauls* | Church-yard. 1654.

1619:1p 1663 (Wing: E25): pp. 109, 214, 214, 246

1619:1q 1667 (Wing: E25A): pp. 109, 214, 214, 246

1619:1r 1682 (Wing: E25B): pp. 69, 137, 138, 160

---

1. Earliest printing of any part of "Satyre V."

1619:2a
Author: William Drummond of Hawthornden
Title [within double rules]: A | MIDNIGHTS | *Trance:* [swash T] | Wherin is difcour- | fed of DEATH, the | *nature of* SOVLES, | *and estate of Im-* | *mortalitie.* | [rule] | As it was Written at the | defire of a Nobleman, | *By* W. D. | [rule] | LONDON, | Printed by *George Purflow,* for [swash G] | *Iohn Budge,* and are to be fold | at the figne of the Greene- | Dragon in *Paules* Church- | yard. 1619.
Collation: 12°. A–D¹² E⁶ ($5: A1, blank; A2, title, unsigned; E3, unsigned; E4, unsigned; E5, blank, unsigned; E6, blank)
STC: 7252.5
Copy: O 8° D.48(1)Th.
Verse: *A*"The second Anniversarie" (l. 288), p. 33; "The first Anniversary" (l. 206), p. 33; "The first Anniversary" (l. 207), p. 33; "The second Anniversarie" (l. 18), p. 42; *A*"The second Anniversarie" (l. 82), p. 48; *A*"The second Anniversarie" (l. 293), p. 65; "The second Anniversarie" (l. 171), p. 67; *A*"The second Anniversarie" (l. 184), p. 67; *A*"The first Anniversary" (l. 454), p. 81

1621:1a
Compilers: William Basse and E. Philips?
Title [within single rules]: A | HELPE TO | MEMORIE | *AND* |

DISCOVRSE. | *The two Syrens of the Eare, and* | *ioynt Twins of Mans perfection.* | Extracted from the ſweating | braines of *Phyſitians, Philoſophers,* [swash 1st *P*] | *Orators* and *Poets.* | Diſtilled in their Aſſiduous, and witty | *Collections: And which for the Method,* | Manner, and Referent handlings may be | fitly termed: A ſecond Miſſelany, | or Helpe to Diſcourſe. | The ſecond Impreſſion, corrected and | enlarged by the Author. | Imprinted at London, by *B.A.* for | L.B. *and are to be ſold at his Shop, in* | the Temple, neere the Church. | 1621.

Collation: 12°. A⁸ B–G¹² H⁴ ($5: A1, blank, unsigned; A2, blank, unsigned; A3, title, unsigned; A5, unsigned; H1, unsigned; H2, unsigned; H3, unsigned)

STC:[1] 13051

Copy: L C.40.a.41

Verse:[2] "The first Anniversary" (ll. 343–44), f. 44

Additional seventeenth-century edition:

1621:1b 1630

Title: A | HELPE TO | MEMORY AND | DISCOVRSE: | *WITH* | TABLE-TALKE, | as Muſicke to a Banquet | of Wine. | Being a Compendium of witty, | *and vſefull Propoſitions, Problemes, and* | Sentences, Extracted from the larger | Volumes of *Phyſicians, Philoſophers,* | *Orators and Poets:* | Diſtilled in their aſſiduous and lear- | ned Obſeruations: | *And which for Method, Manner, and Referent* | *Handling, may be fitly tearmed, A Second* | MISSELANY; Or, | Helpe to Diſcourſe. | [double rule] | LONDON: | Printed by *T. B.* for *Leonard Becket,* and are [swash *B, B, k*] | to be ſold at his Shop in the *Temple,* neere | the Church. 1630.

Collation: 12°. A–H¹² ($5: A1, title, unsigned; D6 and D7, bound between E6v and E7; F3, separate title, unsigned; F4, unsigned; H12, blank?, wanting)

STC: 13051.3; Keynes: 73b

Copy: DFo STC 13051.2

Verse:[3] "The broken heart" (ll. 1–16), pp. 45–46; "The first Anniversary" (ll. 106–7), p. 48; "The first Anniversary" (ll. 109–10), p. 48; "The first Anniversary" (ll. 343–44), p. 98

Separate title: Table-Talke, | *AS* [swash *A*] | MVSICKE | TO A BANQVET | of Wine: | Serued in, in witty propoſitions, | Seaſoning and Queſtions: To- | gether with their Reſoluti- | ons and Anſwers: | To exhilarate and recreate the bodies | and mindes both of our ſelues and | *our friends at our Tables* | and Meetings. | *Singula cum*

valeant, ſunt melior a ſimul. | [ornament] | *LONDON,* | Printed by
Tho. Brudenell, for *Leonard* | *Becket,* and are to be ſold at his ſhop in
[swash *k*] | the Temple neere the Church. | 1630.

Verse:[4] "Song. 'Go, and catch a falling star'" (ll. 1–4, 10–18), p.
143

---

1. The 1620 1st ed. (STC: 13050.5) contains no Donne verse.
2. The text and context of these lines from "The first Anniversary"
very likely derive from 1614:1a.
3. Earliest printing of any part of "The broken heart."
4. Earliest printing of any part of "Song. 'Go, and catch a falling star.'"
Keynes (p. 168) notes the likelihood that "Song. 'Go, and catch a falling
star'" (ll. 1–4, 10–18) first appeared in a 1620 or 1621 separate publication
of *Table-Talke, as Mvsicke to a Banqvet of Wine.*

1623:1A

Author: William Drummond of Hawthornden
Title: [ornament] | FLOVVRES | OF SION. | BY | William
Drvmmond | of Hawthorne-denne. | *TO WHICH IS ADJOYNED
HIS* [swash *D, J, Y, N, E, D*] | CYPRESSE GROVE. | [double rule] |
Printed 1623. [swash *P*]

Collation: 4°. π¹ a–e⁴ F–K⁴ ($3: π1, title; F2, separate title, un-
signed; H4, signed; I4, signed; K3, unsigned)

STC: 7247
Copy: CSmH 49012
Separate title [within double rules]: A [swash] | CYPRESSE |
GROVE. | BY | *W. D.* [swash *D*]

Verse: A"The second Anniversarie" (l. 288), p. 54; "The first
Anniversary" (l. 206), p. 54; "The first Anniversary" (l. 207), p. 54;
"The second Anniversarie" (l. 18), p. 58; A"The second Anniversarie" (l. 82), p. 60; A"The second Anniversarie" (l. 293), p. 66; "The
second Anniversarie" (l. 171), p. 67; A"The second Anniversarie"
(l. 184), p. 67; A"The first Anniversary" (l. 454), p. 72

Large-paper (220 × 167 mm) copy. The DFo copy (shelfmark:
STC 7247) measures 220 × 160 mm. The priority of 1623:1A,
1623:1B, and 1623:1C is uncertain; except for their title pages
(printed on separate leaves rather than as part of sheet a), the
issues are identical.[1] *A Cypresse Grove* is an expanded version of
1619:2a.

Additional seventeenth-century issues/editions:

1623:1a 1623 (STC: 7247. L, shelfmark: C.39.f.21): pp. 54, 54, 54, 58, 60, 66, 67, 67, 72

Kastner (1:lxxii–lxxv) lists this as a small-paper copy even though it measures 207 × 160 mm.

1623:1B 1623 (STC: 7248. AU, shelfmark: 82136 f.): pp. 54, 54, 54, 58, 60, 66, 67, 67, 72

Title [typeset within engraving]: FLOWRES | OF SION. | BY | WILLIAM DRVMMOND | of *Hawthorne-denne.* [swash third *e*] | *To which is adjoy-* | *ned his* | CYPRESSE | GROVE. | [double rule] | *Printed* 1623.

Large-paper (217 × 163 mm) presentation copy: according to a note in seventeenth-century hand on the title page, the copy was "Giuen to the Librarie of Mr Thomas Rheid in Aberdone by the Author 1627." The engraving features a *P* at the top and a *B* at the bottom of a ribbon on the right-hand side.

1623:1C 1623 (STC: 7249. E, shelfmark: De.4.53): pp. 54, 54, 54, 58, 60, 66, 67, 67, 72

Large-paper (221 × 164 mm) presentation copy: according to a note in seventeenth-century hand on the title page, the copy was "Giuen to the colledge of king James Edenbrough by the Author 1624." The typeset portion of the title page is identical with that in 1623:1B; however, the *P* and *B* lie horizontally at the mid-left of the engraving.

1623:1D 1630 (STC: 7250. E, shelfmark: De.4.113): pp. 74, 74, 74, 78, 81, 88, 88, 88, 93

This imperfect copy may be an example of a large-paper (208 × 154 mm) copy of the 2d ed., 1st issue. Although it lacks the title page, it also lacks the errata leaf present in copies of the second issue; and Jean Archibald, Special Collections Librarian at Edinburgh University Library, informs me that if the errata leaf had ever been present "it has certainly been absent for a long time." The sheets of this copy are identical with those of 1623:1E.

1623:1d 1630

Title: [ornament] | FLOWRES OF | SION: | BY [swash *B, Y*] | WILLIAM DRVMMOND | of Hawthorne-denne. | *TO WHICH IS AD-JOYNED HIS* [swash *D, J, Y, N, D*] | CYPRESSE GROVE. | [ornament] | Printed at *Eden-Bourgh*, by the Heires of ANDRO | HART. Anno 1630.

Collation: 4°. A–O⁴ ($4: B4, unsigned; D3, unsigned; D4, unsigned; F4, unsigned; N4, unsigned; O4, bound as title before A1, unsigned)²

STC: 7250

Copy: L C.71.b.16

Separate title [within ornamental border]: A | CYPRESSE | GROVE: [swash G, R, V] | BY | W.D. [swash D]

Verse: A"The second Anniversarie" (l. 288), p. 74; "The first Anniversary" (l. 206), p. 74; "The first Anniversary" (l. 207), p. 74; "The second Anniversarie" (l. 18), p. 78; A"The second Anniversarie" (l. 82), p. 81; A"The second Anniversarie" (l. 293), p. 88; "The second Anniversarie" (l. 171), p. 88; A"The second Anniversarie" (l. 184), p. 88; A"The first Anniversary" (l. 454), p. 93

Small-paper (171 × 133 mm) copy of the 1st issue. The DFo (shelfmark: STC 7250) and MH (shelfmark: STC 7250) small-paper copies are slightly larger, 184 × 138 mm and 185 × 135 mm respectively.

1623:1E 1630 (STC: 7251. MH, shelfmark: HEW 6.10.5): pp. 74, 74, 74, 78, 81, 88, 88, 88, 93

Large-paper (255 × 195 mm) copy (the E copy [shelfmark: De.4.54/1] measures 267 × 204 mm) of the 2d ed., 2d issue, having the cancel title page and usual additional leaf with the errata list.

1623:1e 1630 (STC: 7251. CSmH, shelfmark: 59136): pp. 74, 74, 74, 78, 81, 88, 88, 88, 93

Small-paper (215 × 163 mm) copy.

---

1. For reproductions of the title pages of 1623:1A, 1623:1B, 1623:1C, 1623:1d, and 1623:1E respectively, see L. E. Kastner's two-volume *The Poetical Works of William Drummond of Hawthornden With 'A Cypresse Grove'* also printed as vols. 5 and 6 of the English Series by the University of Manchester Press in 1913: vol. 1, plates 10, 11, 12, 13, and vol. 2, plate 8.

2. The stub of leaf O4 remains in the L copy (shelfmark: C.71.b.16).

1624:1a

Author: John Donne

Title [within double rules]:¹ DEVOTIONS | VPON | Emergent Occaſions, and ſe- | uerall ſteps in my Sicknes: | Digeſted into | 1. MEDITATIONS *vpon our Hu-* | *mane Condition:* | 2. EXPOSTVLATIONS, *and De-* | *batements with God.* | 3. PRAYERS, *vpon the ſeuerall Oc-* |

cafions, to him. | [rule] | By Iohn Donne, Deane of | *S. Pauls*, London. | [rule] | London, | Printed for Thomas Iones. | 1624.

Collation: 12°. A⁶ B–2D¹² 2E⁴ ($5: A1, title, unsigned; A2, missigned A3; A4, unsigned; A5, unsigned; 2E4, blank, unsigned)

STC: 7033a; Keynes: 35

Copy: CSmH 53918

Verse:² "Insultus morbi primus," sigs. A5–6; "Insultus morbi primus," in segments (sigs. B1, B11, C8v, D8v, E10v, F10, H1, I4, K5, L5v, M6v, N10v, O12v, P10, R3, S2v, T1v, V2v, X7, Z3, 2A5, 2B9, 2C10v)

Text:

Stationes, *siue* Pe-
riodi *in* Morbo, *ad*
  quas referuntur Me=
  ditationes se-
  quentes.

1 INsultus *Morbi primus;*
  2 *Post,* Actio læsa;
3 Decubitus *sequitur tandē;*
4 Medicusq; *vocatur;*
5 Solus *adest;* 6 Metuit;
  7 Socios *sibi iungier instat;*
8 *Et* Rex *ipse suum mittit;*
  9 Medicamina scribunt;
10 Lentè *& Serpenti* sata-
  gunt *occurrere Morbo.*
11 *Nobilibusq; trahunt,*
  a cincto corde, venenum,
Succis, *&* Gemmis; *&*
  quæ *Generosa, ministrant*
Ars, *& Natura, instillant;*
  12 *Spirante* Columbâ,
Suppositâ pedibus, reuocan-
  tur ad ima vapores;
13 *Atq;* Malum Genium,
  numeroso stigmate, *fassus,*
Pellitur ad pectus, Morbiq;
  Suburbia, Morbus:
14 *Idq; notant* Criticis,
  Medici, euenisse diebus.

15 *Interea* insomnes *Noctes*
  ego duco, Diesq;:
16 *Et properare* meum, *cla-*
  mant, e turre propinqua
Obstreperæ Campanæ, alio-
  rum *in funere, funus.*
17 *Nunc* lento sonitu *dicunt,*
  Morieris; 18 *At inde,*
Mortuus *es, sonitu* celeri,
  pulsuq; agitato.
19 Oceano *tandem emenso,*
  aspicienda resurgit
Terra; *vident, iustis,* Medici,
  iam cocta *mederi*
Se posse, indicijs; 20 Id agunt;
  21   *Atq; annuit* Ille,
Qui per eos *clamat, linquas*
  iam Lazare *lectum;*
22 *Sit* Morbi Fomes *tibi*
  Cura; 23 Metusq; Relabi.

Additional seventeenth-century states/issues/editions:

1624:1b 1624 (STC: 7033; Keynes: 34. C, shelfmark: Syn.8.62.69):
sigs. A5–6, B1, B11, C8v, D8v, E10v, F10, H1, I4, K5, L5v, M6v,
N10v, O12v, P10, R3, S2v, T1v, V2v, X7, Z3, 2A5, 2B9, 2C10v
  Title [within double rules]: DEVOTIONS | VPON | Emergent
Occaſions, and ſe- | uerall ſteps in my Sicknes: | Digeſted into | 1.
MEDITATIONS *vpon our Hu-* | *mane Condition:* | 2. EXPOSTVLATIONS,
and De- | *batements with God.* | 3. PRAYERS, *vpon the ſeuerall Oc-* |
caſions, to him. | [rule] | By IOHN DONNE, Deane of | *S. Pauls,* Lon-
don. | [rule] | LONDON, | Printed by *A.M.* for THOMAS [swash *A*] |
IONES. 1624.
  The priority of 1624:1a and 1624:1b is ambiguous.[3] The texts of
the verses in the CSmH copy (shelfmark: 53918) of 1624:1a and the
C copies (shelfmarks: Syn.8.62.69 and Keynes B.4.27) of 1624:1b
differ only in a comma added after "Ministrant" (sig. M6v) in
1624:1b; the CT (shelfmark: C.34.32) and C (shelfmark: Peterborough H.2.41[3]) copies of 1624:1b lack the comma.[4] Keynes notes
that the title page differences (see n. 1 below) are likely a "press
correction made early in the series" (p. 85), and Anthony Raspa
argues that the differences between the title pages result from

stop-press corrections and do not indicate the existence of two issues (*John Donne: Devotions Upon Emergent Occasions*, p. xliv). The facts that the two C copies (shelfmarks: Keynes B.4.26 [1624:1a] and Syn.8.62.69 [1624:1b]), both in their original vellum binding, have their title pages conjugate with leaf A6 and that their half-sheet A typesettings are identical confirm that the title page differences are stop-press corrections. Comparison of the CSmH and C copies of 1624:1a with the C and CT copies of 1624:1b shows that only the type below "London" was disturbed. Further, Raspa's inference that 1624:1a has the earlier state of the title page seems logical ("The exclusion of Mathewes' initials appears to have been an oversight rectified during publication" [p. xlvi]), particularly in light of the fact that the 1624 2d ed. (1624:1c) prints the initials exactly as in 1624:1b; thus, I have reversed the priority of 1624:1a and 1624:1b found in STC and Keynes.

1624:1c 1624 (STC: 7034; Keynes: 36): sigs. A5r–v, pp. 1, 20, 38, 60, 87, 109, 137, 166, 166[190], 215, 239, 269, 295, 314, 346, 368, 389, 389[413], 443, 480, 505, 534, 558

1624:1d 1626 (STC: 7035; Keynes: 37): sigs. A5r–v, pp. 1, 20, 38, 61[60], 87, 109, 137, 166, 190, 215, 239, 269, 295, 314, 346, 368, 389, 413, 443, 480, 505, 534, 558

1624:1e 1627 (STC: 7035a; Keynes: 38): sigs. A5r–v, pp. 1, 20, 38, 61[60], 87, 109, 137, 166, 190, 215, 239, 269, 295, 314, 346, 368, 389, 413, 443, 480, 505, 534, 558
   Raspa concludes that 1624:1d and 1624:1e may not constitute separate issues despite the differently dated title pages: "It is not possible, moreover, to ascribe a separate issue to each title page, because textual errors occur among the surviving copies without pattern" (p. xlix). I consider them separate issues because their title pages were printed separately.

1624:1f 1634 (STC: 7036; Keynes: 39): sigs. A4r–v, A5, B1, B8, C5, D4v, E2, F2, G2, G12v, H11v, I10, K10v, L9, M5, N6v, O4, O12v, P10v, Q12, S4, T3, V4v, X6

1624:1g 1638 (STC: 7037; Keynes: 40): sigs. A3r–v, A4, A11, B5v, C1v, C11v, D8, E7, F5v, G3, G12v, H10, I9, K6v, L1v, M2, M10, N6, O3v, P3v, Q5v, R3, S1v, S10v

1. The reproductions of the title pages of 1624:1a and 1624:1b in Keynes (items 35 and 34) show a period, rather than an italic colon, after "*Condition*"; however, the described copy and the C copy (shelfmark: Keynes B.4.26) of 1624:1a as well as the CT copy (shelfmark: C.34.32) and C copies (shelfmarks: Syn.8.62.69; Peterborough H.2.41³; and Keynes B.4.27) of 1624:1b have the italic colon.

2. Earliest printing of "Insultus morbi primus." Joan Webber first recognized "Insultus morbi primus" as "a Latin poem in dactylic hexameters" (*The Eloquent "I"* [Madison: University of Wisconsin Press, 1968], p. 19), though Chambers had published the Latin lines in 1896 without explicitly identifying them as verse in his "Appendix F" (2:315–18) in conjunction with a manuscript English verse translation discovered by Alexander B. Grosart (and thought by Grosart to be in Donne's hand) in a copy of 1624:1e (Keynes, 82). After their initial appearance as a unit on sigs. A5–6, each of the twenty-three segments of "Insultus morbi primus" heads a "Meditation."

3. Yet another state of the 1st ed. may exist: in a review of the 1932 2d ed. of Geoffrey Keynes's *Bibliography*, Evelyn M. Simpson describes the stub of original C2 remaining in the OM copy and suggests that ll. 11–15 were reset (*Review of English Studies* 9 [1933]: 107–8). Gary A. Stringer informs me that the stub of the original leaf C2 remains in the CT copy (shelfmark: C.34.32) of 1624:1b. Examination of the C copy (shelfmark: Keynes B.4.26) of 1624:1a, still in its original binding, shows that cancel C2 is a single leaf with its stub following sig. C11v, that C11 is a single leaf with its stub following sig. C2v, and that sig. C2 is mispaginated 393 (for 27); thus, original C2 was cut off original C11 and replaced with the present cancel, probably during the setting of sheet Q (sig. C2 was set in the same skeleton forme as was sig. Q11 [p. 393]). Through the 4th ed. of his *Bibliography*, Keynes had not found a copy with original C2 (p. 83).

4. The C copy of 1624:1a (shelfmark: Keynes 4.26) lacks sheet M.

1632:1a

Author: John Donne

Title [within double rules]: DEATHS | DVELL, | *OR,* | A Conſol-ation to the Soule, againſt | the dying Life, and liuing | Death of the Body. | *Deliuered in a Sermon at White Hall, before the* | KINGS MAIE-STY, *in the beginning* | *of Lent,* 1630. | By that late learned and Reuerend Diuine, | IOHN DONNE, Dr. in Diuinity, | & Deane of S. *Pauls,* London. | *Being his laſt Sermon, and called by his Maieſties houſhold* | THE DOCTORS OWNE FVNERALL SERMON. | [ornament] | LONDON, | Printed by THOMAS HARPER, for *Richard Redmer* | and *Beniamin Fiſher,* and are to be ſold at the ſigne | of the Talbot in Alderſ-gate ſtreet. | *M.DC.XXXII.*

Collation: 4°. A–G⁴ ($3: A1, blank, signature within ornament; A2, blank; A2v, portrait; A3, title, unsigned)
STC: 7031; Keynes 24
Copy: O Antiq.e.E.1632.11
Verse:[1] "Corporis haec animae sit syndon syndon Jesu," sig. A2v

Additional seventeenth-century editions/issues:

1632:1b 1633 (STC: 7032; Keynes: 25):[2] sig. A2v

1632:1c 1633 (STC: 7032a; Keynes: 26a. C, shelfmark: Keynes B.5.24): sig. A2
Keynes (p. 56) accepts George R. Potter and Evelyn M. Simpson's argument for the priority of 1632:1c over 1632:1d (*The Sermons of John Donne* [Berkeley and Los Angeles: University of California Press, 1953], 1:23n).

1632:1d 1633 (STC: 7032a; Keynes: 26. C, shelfmark: Keynes B.5.29²): sig. A2

---

1. Earliest printing of "Corporis haec animae sit syndon syndon Jesu." Gardner first treated the line as verse (*Divine*, pp. 112–13).

2. The leaf containing the frontispiece portrait of Donne on which "Corporis haec animae sit syndon syndon Jesu" appears has been removed from all copies of 1632:1b listed in the *National Union Catalog of Pre-1956 Imprints* and STC, as well as from the L copy (shelfmark: 693.f.11.[11]) listed in Keynes (who reports the presence of the frontispiece in 1632:1b). The other copy listed in Keynes (LP, shelfmark: 47ᴬG:2:) is missing.

1633:1a
Author: Henry Holland
Title: ECCLESIA | SANCTI PAVLI | ILLVSTRATA. | [rule] | THE | MONVMENTS, [swash M, N, M, N] | Inscriptions, and Epitaphs, of | Kings, Nobles, Biſhops, and others, [swash B] | buried in the Cathedrall Church of | Sᵗ. Pavl, London. | Together, with the Foundation of the | ſaid Church: A Catalogue of all the Arch-biſhops [swash A, C, A] | and Biſhops of London, from the beginning. A | Catalogue alſo of all the Deanes of the ſame | Church: and the Monuments conti- | nued vntill this preſent yeere | of Grace 1633. | A Copy of the Popes Pardon, buried with Sᵗ. Gerard | Braybroke, 1390. | To-

gether with a Preface, touching the Decayes | *and for the Repayring of this famous Church.* | [rule] | *By H. H.* [swash *B*] | [rule] | *LON-DON,* | Printed by Iohn Norton, and are to be ſold by | Henry Seyle, at the Tigars head in S*t*. *Pauls* | Church yard, 1633.

Collation: 4°. A⁴ a² B–I⁴ ($3: A1, title, unsigned; A2, unsigned; a2, unsigned; I4, wanting)

STC: 13584

Copy: L 577.c.4.[2]

Verse:[1] "Ioannes Donne Sac: Theol: Profess," sigs. E2v–3

Text:

> *And to come backe to the South Ile, betweene the*
> *doore and Deane* Colets *Monument, is newly*
> *erected a Monument for Deane* Donne, *which*
> *is, his face appearing out of his Winding-sheete,*
> *done in white Marble, standing vpon an Vrne,*
> *and this Inscription following: all done accor-*
> *ding to the will of the sayd Deane* Donne.

Ioannes Donne Sac: Theol: Profess: post
varia studia, quibus ab annis tenerrimis, fideliter
nec infæliciter, incubuit, instinctu et impulsu Spir:
S*ti* monitu et hortatu Regis Iacobi, Ordines Sacros
amplexus, Anno sui Iesu 1614. et suæ ætatis 42. De-
cenatu hujus Eccles: indutus 27. Novembris 1621.
exutus Morte vlt°. die Martii 1631.

> *Hic licet in Occiduo Cinere*
> *Aspicit eum,*
> *Cuius Nomen est Oriens.*

Additional seventeenth-century issues:

1633:1b 1633 (STC: 13584. LG, shelfmark: A.7.6. no. 2 in 32): sigs. E2v–3

Title: ECCLESIA | SANCTI PAVLI | ILLVSTRATA. | [rule] | THE | *MONVMENTS,* [swash *M, N, M, N*] | Inscriptions, and Epi-taphs, of | *Kings, Nobles, Biſhops,* and others, [swash *B*] | buried in the Cathedrall Church of | S*t*. Pavl, *London.* | Together, with the Foundation of the | *ſaid Church. A Catalogue of all the Arch-biſhops* [swash *A, C, A*] | and Biſhops of *London,* from the beginning. A | *Catalogue alſo of all the Deanes of the ſame* | Church: and the Monu-ments conti- | *nued vntill this preſent yeere* | of Grace 1633. | *A Copy of*

Pope Boniface *the fecond, his Pardon, buried with* | St. Gerard Braybroke, 1390. | Together with a Preface, touching the Decayes | *and for the Repayring of this famous Church.* | [rule] | *By H. H.* [swash *B*] | [rule] | *LONDON,* | Printed by Iohn Norton, and are to be fold by | Henry Seyle, at the Tigars-head in *S*ᵗ. *Pauls* | Church-yard, 1633.

Collation and text of "Ioannes Donne Sac: Theol: Profess" identical with 1633:1a. Its identification of the "Pope" in the 1633:1a title page as "Pope Boniface the second" suggests that this title page may postdate that of 1633:1a.

1633:1c 1634 (STC: 13585): sigs. E2v–3

----

1. Earliest printing of "Ioannes Donne Sac: Theol: Profess."

1633:2a
Author: John Stow
Title [within double rules]: THE | SURVEY | OF | *LONDON*: [swash *L, N, D, N*] | Contayning | The Originall, Increafe, Moderne | Eftate, and Government of that City, | Methodically fet downe. | *With a memoriall of thofe famoufer Acts of Charity, which for* [swash *A, C*] | *Publicke and Pious Vfes have beene beftowed by many Worfhipfull* [swash 1st *P, V, v*] | *Citizens and Benefactors.* | As alfo all the Ancient and Moderne Monuments erected in the | Churches, not onely of thofe two famous Cities, London and | Westminster, but (now newly added) | Foure miles compaffe. | [rule] | Begunne firft by the paines and induftry of Iohn Stovv, | in the yeere 1598. | Afterwards inlarged by the care and diligence of *A.M.* [swash *A, M*] | in the yeere 1618. | And now completely finifhed by the ftudy and labour of *A.M. H.D.* [swash *A, M*] | and others, this prefent yeere 1633. | *Whereunto, befides many Additions (as appeares by the Contents)* [swash *A, C*] | *are annexed divers Alphabeticall Tables; efpecially two:* | The firft, an Index of Things. | The fecond, a Concordance of Names. | [rule] | London, | Printed by Elizabeth Pvrslovv, and are to be fold by | Nicholas Bovrne, at his Shop at the South Entrance of | the Royall Exchange. 1633.

Collation: 2°. A⁸ B–2Y⁶ (2Y)⁴ X¹ 2Z–4K⁶ 4L–M⁴ 4N⁶ ($3: A1, blank, unsigned; A2, title, unsigned; A4, signed; 4L3, unsigned; 4M3, unsigned)

STC: 23345
Copy: L 579.k.23
Separate title [within double rules]: [ornament] | THE | RE-

MAINES | OR | REMNANTS | OF | DIVERS | WORTHY THINGS, | which ſhould have had their due place and honour | in this Worke, if promiſing friends had kept | their words. | But they failing, and part of them comming to my hands | by other good meanes, they are here inſerted, to accompany | my Perambulation foure miles about *London*. | (***) | [rule] | [ornament] | [rule] | London, | Printed by *Elizabeth Purſow*, and are to bee ſold by [swash *z, P*] | *Nicholas Bourne*, at his Shop, at the South Entrance [swash *B*] | of the Royal Exchange. | 1633.

Verse:[1] "Ioannes Donne Sac: Theol: Profess," p. 776; "Annae Georgii More de Filiae," p. 889

Text:

A faire Monument in the Chancell, on
the North side, at the upper end,
with this Inscription.

	Annæ	
Georgii	*More de*	*Filiæ.*
Roberti	*Lothesley*	*Soror:*
Wilelmi	*Equit:*	*Nept:*
Christopheri	*Aurat:*	*Pronep:*

Fœminæ Lectissimæ, Dilectissimæque,
Conjugi Charissimæ Castissimæque,
Matri Piissimæ Indulgentissimæque,
XV. *Annis in Conjugio Transactis,*
VII. *post* XII. *partum (quorum* VII.
superstant) dies
Immani Febre Correptæ
(Quod hoc saxum Fari jussit,
Ipse præ dolore infans)
Maritus (miserrimum dictu) olim
Charæ Charus
Cineribus Cineres spondet suos,
Novo Matrimonio (Annuat deus) Hoc
loco sociandos,
Ioannes Donne,
Sacr. Theolog. Profess.
Secessit,
Anno XXIII. *Ætat. suæ & sui Iesu*
CIↃ.DC.XVII.
Aug. XV.

Additional seventeenth-century edition:

1633:2b 1640+ (STC: 23345.5): pp. 776, 889

---

1. Earliest printing of "Annae Georgii More de Filiae."

1635:1a
Author: John Swan, Jr.
Title [within single rules, ornamental border, and single rules]:
SPECVLVM | MUNDI | OR | A GLASSE RE- | PRESENTING THE
FACE | OF THE WORLD; SHEWING | both that it did begin, and
muſt alſo end: | The manner How, and time When, | being largely
examined. | WHEREUNTO IS JOYNED | an Hexameron, or a
ſerious diſcourſe of the | cauſes, continuance, and qualities of
things | in Nature; occaſioned as matter pertinent | to the work
done in the ſix dayes of | the Worlds creation. | [double rule] | AUG.
in Ser. de Aſcen. | *Qui ſe dicit ſcire quod neſcit, temerarius eſt.* | *Qui ſe*
negat ſcire quod ſcit, ingratus eſt. | [double rule] | ¶ Printed by the
Printers to the | *Vniverſitie* of *Cambridge.* 1635.
    Collation: 4°. ¶⁴ 2¶⁴ A–3V⁴ 3X² ($3: ¶1, ornament, unsigned; ¶2,
title, unsigned; 3R3, unsigned; 3X2, blank?, wanting)
    STC: 23516
    Copy: CSmH 22316
    Verse:[1] "The first Anniversary" (ll. 343–44), p. 296

Additional seventeenth-century issues/editions:

1635:1b 1643 (Wing: S6238): p. 290

1635:1c 1643[4] (Wing: S6238A): p. 290
    The engraved title page has a 1644 date.

1635:1d 1665 (Wing: S6239): p. 259

1635:1e 1670 (Wing: S6240): p. 259

1635:1f 1698 (Wing: S6240A): p. 259

---

1. The context and text probably derive from 1614:1a or 1621:1b.

1640:1a
Author: Anonymous
Title [within double rules]: HORTI | CAROLINI | *ROSA AL-
TERA*. [swash *R*, 2d *A*, *R*] | [printer's device] | *OXONIÆ* [swash *A*] |
Excudebat LEONARDUS LICHFIELD | *Academiæ Typographus*. 1640.
    Collation: 4º. π² *⁴ 2*⁴ A–E⁴ F² a–c⁴ 2c² d–e⁴ ($3: π1, title; F2,
unsigned; 2c2, unsigned)
    STC: 19039; Case: 94
    Copy: CSmH 29091
    Verse: "Elegie. Death" (l. 1), sig. b3v

Additional seventeenth-century issue:

1640:1b 1640 (STC: 19039.5): sig. b3v

1640:2a
Author: John Donne
Title [within double rules]: [rule] | LXXX | SERMONS |
PREACHED | BY THAT LEARNED AND | REVEREND DIVINE, |
IOHN DONNE, | Dʳ IN DIVINITY, | Late Deane of the Cathedrall |
Church of S. PAULS *London*. | [rule] | [ornament] | [rule] | *LONDON*,
[swash *N*, *D*, *N*, | Printed for RICHARD ROYSTON, in Ivie-lane, and
RICHARD | MARRIOT in S. *Dunʃtans* Church-yard in Fleetʃtreet.
[swash *D* | [rule] | *M DC XL*. [swash *M*]
    Collation: 2º. A–B⁶ ($3: A1, engraved title, unsigned; A2, title,
unsigned) C⁴ ($2) B–Z⁶ ($3: B1, unsigned) 2A–4A⁶ ($3: 2I2, mis-
signed I2) 4B⁴ ($3) 4C⁸ ($4: 4C8, blank)
    STC: 7038; Keynes: 29
    Copy: C Keynes B.7.31
    Verse: "A Hymne to God the Father," sig. B4; "Hymne to God
my God, in my sicknesse" (heading only), sig. B4; "Ioannes Donne
Sac: Theol: Profess," sig. C1v

1640:3a
Compiler:[1] John Mennes
Title: Wits | RECREATIONS. | [rule] | Selected from the fineʃt
Fancies | of Moderne MUSES. | [rule] | [ornament] | *LONDON*,
[swash *N*, *N*] | Printed by *R. H.* for *Humphry Blunden* | at the Caʃtle
in Corn-hill 1640.
    Collation: 8º. π⁶ B–L⁸ M⁴ 2A–2C⁸ ($4: π1, blank; π2v, explana-

tion of frontispiece; π3, frontispiece; π4, title; D4, unsigned; E4, unsigned; F4, unsigned; G4, unsigned; H3, unsigned; K3, missigned R3; L4, unsigned; M3, unsigned; M4, blank, unsigned; 2B2, missigned 2A2) A–D⁸ E⁴ ($4: A1, separate title, unsigned; E2, missigned D2; E3, unsigned; E4, unsigned)

STC: 25870; Case: 95

Copy: CSmH 61435

Verse: *A*"Song. 'Go, and catch a falling star,'"² sig. E3; *A*"The Dampe,"³ sig. G3r–v; "Song. 'Go, and catch a falling star'"⁴ (ll. 10–18), sig. L2

---

1. In his introduction to *Witts Recreations* (Hants, England: Scolar Press, 1990), Colin Gibson notes Timothy Raylor's arguments (*"Wit's Recreations* not by Sir John Mennes or James Smith?," *Notes & Queries* 230 [1985]: 2–3) that no direct evidence links either John Mennes or James Smith to *Wits Recreations* and suggests Thomas Jordan, compiler of several verse miscellanies in the mid-seventeenth century, as the likely compiler of *Wits Recreations* (pp. xi–xii).

2. The poem is Francis Beaumont's "Womans Mutability."

3. The poem is Thomas Carew's "Secresie protested." Dunlap notes that the idea in ll. 12–16 "is borrowed from Donne, *The Dampe*, lines 1–4" (p. 219).

4. 1621:1b also prints a segment of ll. 10–18 of "Song. 'Go, and catch a falling star.'"

1645:1a

Compiler: John Gough

Title [within ornamental border]: THE | ACADEMY | OF | Complements. | Wherein *Ladies, Gentlewomen,* | *Schollers,* and *Strangers* may accommo- | date their Courtly practice with | gentile Ceremonies, Comple- | mentall amorous high expreſſions, | and formes of ſpeaking or | writing of Letters moſt | in faſhion. | A worke per-uſed, exactly perfected, every | where corrected and inriched, by the | Author, with additions of witty Poems, | and pleaſant Songs. | [rule] | The ſixt Edition, with two Tables, the | one expounding the moſt hard Engliſh | words, the other reſolving the moſt de- | lightfull fictions of the | Heathen Poets. | [rule] | *London,* Printed by *T. Badger,* for *H. Moſley,* | and are to be ſold at his ſhop at the Princes Armes | in *Pauls* Church-yard. 1645. [swash *P*]

Collation: 12°. A–N¹² ($5: A1, blank, unsigned; A1v, illustrated title; A2, title, unsigned; E3, unsigned; G3, missigned F3; I3, un-

signed; I5, unsigned; M3, missigned L3; N3, missigned M3; N4, missigned M4)
Wing:[1] G1401A
Copy: CtY 1974 262
Verse: "Breake of day" (ll. 1–2, 4–3, 5–6), p. 166

Additional seventeenth-century editions/issues:

1645:1b 1646
Title [within ornamental border]: THE | ACADEMY | OF | Complements. | Wherein, | *Ladies, Gentlewomen, Schollers,* and | *Strangers* may accommodate their | Courtly practice with gentile Ceremo- | nies, Complementall amorous high | expreſſions, and forms of ſpeaking | or writing of Letters moſt | in faſhion. | [rule] | A worke peruſed, exactly perfected, every | where corrected and inriched by the | Author, with additions of witty Poems, | and pleaſant Songs. | [rule] | The ſeventh Edition, with two Tables; the one | expounding the moſt hard Engliſh words, the other | reſolving the moſt delightfull fictions of | the Heathen Poets. | With an Addition of a new Schoole of Love, | and a Preſent of excellent Similitudes, Compariſons | Fancies, and Devices. | [rule] | *London,* Printed by *M. Bell,* for *Hum. Moſeley,* | and are to be ſold at his ſhop at the Princes Armes | in *Pauls* Church-yard. 1646.
Collation: 12⁰. A–L¹² ²L–²N¹² ($5: A1, title, mounted, unsigned; K5, missigned K9; ²N3, unsigned; ²N12, wanting)[2]
Wing: G1401B
Copy: O Firth f.52
Verse: "Breake of day" (ll. 15–18), p. 135; *A*"The Dampe,"[3] p. 191; "Breake of day" (ll. 1–2, 4–3, 5–6), pp. 202–3

1645:1c 1650
Title [within ornamental border]: THE | ACADEMY | OF | COMPLEMENTS. | WHEREIN | Ladies, Gentlewomen, | Schollers, and Strangers, may | accommodate their Courtly practice | with gentile Ceremonies, Complemental | amorous high expreſſions, and Forms of | ſpeaking or writing of Letters | moſt in faſhion. | A Work peruſed, exactly per- | fected, every where corrected and inlarged, | and inriched by the Author, with Additions of | many witty Poems, and pleaſant Songs. | With an Addition of a new School of | Love, and a Preſent of excellent Similitudes, | Compariſons, Fancies, and Devices, | The Ninth Edition, with two Tables; the | one expounding the moſt hard Engliſh words, | the

other refolving the moft delightful | fictions of the Heathen Poets. | [rule] | *London*, Printed for *Humphrey Mofely*, at the Princes | Armes in St. *Pauls* Church-yard. 1650.

Collation: 12°. A–P¹² ($5: A1, blank; A1v, engraved title; A2, typeset title, unsigned; A2v, missigned A3; A3, unsigned; A5, unsigned; sheet D, wanting; F5, unsigned; K6–7v, wanting; P3, unsigned)

Wing: G1401C

Copy:⁴ IU uncataloged

Verse: "Breake of day" (ll. 15–18), p. 122; A"The Dampe," pp. 182–267[183]; "Breake of day" (ll. 1–2, 4–3, 5–6), pp. 194–95; "The Indifferent," pp. 233[231]–232

1645:1d 1650 (Wing: G1402; Case 92[b]): pp. 122, 182–83, 194–59[195], 233[231]–32

Title [within ornamental border]: THE | ACADEMY | OF | COMPLEMENTS. | WHEREIN, | Ladies, Gentlewomen, | Schollers, and Strangers, may | accommodate their Courtly practice | with gentile Ceremonies, Complementall | amorous high ex-preffions, and Formes of | fpeaking or writing of Letters | moft in fafhion. | A work perufed, exactly per- | fected, every where corrected and inlarged, | and inriched by the Author, with Additions of | many witty Poems, and pleafant Songs. | With an addition of a new Schoole of | Love, and a Prefent of excellent Similitudes, | Comparifons, Fancies, and Devices. | The Laft Edition, with two Tables; the | one expounding the moft hard Englifh words, | the other refolving the moft delightfull | Fictions of the Heathen Poets. | [rule] | *London*, Printed for *Humphrey Mofeley*, at the | *Princes Armes* in St *Pauls* Church-yard. 1650.

The reading "The Laft Edition" on the title page of this edition suggests that it postdates 1645:1c.

1645:1e 1654 (Wing: G1403): pp. 122, 182–83, 194–95, 231–32

1645:1f 1658 (Wing: G1404): pp. 122, 182–83, 194–95, 231–32

1645:1g 1663 (Wing: G1405; Case: 92[c]): pp. 122, 182–83, 194–95, 231–32

1645:1h 1670

Title [within single rules]: THE | Academy | OF | COMPLE-MENTS | Newly Refin'd. | WHEREIN | Ladies, Gentlewomen, and

Scholars, | may accommodate their Courtly practiſe | with gentile Ceremonies, Complemen- | tal expreſſions, and Forms of ſpeaking or | writing Letters moſt in Faſhion. | ALSO | A New School of Love, and a Preſent of ex- | cellent Similitudes, Compariſons, Fancies | and Devices. | WITH | An Interpretation of the moſt delightful | Fictions of the *Heathen* Poets. | This new impreſſion is exactly reviſed, and | Enlarged with Additions of choiceſt Catches | and Songs *A-la-mode*. | [rule] | *London*, Printed for *A. M.* and are to be ſold | by moſt Bookſellers. 1670.

Collation: 12°. πA A⁶ B–O¹² P⁶ ($5: πA, engraved title page; A1, title, unsigned; A2, unsigned; A4, unsigned; A5, unsigned; D3, unsigned; G3, missigned G8; P3, unsigned; P4, unsigned; P5, unsigned)

Wing:[5] G1405B

Copy: L G.16400

Verse: "Breake of day" (ll. 15–18), p. 122; "Breake of day" (ll. 1–2, 4–3, 5–6), pp. 194–95; "The Indifferent," pp. 231–32

1645:1i 1684

Title [within double rules]: THE | Academy | OF | COMPLE-MENTS | WITH | Many New Additions | OF | Songs and Catches *A-la-mode*. | STORED | With Variety of Complemental and | Elegant Expreſſions, of LOVE and | COURTSHIP. | Alſo Witty and Ingenious Dialogues | and Diſcourſes, | *Amorous and Jovial*. | With Significant LETTERS upon | Several Occaſions. | Compoſed for the uſe of *Ladies* and | *Gentlewomen*. | *By the moſt refined Wits of this Age*. | [rule] | *London*: Printed for *P. Parker* at the | *Leg* and *Star* in *Cornhil*, 1684.

Collation: A² B–H¹² I⁶ K–R¹² ($5: A1, blank; A1v, engraved title; A2, title, unsigned; E6, missigned E5; I4, unsigned; I5, unsigned; K5, unsigned; L3, missigned B3; L4, missigned B4; M12, wanting; N10, wanting; O3, unsigned)

Wing: G1406

Copy: IU Hill 31 Mr.43 Gen.res.

Verse: "Breake of day" (ll. 15–18), p. 94; *A*"Song. 'Go, and catch a falling star,'"[6] pp. 373–74

1645:1j 1684 (Wing: G1406. O, shelfmark: Vet. A3 f. 313): pp. 94, 373–74

Title [within double rules]: THE | Academy | OF | COMPLE-MENTS | WITH | Many New Additions | OF | Songs and Catches *A-la-mode*. | STORED | With Variety of Complemental and | Elegant

Expreſſions of LOVE and | COURTSHIP. | Alſo witty and Inge-
nious Dialogues | and Diſcourſes, | *Amorous and Jovial:* | With Sig-
nificant LETTERS upon | Several Occaſions. | Compoſed for the
uſe of Ladies and | Gentlewomen, | *By the moſt refined WITS of this
Age.* | [rule] | *London:* Printed for *P. Parker,* at the | *Leg* and *Star* in
Cornhil, 1684.

Collation: 12º. *A*² B–H¹² I⁶ K–R¹² ($5: *A*1, blank; *A*1v, engraved
title page; *A*2, title, unsigned; E6, missigned E5; I4, unsigned; I5,
unsigned; K5, unsigned; L3, missigned B3; L4, missigned B4; O3,
unsigned)

The priority of 1645:1i and 1645:1j is uncertain. Their texts of
"Breake of day" (ll. 15–18) and *A*"Song. 'Go, and catch a falling
star'" are identical. The 1685 edition (Wing: G1407) lacks Donne
verse.

----

1. The four previous editions lack Donne verse: 1639 (STC: 19882.5),
1640 (STC: 19883 and 19883.5), and 1641 (Wing: G1401).

2. The first pagination sequence ends at p. 248 (sig. L12v); the second
begins at p. 219 (sig. ²L1) and consists of sheets from another edition.
This copy of 1645:1b would seem unique.

3. The poem is Thomas Carew's "Secresie protested."

4. No copy of an "Eighth" edition has been located; however, an
engraved title page dated 1648 tipped into this copy of the 1650 "Ninth"
edition suggests that an eighth edition may have been published in 1648.

5. A 1664 copy listed by Wing (G1405A) at O does not exist.

6. Ll. 17–20 also recall ll. 7–8 of Donne's "The broken heart," particularly in its relatively common version with "flash" for "flask" (l. 8). I am
unable to identify the poem or its author; its first sixteen lines appear
without attribution on fol. 12v of L MS.Add.27989.

1650:1a

Compiler: Anonymous

Title [within ornamental border]: THE | MIRROUR | OF | Com-
plements. | OR, A MANUALL OF | Choice, requiſite, and com-
pendious Cu- | rioſities, wherein Gentlemen, Ladies, ⌈Gentlewom-
en, and all others, may prac- | tiſe Complementall and amorous |
expreſſions, in ſpeaking or writing | Letters, upon any ſubject or |
occaſion. | EXACTLY PERFORMED, | with Addition of witty
Songs, Sonnets, | Poems, Epigrams, Eſſays, Characters, &c. | [rule]
| The fourth Edition, with very many Addi- | tions: Alſo a Dictio-
nary and Explana- | tion of hard Words frequently in uſe, | taken out
of the Greeke, Latine, | French, and other Tongues. | [rule] | *LON-
DON,* [swash *N, D, N*] | Printed by *T. H.* and are to bee ſold by |

F. Coles, R. Harper, and *W. Gilbertſon,* [swash C] | at their ſhops, 1650.

    Collation: 12°. A–M¹² ($5: A1, wanting; A2, title, unsigned; G4, unsigned; I5, unsigned; L3, unsigned)

    Wing: M2223

    Copy: CSmH 146914

    Verse: *A*"The Dampe" (heading only),[1] sig. A8v; "The Canonization" (heading only), sig. A9; "Womans constancy" (heading only), sig. A9v; "Fall of a wall" (heading only), sig. A9v; "A lame begger" (heading only), sig. A9v; "Disinherited" (heading only), sig. A9v; "Phryne" (heading only), sig. A9v; "Klockius" (heading only), sig. A9v; "Thou hast made me, and shall thy work decay" (heading only), sig. A10v; "The first Anniversary," "A Funerall Elegie," and "The second Anniversarie" (shared heading only), sig. A11v; "The second Anniversarie" and "A Funerall Elegie" (shared heading only), sig. A11v; *A*"The Dampe," sig. G4; "The Canonization," sigs. G7v–8v; "Womans constancy," sig. H1r–v; "Fall of a wall," sig. H1v; "A lame begger," sig. H2; "Disinherited," sig. H2; "Phryne," sig. H2; "Klockius," sig. H2; "Thou hast made me, and shall thy work decay," sigs. H11v–12; "As due by many titles I resign," sig. H12r–v; "The first Anniversary" (ll. 175–76), sig. L7; "The first Anniversary" (ll. 223–34), sig. L7r–v; "The first Anniversary" (ll. 323–24), sig. L7v; "The first Anniversary" (ll. 309–14), sig. L7v; "The first Anniversary" (ll. 361–66), sigs. L7v–8; "A Funerall Elegie" (ll. 3–6), sig. L8; "A Funerall Elegie" (ll. 59–62), sig. L8; "The second Anniversarie" (ll. 67–72), sig. L8r–v; "The second Anniversarie" (ll. 75–80), sig. L8v; "The second Anniversarie" (ll. 123–25), sig. L8v; "The second Anniversarie" (ll. 137–44), sig. L8v; "The second Anniversarie" (ll. 221–25), sigs. L8v–9; "The second Anniversarie" (ll. 241–46), sig. L9; "The second Anniversarie" (ll. 306–10), sig. L9; "The second Anniversarie" (ll. 376–78), sig. L9; "The second Anniversarie" (ll. 468–70), sig. L9; "The second Anniversarie" (ll. 226–30), sig. L9v; "The second Anniversarie" (ll. 147–48), sig. L9v; "A Funerall Elegie" (ll. 83–90), sig. L9v; "A Funerall Elegie" (ll. 97–102), sigs. L9v–10

    The only extant copies of the 1634 (STC: 17978.5) and 1637 (STC: 17979.3) editions of *The Mirrour of Complements* are imperfect: the CSmH copy of 1634 (shelfmark: 50451) lacks sheet A, and the CtY copy of 1637 (shelfmark: Nkz20 635mc) lacks three of the first four preliminary leaves from sheet A (having only the unsigned title page) and all leaves after G1. Even so, nothing about 1634 suggests the presence of verse in the missing sheet, and the intact table of contents for 1637 lists nothing other than letters; thus, these editions likely did not contain any Donne verse. The complete copy of 1635 (STC: 17979) in L (shelfmark: 1085.a.30) lacks any verse.

---

1. The poem is Thomas Carew's "Secresie protested."

1650:2a

Author: Henry Vaughan

Title [engraved, within single rules] : Silex Scintillans: | *or* | *SACRED POEMS* | *and* | *Priuate Eiaculations* | *By* | Henry Vaughan *Silurist* | LONDON *Printed by T: W. for H: Blunden* | *at y^e Castle in Cornehill.* 1650

Collation: 8°. A–G⁸ ($4: A1, blank, unsigned; A2, title, unsigned; G8, wanting)

Wing: V125

Copy: L 238.b.8

Verse: "The broken heart" (l. 25), p. 12

Additional seventeenth-century edition:

1650:2b 1655 (Wing: V126): p. 12

1651:1a

Author: Falkland, Lucius Cary, Viscount

Title [within single rules]: SIR | LUCIUS | CARY, | LATE LORD | VISCOUNT | OF | FALKLAND, | His Diſcourſe of *INFALLIBILITY*, with [swash *N, A, B*] | an Anſwer to it: And his Lordſhips *REPLY.* | *Never before publiſhed.* [swash *N*] | Together with Mr. *Walter Mountague*'s Letter | concerning the changing his Religion. | [rule] | *Anſwered by my Lord of* FALKLAND. [swash *A*] | [rule] | *LONDON* | Printed by *Gartrude Dawſon,* for *Iohn Hardeſty,* [swash *D*] | and are to be ſold at the Signe of the *Black Spread-* | *Eagle,* in *Duck-Lane,* 1651.

Collation: 4°. ✱✱✱⁴ (✱✱✱)² A⁴ (a)-(c)⁴ (d)¹ B–Z⁴ 2A–2P⁴ 2Q¹ ($3: ✱✱✱1, title, unsigned; ✱✱✱3, unsigned; A3, unsigned; (a)3, unsigned; (b)3, unsigned; (c)3, unsigned; K3, unsigned; L3, unsigned; M3, unsigned; O3, unsigned; P3, unsigned; S3, unsigned; T3, unsigned; V3, unsigned; X3, unsigned; Y3, unsigned; Z3, unsigned; 2A3, unsigned; 2B3, unsigned; 2C3, unsigned; 2D3, unsigned;

2E3, unsigned; 2F3, unsigned; 2G3, unsigned; 2H3, unsigned; 2I3, unsigned; 2K3, unsigned; 2L3, unsigned; 2M3, unsigned; 2N3, unsigned; 2O3, unsigned; 2P3, unsigned)
    Wing: F317
    Copy: CSmH 232168
    Verse: "Satyre II" (ll. 41–42), p. 107

Additional seventeenth-century edition:

1651:1b 1660 (Wing: F318): p. 107

1651:2a
    Author: Henry Vaughan
    Title: *OLOR ISCANUS*. [swash *R, N*] | A COLLECTION | OF SOME SELECT | POEMS, | AND | TRANSLATIONS, | Formerly written by | [rule] | *Mr.* Henry Vaughan *Siluriſt.* | [rule] | Publiſhed by a Friend. | Virg. Georg. | *Flumina amo, Sylvaſq Inglorius*—— | [rule] | LONDON, | Printed by *T.W.* for *Humphrey Moſeley,* | and are to be ſold at his ſhop, at the | Signe of the Prince's Arms in St. *Pauls* | Church-yard, 1651.
    Collation: 8º. A–L⁸ ($4: A1, blank; A1v, "*Ad Posteros*"; A2, frontispiece, unsigned; A3, title, unsigned; E3, unsigned; F1, separate title, unsigned; H1, separate title, unsigned; L8, errata list)
    Wing: V123
    Copy: CSmH 109303
    Verse: "Elegy: The Perfume" (ll. 3–4), p. 42

Additional seventeenth-century edition:[1]

1651:2b 1679 (Wing: V123A): p. 42

---

1. Martin's note that "the errata-list is not found in all copies" (p. xxiii) very likely does not imply the existence of yet another state of 1651:2a. The CSmH (shelfmark: 109303), O (shelfmarks: 8º.M.5.Art.B5[4] and Antiq.f.E.4[1]), CLU-C (shelfmark: *PR 3742 O51), and LV (shelfmark: Dyce 10,164) copies have the six-line errata list on sig. L8; and the L copy (shelfmark: 238.b.41) listed by Martin as lacking the errata sheet has all its leaves mounted on guards.

1652:1a
    Author: John Donne
    Title [within ornamental border]: PARADOXES, | PROBLEMS, |

ESSAYES, | CHARACTERS, | WRITTEN | By Dʳ *DONNE* | *Dean of* PAULS. | To which is added a Book of | EPIGRAMS, | Written in Latin by the | ſame Author; tranſlated | into Engliſh by | *J. MAINE*, D. D. | As alſo, | *Ignatius his Conclave*, | A SATYR, | Tranſlated out of the Originall | Copy written in Latin by the ſame | *Author*; found lately amongſt | his own Papers. | *De Ieſuitarum diſsidiis:* | Quos pugnare, Scholis, clamant, hi (diſcite Regna) | Non ſunt Vnanimes, conveniuntq; nimis. | [rule] | *London*, Printed by *T.N.* for *Humphrey* | *Moſeley* at the *Prince's Armes* in | St *Paul's* Church yard, 1652.

Collation: 12º. *A*⁸ B–K¹² L⁴ ($5: *A*1, title, unsigned; *A*3, unsigned; *A*5, unsigned; D3, unsigned; F4, unsigned; F5, separate title, unsigned; L2, unsigned; L3, blank, unsigned; L4, blank, unsigned)

Wing: D1866; Keynes: 45, 10

Copy: L G.19723(1)

Verse:¹ *D*"Upon one who for his wives fault took it ill to be called Cuckold," p. 88; *D*"Upon One *Roger* a Rich Niggard, familiarly unacquainted with the Author," p. 89; *D*"Upon a Whore barren and not barren," p. 89; *D*"On the same. 'Thy dowbak'd Lusts,'" p. 89; *D*"On an old Bawd," p. 89; *D*"On the same. 'Though ramage grown,'" p. 89; *D*"On the same. 'She, whose scarce yet quencht lust,'" p. 90; *D*"On a Bawdy-house," p. 90; *D*"Upon an old rich scolding Woman," p. 90; *D*"Another. 'Shut thy purse-mouth, Old Trot,'" p. 90; *D*"On her unpleasing Kisses," p. 90; *D*"Another. 'When thy dry grissels,'" p. 91; *D*"Another. 'Thy senses faile thee,'" p. 91; *D*"On the same old Wife," p. 91; *D*"To the same. 'Be not seen,'" p. 91; *D*"Upon one who saw the Picture of his scolding wife in a Painters shop," p. 91; *D*"Another. 'Say Painter, who's this,'" p. 92; *D*"Another. 'Who's this, Painter,'" p. 92; *D*"Another. '*Venus*, when *Pygmalion* praid,'" p. 92; *D*"Upon a Pipe of Tobacco," p. 92; *D*"Another. 'An Hearb thou art,'" p. 92; *D*"Another. 'A cloud *Ixion* for a Goddess kist,'" p. 92; *D*"To the Tobacco-seller," p. 93; *D*"Another. 'Lothings, stincks, thirst,'" p. 93; *D*"Another. 'I love thee not,'" p. 93; *D*"Another. 'Niggards till dead are Niggards,'" p. 93; *D*"Upon a Town built in the place where a wood grew," p. 93; *D*"Another. 'Falne Okes the Axe doth into Timber hew,'" p. 93; *D*"Another. 'From a Woods ruines,'" p. 94; *D*"Another. 'This naked Beam,'" p. 94; *D*"Another. '*Wood* yeelds to *stone*,'" p. 94; *D*"Upon a navigable River cut through a Town," p. 94; *D*"Another. 'The drownd land,'" p. 94; *D*"Another. 'The tree her womb bred on the back,'" p. 94; *D*"Another. 'The ground whose head was once enricht,'" p. 94; *D*"Another. 'The place where once grew Ash,'" p. 95; *D*"Upon the Medows over-flown there," p. 95; *D*"Another. 'The hungry Cow,'" p. 95; *D*"Another. 'Here Fishes dwell,'" p. 95; *D*"Another. 'Mere pleasant fields,'" p. 95; *D*"Another. '*Dukes-wood* where once thick bushes did appear,'" p. 95; *D*"Upon a piece of ground ore-flown," p. 95; *D*"Another. 'Fishes now quarter where pavilions stood,'" p. 96; *D*"Another. 'Finn'd Soldiers here,'" p. 96; *D*"Another. '*Dutchman*! This Grove once hatcht,'" p. 96; *D*"Another. 'Gudgeons, where soldiers lay,'" p. 96; *D*"A *Dutch* Captain of Foot," p. 96; *D*"Another. 'We've conquer'd Boys,'" p. 96; *D*"Another. 'Thus conquering kild,'" p. 97; *D*"Another. 'I die well paid,'" p. 97; *D*"Another. 'Me the queld *Spaniard*,'" p. 97; *D*"His Will," p. 97; *D*"To his Fellow Sentinels," p. 101; *D*"In Comædam celeberrimam *Cinthiam* dictam ad instantiam alterius fecit," pp. 101–2; *D*"Idem *Anglicè* versum," p. 102; *D*"On one particular passage of her action, when she was to be stript of her cloaths by *Fulvio*," pp. 102–3

Separate title [within single rules]: *IGNATIVS* [swash *G*, *N*] | HIS | CONCLAVE: | OR, | *His Inthronifation in a late* | *Election in* HELL. | Wherein many Things | are mingled by way of | SATYR. | Concerning | *The difpofition of* Jefuites. | *The Creation of a* new Hell. | *The eftablifhing of a* Church *in the Moon*. | There is alfo added an Apologie for | *JESUITES*. [swash *J*] | All dedicated to the Two ad- | verfary Angels, which are Prote- | ctors of the Papall Confiftory, | and of the Colledge of | SORBON. | [short rules] | *By* JOHN DONNE, *Doctor of Divinity, and* | *late Dean of Saint Pauls.* | [rule] | Printed at *London*, 1653.

Verse: "Resemble *Janus* with a diverse face," p. 107; "My little wandering sportful soul," p. 108; "The lark by busy and laborious ways," p. 109; "With so great noise and horror," pp. 137–38; "That the least piece which thence doth fall," p. 142; "Feathers or straws swim on the water's face," pp. 176–77; "As a flower wet with last night's dew, and then," pp. 215–16

Additional seventeenth-century issue:

1652:1b 1652 (Wing: D1867; Keynes: 46, 10): pp. 88, 89, 89, 89, 89, 89, 90, 90, 90, 90, 90, 91, 91, 91, 91, 91, 92, 92, 92, 92, 92, 92, 93, 93, 93, 93, 93, 93, 94, 94, 94, 94, 94, 94, 94, 95, 95, 95, 95, 95, 95, 95, 96, 96, 96, 96, 96, 96, 97, 97, 97, 97, 101, 101–2, 102, 102–3, 107, 108, 109, 137–38, 142, 176–77, 215–16

Title [within ornamental border]: PARADOXES, | PROBLEMES, | ESSAYES, | CHARACTERS, | Written | By Dr *DONNE* |

Dean of PAULS: | To which is added a Book of | EPIGRAMS: | Written in Latin by the ſame | Author; tranſlated into | Engliſh by | J: *MAINE,* D.D. [swash J] | As alſo | *Ignatius his Conclave,* [swash C] | A SATYR, | Tranſlated out of the Originall | Copy written in Latin by the | ſame *Author;* found lately | amongſt his own Papers. | *De Jeſuitarum diſſidiis.* [swash J] | Quos pugnare, Scholis, clamāt, hi, (diſcite Regna) | Non ſunt Unanimes, conveniuntq; nimis. | [short rules, with italic colon between third and fourth] | *London,* Printed by *T: N:* for *Humphrey* | *Moſeley* at the *Prince's Armes* in | St *Pauls* Churchyard, 1652.

E. M. Simpson argues that 1652:1b may be the earlier issue (*A Study of the Prose Works of John Donne* [Oxford: Clarendon Press, 1924], p. 136). The texts of the Donne dubia and verse in the CSmH (shelfmark: 86647) and L (shelfmarks: E.1359.[2] and 1340.a.17) copies of 1652:1b are identical to those in the copy described of 1652:1a. Keynes (pp. 104–5) notes that the collation is identical for both issues, though the settings of their first sheet differ. The Thomason copy (L, shelfmark: E.1359.[2]) of 1652:1b is dated "Nou. 8 1652."

----

1. Flynn reviews the lengthy controversy over the authorship of the sixty-one epigrams allegedly translated from Donne's Latin by Jasper Mayne and uses biographical and bibliographical evidence to argue that Donne could have written originals for all except numbers 53–57 ("Epigrams," 121–30). Flynn does not specifically discuss epigram 59, D"In Comædam celeberrimam *Cinthiam* dictam ad instantiam alterius fecit," printed in Latin. The subsequent unnumbered epigram, D"Idem *Anglicè* versum," translates D"In Comædam celeberrimam *Cinthiam* dictam ad instantiam alterius fecit"; thus, D"In Comædam celeberrimam *Cinthiam* dictam ad instantiam alterius fecit" could be an original Latin poem by Donne.

1653:1a Author: Francis Beaumont
   Title: POEMS: | BY | *FRANCIS BEAVMONT,* | Gent. |

Viz. {
The Hermaphrodite.
The Remedy of Love.
Elegies.
Sonnets, with other Poems.
}

| [rule] | *LONDON,* | Printed for *Laurence Blaiklock,* [swash k, k] | and are to be ſold at his Shop | neare the middle Temple Gate | in *Fleet-ſtreet.* 1653.

Collation: 8°. π¹ A–N⁸ ($4: π1v, portrait; A1, title, unsigned; A3, unsigned; C1, missigned G; L4, missigned K4)
Wing: B1602
Copy: CLU-C *PR 2422 P74 1653a
Verse: "Song. 'Go, and catch a falling star'" (stanzas 1 and 2), sig. G4r–v; A"The Dampe,"[1] sig. G4v
The Thomason copy (L, shelfmark: E.1236.[3]) is dated "ffebr. 10 1652." The 1640 1st ed. A1640:1a contains an adaptation of "Song. 'Go, and catch a falling star'" omitted from subsequent editions.

Additional seventeenth-century issue and edition:

1653:1b 1653 (Wing: B1603): sigs. G4r–v, G4v
The Thomason copy (L, shelfmark: E.1455.[3]) is dated "Nou. 22 1653." The settings of "Song. 'Go, and catch a falling star'" (stanzas 1 and 2) and A"The Dampe" in 1653:1a and 1653:1b are identical.

1653:1c 1660 (Wing: B1604): sigs. G4r–v, G4v

---

1. The poem is Thomas Carew's "Secresie protested."

1653:2a
Author: Samuel Sheppard
Title: see 1653:2b. The title page in this, the only copy of 1653:2a, is that of 1653:2b and has been tipped in.
Collation: 8°. A–C⁸ ($4: A1, title, unsigned, supplied from a copy of 1653:2b; A4, unsigned; A8, misbound after B8; C2, separate title, unsigned; C8, blank?, wanting)
Wing: A1588
Copy: DFo A1588
Verse: "Vpon Mr. Thomas Coryats Crudities" (ll. 57–72), sig. A2; "Satyre II" (ll. 5–6), sig. A3; "Elegy: The Bracelet" (ll. 59–64), sig. A3; "Satyre II" (ll. 39–48), sig. A4v; "Satyre II" (ll. 111–12), sig. A4v; "The Calme" (ll. 1–6), sig. A5; "Satyre V" (ll. 35–36), sig. A5v; "The Calme" (ll. 27–28), sig. A5v; "The Calme" (ll. 31–34), sig. A5v; "The Calme" (ll. 15–16), sig. A5v; "The Calme" (ll. 49–56), sig. A6v; "To Sʳ Edward Herbert. at Julyers" (ll. 43–44), sig. A6v; "The first Anniversary" (ll. 91–94), sig. A7; "Satyre IIII" (ll. 225–28), sig. A7; "To the Countesse of Bedford. T'have written then"

(ll. 83–90), sig. A7v; "To the Countesse of Bedford. Madame, You have refin'd" (ll. 41–42), sig. A7v; "To Sʳ Henry Wotton. Sir, more then kisses" (ll. 39–46), sig. A8v; "Satyre II" (ll. 19–20), sig. A8v; "Satyre I" (ll. 59–62), sig. B1v; "The first Anniversary" (ll. 283–84), sig. B1v; "The first Anniversary" (ll. 279–80), sig. B1v; "To Sʳ Henry Wootton. Here's no more newes" (ll. 13, 15), sig. B1v; "To the Countesse of Salisbury. August. 1614" (ll. 27–30), sig. B2; "The first Anniversary" (ll. 201–8), sig. B2v; "Elegy: On his Mistris" (ll. 31–32), sig. B2v; "To the Countesse of Bedford. T'have written then" (ll. 59–66), sig. B3v; "To the Countesse of Bedford. T'have written then" (ll. 35–36), sig. B3v; "To the Countesse of Bedford. T'have written then" (ll. 37–38), sig. B3v; "The first Anniversary" (ll. 211–18), sig. B4v; "To the Countesse of Huntingdon. Madame, Man to Gods image" (ll. 5–8), sig. B4v; "The first Anniversary" (ll. 295–302), sig. B5v; "To Mʳ R. W. If, as mine is" (ll. 29–32), sig. B5v; "The first Anniversary" (ll. 127–32), sig. B6v; "The first Anniversary" (ll. 143–44), sig. B6v; "The first Anniversary" (ll. 397–98), sig. B6v; "Epithalamion made at Lincolnes Inne" (ll. 49–50), sig. B7v; "To Sʳ Henry Wotton. Sir, more then kisses" (ll. 17–18), sig. B7v; "The Calme" (ll. 23–26), sig. B7v; "The Calme" (ll. 37–38), sig. B7v; "Obsequies to the Lord Harrington" (ll. 111–18), sig. B8v; "Satyre II" (ll. 109–10), sig. B8v

Separate title: A | GENERAALL | PRONOSTICATION. | FOR THE YEAR | 1653. | [rule] | By | Raphaell Desmus. | [rule] | [ornament] | *LONDON:* Printed for the Year 1653.

Verse: "To Mʳ T. W. All haile sweet Poët" (ll. 5–8), sig. C2v; "To Sir H. W. at his going Ambassador to Venice" (ll. 33–36), sig. C2v; "Satyre IIII" (ll. 18–20), sig. C3; "Satyre IIII" (ll. 23–27), sig. C3; "Satyre IIII" (ll. 31–33), sig. C3; "Satyre IIII" (ll. 47–48), sig. C3; "Satyre IIII" (ll. 52–54), sig. C3v; "Satyre IIII" (ll. 96–97), sig. C3v; "Satyre IIII" (ll. 129–30), sig. C3v; "Satyre IIII" (ll. 138–44), sigs. C3v–4; "Satyre IIII" (ll. 145–49), sig. C4

Additional seventeenth-century editions:

1653:2b 1653 (Wing: A1588. L, shelfmark: E.1348.[1]): sigs. A2, A3, A3, A4v, A4v, A5, A5v, A5v, A5v, A5v, A6v, A6v, A7, A7, A7v, A7v, A8v, A8v, B1v, B1v, B1v, B1v, B2, B2v, B2v, B3v, B3v, B3v, B4v, B4v, B5v, B5v, B6v, B6v, B6v, B7v, B7v, B7v, B7v, B8v, B8v, C2v, C2v, C3, C3, C3, C3, C3v, C3v, C3v, C3v–4, C4

Title [within single rules]: *MERLINVS ANONYMVS.* [swash initial *M*] | An | ALMANACK, | And no *Almanack.* | A KALENDAR,

| And no *Kalendar*. | An EPHEMERIS (between jeſt, and | earneſt) for the year, 1653. | Monthly Obſervations, and Chronolo- | gicall Annotations, on things paſt, | preſent, and to come. | WITH | A Prognoſtication, and Plenary Prediction | as well on the Eclipſes of Divers, as the aſpects | of the Planets, *(Peregrine)* and the mo- | tions of tereſtiall Bodies. | ALSO | A Meteorologicall Diary, fitted for the uſe of | Citizen, and Country-man, in a novell, | but pleaſing meth- od. | Intended eſpecially for the Horizon of Saint | *George-ſtreet Southwark*, where the Pole [swash k] | is elevated 1200 inches from that | of *China*, but may indifferent- | ly ſerve for all Climates, | Countries, and Con- | tinents. | [rule] | By *RAPHAEL DESMVS*, PHILOLOGIST. | [rule] | *Lætitia Cœlum vos creavit ſua.* | *Lætitia Cœlum vos ſervabit veſtra.* | *LONDON:* Printed by *F: N:* 1653.

The L Thomason copy, dated "Jan. 3 1652," may be the only surviving copy of 1653:2b. Its sheet A (l. 33 from "The Calme" on sig. A5v reads "*Like* Bajacet the shepherds scoffe,") is a line-for-line, error-ridden, resetting of 1653:2a; its sheet B (l. 35 from "To the Countesse of Bedford. T'have written then" on sig. B3v reads "*Lightnesse depresse us, emp*") has stop-press corrections but has not been reset; and the line-for-line resetting in its sheet C (a separate title page on sig. C2 reads "GENERALL") corrects some obvious errors in 1653:2a while introducing some new errors. Despite the fact that its title page is part of its sheet A, the following omissions in the texts of 1653:2b establish the priority of 1653:2a: "*draw*" at the end of the thirteenth line of the selection on sig. A4v; "*or*" following "*Chance*," on l. 6 of the selection on sig. A6v; "*greet themselves*" following "*strangers*" on l. 7 of the selection from sig. A8v; and "*respect;*" following "*devout*" in l. 2 of the selection from sig. C2v.

1653:2c 1654

Title [within single rules]: *MERLINVS ANONYMVS.* [swash *M, A*] | An *Almanack*, and no *Almanck.* [swash *k, k*] | A *Kalendar*, and no *Kalendar.* | An *Epemeris* (between jeſt, and earneſt) for | the Year 1654. | Lunacious Obſervations, monethly Prognoſti- | cations, and chronological Annotations, pointing to | a clear diſcovery of vvhat *was, is,* and *ſhall be.* | With a Prophylatical Prediction, as well on di- | vers dreadful Eclipſes, as the mutual aſpects of thoſe Sa- | turine, Joviall, Solar, Venerious, Witty, Warlike, Watry, | (Pegaſian) Plan- ets, vvho govern mens bodies, and | the magnetick motions of terreſtial carcaſes. | ALSO, | A Meteorogical Diary fitted for the uſe of Citi- | zen, and Countriman, the times, and tides that vvill | ſtay

for any man, Phyſical Aphoriſm's of the | famous man-curer *Sig-
nior Alphonſo Mon-* | *tibanco Egregio,* vvith other (contami- | nated)
curious crotchets, | vvorthy devout notice. | Intended eſpecially for
the Horizon of Saint *An* | *drews Holburn,* viz: *Grayes-Inn-lane,*
vvhere the pole | is elevated 1600 cubits from that of *Comſmopo-* |
lis, and may indifferently ſerve for all cli- | mats, Countries, and
continents. | [rule] | By *Raphael Deſmus* Philologiſt. | [rule] | *Lætitia
Cælum vos creavit ſua,* | *Lætitia Cælum vos ſervabit veſtra.* | [rule] |
LONDON: | Printed by *F. Neile* in Alderſgate-ſtreet: 1654.

Collation: 8º: A–C⁸ ($4: A1, title, unsigned; B3, unsigned)
Wing:[1] A1589
Copy: L E.1487.(1)
Verse: "The first Anniversary" (ll. 251–58), sig. B3v; "The first
Anniversary" (ll. 259–66), sig. B7v
This Thomason copy is dated "Nou. 18 1653."

---

1. The 1655 edition (Wing: A1590) lacks any Donne verse.

1653:3a

Author: Izaak Walton
Title [engraved and typeset]: *The* | *Compleat Angler* | *or the* |
Contemplative Man's | *Recreation.* | Being a Diſcourſe of | FISH and
FISHING, | Not unworthy the peruſal of moſt *Anglers.* | [short
rules] | Simon Peter ſaid, I go a fiſhing: *and they ſaid, We* | *alſo wil go
with thee.* John 21.3. | [short rules] | *London,* Printed by *T. Maxey* for
Rɪᴄʜ. Mᴀʀʀɪᴏᴛ, in | S. *Dunſtans* Church-yard Fleetſtreet, 1653.

Collation: 8º. A–Q⁸ R⁴ ($4: A1, title, unsigned; G4, missigned
F4; P5, signature inverted; R3, unsigned; R4, blank, unsigned)
Wing: W661
Copy: CSmH 105478
Verse: "The Baite," pp. 184–86
The Thomason copy (L, shelfmark: E.1488.[1]) is dated "May.
20. 1653."

Additional seventeenth-century issues/editions:[1]

1653:3b 1655 (Wing: W662): pp. 256–57

1653:3c 1661 (Wing: W663): pp. 186–87

1653:3d 1664 (Wing: W664): pp. 186–87

1653:3e 1668 (Wing: W665): pp. 186–87

1653:3f 1676 (Wing: W666): pp. 194–95

---

1. For reproductions of the title pages for these editions and issue, see Jonquil Bevan, ed., *Izaak Walton: The Compleat Angler 1653–1676*, pp. 41–45.

1654:1a
Compiler: R. C. [Robert Chamberlain]
Title [within ornamental border]: THE | HARMONY | OF THE | MUSES: | OR, | The Gentlemans and Ladies | Choiʃeʃt Recreation; Full of various, pure, | and tranʃcendent Wit. | Containing ʃeverall excellent Poems; Some, | Fancies of Love, ʃome of Diʃdain, and all the | ʃubjects incident to the paʃʃionate Affecti- | ons either of men or women. | Heretofore written by thoʃe unimitable Ma- | ʃters of Learning and Invention, |

Dr. *Joh. Donn*	Sr. *Kenelm Digby*	*J. Cleveland*
Dr. *Hen. King*	Mr. *Ben. Johnʃon,*	*T. Randolph*
Dr. *W. Stroad*	Mr. *Fra. Beamont*	*T. Carew.*

[swash *J, J, J*] | And others of the moʃt refined Wits of thoʃe | TIMES. | [rule] | *Never before Publiʃhed.* | [rule] | *London,* Printed by *T. W.* for *William Gilbertʃon* | at the ʃign of the Bible in *Giltʃpur-ʃtreet* | without *Newgate.* 1654.
Collation: 8º. A–G⁸ ($4: A1, blank, unsigned; A2, title, unsigned)
Wing: C105; Keynes: 107
Copy: CSmH 55252
Verse:[1] "Elegy: Going to Bed," pp. 2–3; "Elegy: Loves Warr" (ll. 29–46), pp. 6–7; "Elegy: Loves Progress," pp. 36–39; "Elegy: The Autumnall," pp. 47–49; "A Valediction: forbidding mourning," pp. 97–98; "The Prohibition," pp. 98–99; "Loves diet," pp. 99–100; "The Will," pp. 102–3

The CSmH copy may not be unique and may not represent the only state of the text. Although sig. A1 is blank, sig. A1v describes "The Frontispiece," and W. Carew Hazlitt lists a copy "With a frontispiece" (*Hand-Book to the Popular, Poetical, and Dramatic Literature of Great Britain, from the Invention of Printing to the Restoration* [1867; rpt. New York, 1961], p. 81). For a fuller description of 1654:1a, see my edition.

---

1. Earliest printing of "Elegy: Going to Bed," any part of "Elegy: Loves Warr," and "Elegy: Loves Progress."

1654:2a
Author: Edmund Gayton
Title [within double rules]: PLEASANT | NOTES | UPON | Don Quixot. | [rule] | By EDMUND GAYTON, Eſq; | [rule] | JUVENAL. | ═══════lætam fecit cum Statius Vrbem, | Eſurit, intactam Paridi niſi vendat Agauen. | Authors muſt ſell *Romances*, or such *Books*, [swash k] | Or elſe they will want money for the *Cooks*. [swash k] | [rule] | [inverted ornament] | [rule] | LONDON, | Printed by *William Hunt*. MDCLIV.
Collation: 2°. π¹ *⁴ *² B–Z⁴ 2A–2O⁴ ($2: π1, title)
Wing: G415
Copy: CSmH 148580
Verse: "The Storme" (ll. 3–5), p. 35

Additional seventeenth-century issue:

1654:2b 1654 (Wing: G415. CSmH, shelfmark: 148581): p. 35
The priority of 1654:2a and 1654:2b is uncertain: both title pages have the same type, rules, and bunch of grapes watermark (the paper other than that in the title pages in both copies has a tall vase watermark). Their texts of "The Storme" (ll. 3–5) are identical. The title page of 1654:2b reads:
Title [within double rules]: PLEASANT | NOTES | UPON | Don Quixot. | [rule] | By EDMUND GAYTON, Eſq; | [rule] | JUVENAL. | ═══════lætam fecit cum Statius Vrbem, | Eſurit, intactam Paridi niſi vendat Agauen. | [rule] | [ornament] | [rule] | LONDON, | Printed by *William Hunt*. MDCLIV.

1654:3a
Author: Henry Wotton
Title [within ornamental border]: *Reliquiæ Wottonianæ*. [swash R, W] | [rule] | OR | A COLLECTION
of { LIVES, LETTERS, POEMS;
With | CHARACTERS | OF | Sundry PERSONAGES: | *And other* | Incomparable PIECES | of *Language* and *Art*. | [rule] | *By* The curious PENCIL of | the Ever Memorable | Sʳ *Henry Wotton* Kᵗ, [swash W] | Late | Provoſt of *Eton Colledge*. | [rule] | The ſecond *Edition* with large *Additions*. | [rule] | LONDON, | Printed by *Thomas Maxey*, for R. *Marriot*, | G. *Bedel*, and T. *Garthwait*. 1654.
Collation: 12°. A⁶ B–D¹² d¹² E–2C¹² ($5: A1, wanting; A2, title,

unsigned; A5, unsigned; E1, blank, signed; G11, wanting; *S⁸ inserted between S2v and S3; S4, unsigned; T1, unsigned)
    Wing: W3649
    Copy: L 635.c.11
    Verse:[1] "To Sir H. W. at his going Ambassador to Venice," sigs. C6v–7v

Additional seventeenth-century editions:

1654:3b 1672 (Wing: W3650): sigs. c2r–v

1654:3c 1685 (Wing: W3651): sigs. c2r–v

---

1. Izaak Walton's *The Life of Sir Henry Wotton* in the 1651 1st ed. of *Reliquiæ Wottonianæ* (Wing: W3648) lacks "To Sir H. W. at his going Ambassador to Venice."

1654:4a
    Author: Richard Whitlock
    Title [within double rules]: ΖΩΟΤΟΜΙΑ, | OR, | OBSERVATIONS | ON THE | PRESENT MANNERS | OF THE | ENGLISH: | *Briefly Anatomizing the Living* [swash B, A] | *by the Dead.* | WITH | AN USEFULL DETECTION | OF THE | Mountebanks of both Sexes. | [rule] | By *Richard Whitlock*, M. D. Late Fellow of [swash k] | *All-Souls* Colledge in *OXFORD*. | [rule] | *LONDON*, | Printed by *Tho. Roycroft*, and are to be ſold by | *Humphrey Moſeley*, at the Princes Armes in [swash M] | St. *Pauls* Church-yard, 1654.
    Collation: 8°. A⁸ ($5: A1, blank, unsigned; A1v, explication of frontispiece; A2, blank, unsigned; A2v, frontispiece; A3, title, unsigned) a⁸ ($4) A² (original A4 and A5 replaced by current A5 and moved to follow a8) B–2O⁸ ($4) 2P⁴ ($2: 2P4, blank)
    Wing: W2030
    Copy: CSmH 148368
    Verse: "Satyre III" (ll. 77–79), p. 218; "The second Anniversarie" (ll. 241–46), p. 336[339]; "The second Anniversarie" (ll. 341–42), p. 350
    The Thomason copy (L, shelfmark: E.1478.[2]) is dated "Jan. 24 1653."

1655:1a
    Compiler: John Cotgrave
    Title: WITS INTERPRETER, | THE | *ENGLISH PARNASSVS.*

[swash *N, G, P, R, N, V*] | OR, | A ſure Guide to thoſe Admirable Accom- | pliſhments that compleat our Engliſh *Gentry*, in | the moſt acceptable Qualifications of *Diſcourſe*, or | *Writing*. | In which brief- ly the whole Myſtery of thoſe plea- | ſing *Witchcrafts* of *Eloquence* and *Love* are made eaſie | in the following Subjects. |

1. *The Art of Reaſoning, A new Logick.*

2. *Theatre of Court ſhip, Ac- curate Complements.*

3. *The Labyrinth of Fancies, New Experiments and In- ventions.*

4. *Apollo and Orpheus ſeve- rall Love-Songs, Epigrams, Drolleries, and other Verſes.*

5. Cyprian *Goddeſs, Deſcrip- tion of Beauty.*

6. *The Muſes* Elizium, *ſeve- rall Poeticall Fictions,*

7. *The perfect Inditer, Letters Ala-mode.*

8. Cardinal Richeleiu's *Key to his manner of writing of Letters by Cyphers.*

| As alſo an Alphabeticall Table of the first Deviſers of | Sciences and other Curioſities; All which are collected with In- | duſtry and Care, for the benefit and delight of thoſe that love in- | genious Enterpriſes. | [rule] | By *I. C.* | [rule] | *Trahit ſua quemque voluptas.* | [rule] | *LONDON,* | Printed for *N: Brooke*, at the Angel in *Cornhill*. 1655. [swash *k*]

Collation: 8°. A–M⁸ O–Z⁸ 2A–2E⁸ 2F⁴ ($4: A1, engraved title, unsigned; A2, title, unsigned; A7–8, advertisements; H3, un- signed; L3, unsigned; 2D4, unsigned; 2E4, unsigned; 2F3, un- signed; 2F4, half-title, unsigned) 2A–2H⁸ ($4: 2A3, unsigned; 2A4, unsigned; 2B3, unsigned; 2B4, unsigned; 2D3, missigned D3; 2G4, unsigned)

Wing: C6370; Case: 110

Copy: CSmH 120919

Half title: VVɪᴛꜱ Iɴᴛᴇʀᴘʀᴇᴛᴇʀ: | OR, | *Apollo* and *Orpheus*: Sev- eral [swash *A*] | Love-Songs, Drollery, and | other Verſes.

Verse: "A Feaver," sigs. O2v–3; "Breake of day" (ll. 1–6), sig. O7v; "Breake of day" (ll. 1–6), sig. P5r–v; *A*"The Dampe,"[1] sig. P6r–v; "Elegy: Loves Warr" (ll. 29–32), sig. T4v; "Elegy: Loves Warr" (ll. 35–36), sig. T4v; "Elegy: Loves Warr" (ll. 39–40), sig. T4v; "Elegy: Loves Warr" (ll. 43–46), sig. T4v

The Thomason copy (L, shelfmark: E.1448) is dated "May 7" 1655.

Additional seventeenth-century editions:

1655:1b 1662 (Wing: C6371; Case: 110[b]): pp. 109–10, 118–19, 130– 31, 133, 193, 194, 194, 194

1655:1c 1671 (Wing: C6372; Case: 110[c]): pp. 109–10, 118–19, 130–31, 133, 193, 194, 194, 194

---

1. The poem is Thomas Carew's "Secresie protested."

1655:2a

Author: Johann Grindal

Title: Aendachtige | BEDENCKINGEN, | Op de voorvallende gelegenthe- | den, en befondere trappen in des | Autheurs fieckte. | *Beftaende* | I. 𝕴𝖓 𝕭𝖊𝖉𝖊𝖓𝖈𝖐𝖎𝖓𝖌𝖍𝖊𝖓 𝖔𝖕 𝖉𝖊𝖘 𝕸𝖊𝖓𝖘𝖈𝖍𝖊𝖓 | 𝖘𝖙𝖆𝖓𝖙 𝖊𝖓 𝖈𝖔𝖓𝖉𝖎𝖙𝖎𝖊. | II. 𝕴𝖓 𝖇𝖗𝖆𝖌𝖊𝖓/ 𝖊𝖓 𝖉𝖊𝖇𝖆𝖙𝖊𝖗𝖎𝖓𝖌𝖊𝖓 𝖒𝖊𝖙 𝕲𝖔𝖉𝖙. | III. 𝕴𝖓 𝕲𝖊𝖇𝖊𝖉𝖊𝖓/ 𝖔𝖕 𝖇𝖊𝖘𝖔𝖓𝖉𝖊𝖗𝖊 𝖔𝖈𝖈𝖆𝖘𝖎𝖊𝖓 𝖉𝖊𝖓 | 𝕬𝖚𝖙𝖍𝖊𝖚𝖗 𝖘𝖊𝖑𝖋𝖘 𝖛𝖔𝖔𝖗𝖌𝖊𝖐𝖔𝖒𝖊𝖓. | In't Engelfch befchreven door den ver- | maerden en hoog-geleerden | D. JOANNEM DONN. | 𝕰𝖓 𝖔𝖒 𝖋𝖎𝖏𝖓𝖊 𝖛𝖔𝖔𝖗𝖙𝖗𝖊𝖋𝖋𝖊𝖑𝖎𝖏𝖈𝖐𝖍𝖊𝖞𝖉𝖙𝖘 𝖜𝖎𝖑𝖑𝖊 𝖛𝖎𝖏𝖙= | 𝖒𝖆𝖊𝖑 𝖎𝖓 '𝖙 𝕰𝖓𝖌𝖊𝖑𝖘 𝖍𝖊𝖗𝖉𝖗𝖚𝖈𝖐𝖙. | *En nu in 't Nederlandts vertaelt, door* J. G. | [ornament] | t'AMSTERDAM, | [rule] | 𝕭𝖞 Abram de Wees, 𝕭𝖔𝖊𝖈𝖐-𝖛𝖊𝖗𝖐𝖔𝖔𝖕𝖊𝖗 𝖎𝖓 𝖉𝖊 | 𝕲𝖆𝖘𝖙-𝖍𝖚𝖞𝖘 𝕸𝖔𝖑𝖊𝖓-𝖘𝖙𝖊𝖊𝖌𝖍. 𝕬𝖓𝖓𝖔 1655.

Collation: 12°. π⁴ A–D¹² F–I¹² K⁸ ($7: π1, title; K6, unsigned; K7, unsigned)

Wing: none

Copy:[1] xerox of copy at Universiteits-Bibliotheek, Universiteit van Amsterdam 2328 F 28

Verse: "Insultus morbi primus," sig. π4r–v; "Insultus morbi primus," segments on pp. 1, 9, 15, 24, 34, 43, 54, 65, 75, 85, 94, 105, 115, 122, 135, 143, 151, 161, 173, 188, 197, 209, 219

---

1. This copy wants sheet E. The verse on sheet E (pp. 97–120) is supplied from xerox of sheet E in a copy owned by W. van Gent. For a description of the Gent copy, see Paul R. Sellin, *John Donne and 'Calvinist' Views of Grace* (Amsterdam: VU Boekhandel /Uitgeverij, 1983), pp. 59–60.

1655:3a

Author: Samuel Sheppard

Title [within single rules]: THE | MARROVV | OF | COMPLE-MENTS. | *OR,* | A moft Methodicall and accu- | rate forme of Inftructions for all Va- | riety of Love-Letters, Amorous Dif- | courfes, and Complementall En- | tertainements. | Fitted for the ufe of all forts of perfons from | the Noblemans Palace to the | Artizans Shop. | *With many delightfull Songs, Sonnetts,* | *Odes, Dia-logues, &c.* | Never before publifhed. | [rule] | *LONDON,* | Printed for *Humphrey Moʃeley*, and are to be | ʃold at his ʃhop at the *Princes Armes* in St. *Pauls* | Church-yard. 1655.

Collation: 12°. A–H¹² ($5: A1, title, unsigned; B4, unsigned; C4, unsigned; D5, unsigned; F2, missigned F3)

Wing: M719; Case: 109

Copy: L E.1530

Verse: "Elegy: The Expostulation" (ll. 1–11), pp. 41–42; "Elegy: The Expostulation" (ll. 13–21), p. 42; "Elegy: The Expostulation" (ll. 27–30), p. 42; "Elegy: The Expostulation" (l. 39), p. 42; "Elegy: The Expostulation" (ll. 42–44), p. 42

This Thomason copy (L, shelfmark: E.1530) is dated "July 15 1654."

1656:1A

Author: Abraham Cowley

Title [within double rules]: POEMS: |

Viz. { I. *MISCELLANIES.* [swash *M, N*]

II. *The Miʃtreʃs, or, Love Verʃes.* [swash *M*]

III. *PINDARIQUE ODES.* [swash *N, R, Q, U,* last *E*]

| And IV. | Davideis, | OR, A | SACRED POEM | OF THE | TROU-BLES | OF | DAVID. | [rule] | Written by *A. COWLEY.* [swash *A, C, E*] | [rule] | Virg. Georg. 3. | ———*Tentanda via eʃt quà me quoq; poʃsim* [swash *v*] | *Tollere humo, victorq virûm volitare per ora.* | [rule] | *LONDON,* | Printed for *Humphrey Moʃeley,* at the Prince's | Arms in St *Pauls* Church-yard, M.DC.LVI.

Collation: 2°. π¹ A² (a)-(b)⁴ B–F⁴ 2A–2K⁴ 3A² 3B–3I⁴ 3K² 4A–4T⁴ ²π¹ 5A–5C⁴ ($2: π1, title; A1, blank, unsigned; A2, unsigned; 2A1, separate title, unsigned; 2B1, missigned B1; 2B2, missigned B2; 3A1, separate title, unsigned; 3G1, missigned G1; 3H1, missigned H1; 3K2, unsigned; 4A1, separate title, unsigned; 5A1, missigned A1; 5A2, missigned A2)

Wing: C6682; Perkin: A19[1]

Copy: CSmH 120869

Verse: "The Will" (l. 51), sig. (a)3v

Large-paper (329 x 212 mm) copy.

1656:1a 1656 (Wing: C6682. C, shelfmark: Keynes 0.3.3): sig. (a)3v

Small-paper (270 x 170 mm) copy. The text of "The Will" (l. 51) is identical to that in 1656:1A.

---

1. M. R. Perkin, *Abraham Cowley: A Bibliography.*

1656:2a

Compiler: John Mennes

Title: WIT | AND | DROLLERY, | JOVIAL POEMS. | Never before Printed. | [rule] | By Sir *J.M. Ja: S.* Sir *W.D. J.D.* | And other admirable Wits. | [rule] | *Vt Nectar Ingenium.* [swash N] | [rule] | *LONDON,* | Printed for Nath: Brook, at the | Angel in Cornhil, 1656.

Collation: 8º. A⁴ B–G⁸ H⁴ F⁸ H–M⁸ ($4: A1, title, unsigned; A4, unsigned; H4, unsigned; ²F1, missigned G; ²F3, unsigned)

Wing: W3131; Case: 114

Copy: L E.1617.(1)

Verse: "Elegy: Loves Progress," pp. 157–60

This, the Thomason copy, is dated "January 18 1655."

Additional seventeenth-century edition:[1]

1656:2b 1661 (Wing: W3132; Case: 114[b]): pp. 237–40

------

1. The 1682 work *WIT AND DROLLERY. Jovial Poems* (Wing: W3133; Case: 114[c]) lacks Donne verse.

1656:3a

Compiler: Abraham Wright

Title [within double rules]: Parnaſſus Biceps. | *OR* [swash R] | *Severall Choice Pieces* [swash C, P] | OF | POETRY, | Compoſed by the beſt WITS | that were in both the | Univerſities | BEFORE THEIR | DISSOLUTION. | [rule] | *With an* Epiſtle *in the behalfe of* | *thoſe now doubly ſecluded and ſequeſtred* | Members, *by One who* | *himſelfe is none.* | [rule] | *LONDON:* [swash N, D, N] | Printed for | *George Everſden* at the Signe [swash G, E] | of the *Maidenhead* in St. *Pauls* [swash P] | Church-yard. 1656.

Collation: 8º. A–L⁸ M² ($4: A1, title, unsigned; M2, unsigned)

Wing: W3686; Case: 113

Copy: L 1076.a.18

Verse: "Elegy: The Anagram" (ll. 1–52), pp. 86–88; "Elegy: The Autumnall," pp. 118–19

1657:1a

Author: Joshua Poole

Title: The Engliſh | <PARNASSUS:> | OR, | A HELPE | TO | <English Poeſie.> | Containing | A ſhort <Inſtitution> of <that

Art,> | *A COLLECTION* [swash *A, C*] | Of all <Rhyming Monoſyl-
lables,> | The choiceſt <Epithets,> and <Phraſes:> | With ſome |
General <Forms> upon all <Occaſions, Subjects,> | and
<Theams,> Alphabetically digeſted | [rule] | By <*JOSUA
POOLE.*> M.A. *Clare Hall Camb.* [swash <*J*>, <*A*>] | [rule] | *Lon-
don,* Printed for <*Tho. Johnſon,*> at the golden <Key> [swash
<*J*>] | in St. *Pauls* Church-yard. 1657.

Collation: 8°. A⁸ a⁴ B–Z⁸ 2A–2S⁸ 2T⁴ ($4: A1, blank; A2, title,
unsigned; I4, unsigned; V3, unsigned; 2F4, missigned F4; 2T3–4,
unsigned)

Wing: P2814; Case: 115

Copy: ICN CASE X 997.69

Verse: "Satyre IIII" (ll. 129–30), sig. Q6; "Elegie. Death" (l. 19),
sig. R5v; "The second Anniversarie" (ll. 223–25), sig. R5v; "The
second Anniversarie" (l. 176), sig. S4v; "The Progresse of the
Soule" (ll. 502–4), sig. S5v; "The Calme" (ll. 8–9), sig. S8;
"The Sunne Rising" (l. 10), sig. V4v; "Elegie. Death" (l. 19), sig.
X7v; "The Progresse of the Soule" (ll. 381–83), sig. Y2; "The Apparition" (l. 12), sig. 2A1; "The Progresse of the Soule" (ll. 231, 236),
sig. 2B6; "Elegy: The Expostulation" (l. 28), sig. 2H1; "Obsequies
to the Lord Harrington" (ll. 16–17), sig. 2H5; "The Progresse of the
Soule" (ll. 21–26, 29), sig. 2H6; "Elegy: The Autumnall" (l. 2), sig.
2H8; "Song. 'Go, and catch a falling star'" (l. 13), sig. 2H8v; "Elegy: The Autumnall" (ll. 37–44), sig. 2I1v; "The Storme" (ll. 35–36),
sig. 2M3; "Satyre IIII" (ll. 18–23), sig. 2N4v; "The Storme" (ll. 43–
44, 67–68), sig. 2O6v; "Elegy: The Perfume" (ll. 35–36), sig. 2Q7v;
"Satyre II" (ll. 34–36), sig. 2Q7v; "The first Anniversary" (ll. 435–
39), sig. 2S7

Additional seventeenth-century issues/editions:

1657:1b 1657 (Wing: P2814; Case: 115. CSmH, shelfmark: 12886):
sigs. Q6, R5v, R5v, S4v, S5v, S8, V4v, X7v, Y2, 2A1, 2B6, 2H1, 2H5,
2H6, 2H8, 2H8v, 2I1v, 2M3, 2N4v, 2O6v, 2Q7v, 2Q7v, 2S7

Title: The Engliſh | PARNASSUS: | OR, | A HELPE | TO | English
Poeſie. | Containing *A COLLECTION* [swash *A, C*] | Of all Rhym-
ing Monoſyllables, | The choiceſt Epithets, and Phraſes: | With
ſome | General Forms upon all Occaſions, Subjects, | and Theams,
Alphabetically digeſted | [rule] | By *JOSUA POOLE.* M.A. *Clare Hall
Camb.* [swash *J*] | [rule] | Together with | A ſhort Inſtitution to
Engliſh Poe- | ſie, by way of Preface. | [rule] | *London,* Printed for

Tho. Johnſon, at the golden Key [swash J] | in St. *Pauls* Church-yard. 1657.

The order of 1657:1a and 1657:1b is uncertain; however, the addition of "A short Institution to English Poesie, by way of Pref-ace" on the title page would suggest that 1657:1b is the later issue. The texts of the Donne verses in 1657:1b are identical to those in 1657:1a.

1657:1c 1677 (Wing: P2815; Case: 115[b]): sigs. Q2, R1v, R1v, R8v, S1v, S4, T8v, X3v, X6, Z5, 2B2, 2G5, 2H1, 2H2, 2H4, 2H4v, 2H5v, 2L7, 2M8v, 2O2v, 2Q3v, 2Q3v, 2S2

1657:1d 1678 (Wing: P2816): sigs. Q2, R1v, R1v, R8v, S1v, S4, T8v, X3v, X6, Z5, 2B2, 2G5, 2H1, 2H2, 2H4, 2H4v, 2H5v, 2L7, 2M8v, 2O2v, 2Q3v, 2Q3v, 2S2

1658:1a

Author: Aston Cokayne

Title: Small | POEMS | OF | Divers ſorts | [rule] | Written by | Sir *ASTON COKAIN.* [swash N, N] | [rule] | [three rows of ornaments] | *LONDON* Printed by *WIL. GODBID*, 1658.

Collation: 8°. A–2L⁸ ($4: A1v, portrait; A2, title, unsigned; A4, unsigned; B3, unsigned; T7, blank; T8, blank; V1, separate title, unsigned; V3, missigned X3; 2A3, missigned A3)

Wing: C4898

Copy: CSmH 31338

Verse: "The second Anniversarie" (l. 65), sig. R3

1658:2a

Author: Aston Cokayne

Title: A CHAIN | OF | GOLDEN POEMS | Embelliſhed with | Wit, Mirth, and Eloquence. | Together with two moſt excellent | COMEDIES, | (*viz.*) | *The OBSTINATE LADY,* | AND | TRAPPOLIN | Suppos'd a Prince: | [rule] | Written by | Sʳ *Aſton Cokayn.* [swash k] | [rule] | *LONDON,* Printed by *W.G.* and are to be [swash N, D, N, G] | ſold by *Iſaac Pridmore*, at the *Golden-Falcon* [swash P] | near the *New-Exchange.* 1658.

Collation: 8°. π¹ A–2L⁸ ($4: π1v, portrait; A1, title, unsigned; A2, separate title, unsigned; A4, unsigned; B3, unsigned; T7, blank; T8, blank; V1, separate title, unsigned; V3, missigned X3; 2A3, missigned A3)

Wing: C4894

Copy: CSmH 84862

Separate title: Small | POEMS | OF | Divers ſorts | [rule] | Written by | Sir *ASTON COKAIN*. [swash *N, N*] | [rule] | [three rows of ornaments] | *LONDON* Printed by *WIL. GODBID*, 1658.

Verse: "The second Anniversarie" (l. 65), sig. R3

The same typesetting as 1658:1a but with a collective (and presumably later) title page placed between the portrait and the title page of 1658:1a.

Additional seventeenth-century issue:

1658:2b 1659 (CLU-C, shelfmark: *PR3349 C3C3 1659): sig. R3

A reissue of the sheets of 1658:2a with a cancel title page dated 1659. The CLU-C copy also has the 1658:2a title page.

1658:3a

Author: William Dugdale

Title: THE | <HISTORY> | OF | Sᵗ· <PAULS CATHEDRAL> | IN | <LONDON,> | From its Foundation untill theſe Times: |

Extracted out of { Originall CHARTERS.
RECORDS.
LEIGER BOOKS, and other
MANUSCRIPTS.

| Beautified with ſundry Proſpects of the Church, | Figures of Tombes, and Monuments. | [rule] | By <*WILLIAM DVGDALE.*> [swash <*D*>, <*G*>, <*D*>] | [rule] | Pſalm. 48.12,13. | *Walke about Sion, and go round about her; tell the* [swash *k*] | *Towers thereof: Marke ye well her Bulwarks, conſider her* [swash *k, B, k*] | *Palaces, that ye may tell it to the Generations following.* [swash *P, G*] | [rule] | Tibullus. | *Non ego, ſi merui, dubitem procumbere Templis,* [swash *N*] | *Et dare ſacratis oſcula liminibus.* | [rule] | London, Printed by <*Tho. Warren,*> in the year | of our Lord God <MDCLVIII.>

Collation: 2°. A⁴ B–3Z² χ¹ ($2: A1, unsigned; A1v, portrait; A2, title, unsigned; A3, signed; illustration tipped in between L2v and M1; Q1, missigned 2Q; Q2, separate title, unsigned; 2G2, unsigned; folio illustration tipped in between 2K1v and 2K2; folio illustration tipped in between 2L2v and 2M1; 4 folio illustrations + 1 single-leaf illustration + 5 folio illustrations tipped in between 2N2v and 2O1; 2P1, unsigned; 3P2, unsigned; 3X2, unsigned)

Wing: D2482

Copy: L 673.1.16

Separate title: A | VIEW | OF THE | MONUMENTS, | Situate in and about the | Quire, Side-iles, & Chapels | ADJACENT; | As they ſtood in | SEPTEMBER, Anno D. MDCXLI. | WITH THEIR | EPI-TAPHS | EXACTLY IMITATED; | OF WHICH | In regard that to every Eye, the Character is not ſo | legible, I have added the Cop-ies; with ſuch other Monu- | mentall Inſcriptions, made upon Tab-lets of Marble | or otherwiſe, as were then extant there. | [rule] | [ornament] | [rule] | LONDON, Printed in the year, 1658. [swash N, D, N]

Verse: "Ioannes Donne Sac: Theol: Profess," p. 62; "Ioannes Donne Sac: Theol: Profess," p. 63

1658:4a

Author: Constantin Huygens

Title [typeset]: KOREN-BLOEMEN, | <NEDERLANDSCHE GEDICHTEN> | Van | <CONSTANTIN HUYGENS Ridder;> | Heere van Zuylichem, Zeelhem, ende in Monickeland: | Eerſte Raad ende Rekenmeeſter van S. Hoocheit den | Heere PRINCE van ORANGE. | <IN XIX BOECKEN.> | [ornament] | <IN'S GRAVEN-HAGE> | [rule] | By ADRIAEN VLACK | <M. DC. LVIII.> | Met Privilegie vande Heeren Staten van Hollant ende Weſt-Vrieſlant.

Collation: 4º. *⁴ 2*⁴ 3*⁴ 4*² A–7X⁴ 7Y² 7Z⁴ 8A–8K⁴ ($3: *1, orna-mental title, unsigned; *2, typeset title, unsigned; 2*3, unsigned; 4*2, unsigned; G2, unsigned; 2F3, unsigned; 2G3, unsigned; 2K2, unsigned; 2O1, unsigned; 3B3, unsigned; 3I3, unsigned; 3M3, un-signed; 3P3, unsigned; 3Q2, unsigned; 3T1, missigned T1; addi-tional leaf tipped in between 3T2v and 3T3; 3T3, unsigned; 3Z3, unsigned; 4C1, missigned 3C1; 4D3, unsigned; 4K2, unsigned; 4K3, unsigned; 5C2, missigned Ccecc2; 5T3, unsigned; 6P3, un-signed; 8D3, unsigned)

Wing: none; Keynes: 108

Copy: L 11556.dd.30

Verse: "The Flea" (l. 1), p. 1095; T"The Flea," pp. 1095–96; "The Apparition" (l. 1), p. 1096; T"The Apparition," p. 1096; "Witchcraft by a picture" (l. 1), p. 1097; T"Witchcraft by a picture," p. 1097; "Twicknam garden" (l. 1), p. 1097; T"Twicknam garden," pp. 1097–98; "Song. 'Go, and catch a falling star'" (l. 1), p. 1098; T"Song. 'Go, and catch a falling star,'" pp. 1098–95[99]; "The triple Foole" (l. 1), p. 1095[1099]; T"The triple Foole," pp. 1095[1099]–1100; "A Valediction: of weeping" (l. 1), p. 1100; T"A Valediction:

of weeping," pp. 1100–1101; "The Dreame" (l. 1), p. 1101; *T*"The Dreame," pp. 1101–2; "Elegy: The Anagram" (heading, l. 1), p. 1031[1103]; *T*"Elegy: The Anagram," pp. 1031[1103]–4; "Elegy: Oh, let mee not" (heading, l. 11), p. 1105; *T*"Elegy: Oh, let mee not" (ll. 11–34), pp. 1105–6; "The Extasie" (heading, l. 1), p. 1106; *T*"The Extasie," pp. 1106–9; "The Blossome" (l. 1), p. 1110; *T*"The Blossome," pp. 1110–11; "Womans constancy" (l. 1), p. 1110[1112]; *T*"Womans constancy," p. 1110[1112]; "A Valediction: forbidding mourning" (l. 1), p. 1110[1112]; *T*"A Valediction: forbidding mourning," pp. 1110[1112]–14; "The Sunne Rising" (l. 1), p. 1114; *T*"The Sunne Rising," pp. 1114–15; "Breake of day" (l. 1), p. 1115; *T*"Breake of day," pp. 1115–16; "Loves Deitie" (l. 1), p. 1116; *T*"Loves Deitie," pp. 1116–17; "The Legacie" (l. 1), p. 1117; *T*"The Legacie," pp. 1117–18; "Goodfriday, 1613. Riding Westward" (l. 1), p. 1118; *T*"Goodfriday, 1613. Riding Westward," pp. 1118–20

Additional seventeenth-century edition:

1658:4b 1672 (Wing: none. L, shelfmark: C.134.h.4): 2:538, 538, 539, 539, 539, 539–40, 540, 540–41, 541, 541, 541, 541–42, 542, 542–43, 543, 543–44, 544, 544–45, 545, 545–46, 546, 546–49, 549, 549–51, 551, 551, 551, 551–52, 552, 552–53, 553, 553–54, 554, 554–55, 555, 555–56, 556, 556–57

1658:5a
   Compiler: Henry Stubbs
   Title: DELICIÆ | Poetarum | Anglicanorum | IN *GRÆCVM* [swash *R*] | VERSÆ. | *Quibus accedunt Elogia* Romæ | & Venetiarum. | [rule] | Authore H. Stubbe A.M. *ex æde Chrifti.* | [rule] | [ornament] | [rule] | OXONIÆ, | Excudebat H. Hall, Academiæ Typographus, | impenſis Edvardi Forrest. 1658.
   Collation: 8°. A–C⁸ D² ($4: A1, title, unsigned; C8, blank?, wanting)
   Wing: S6040; Keynes: 109
   Copy: CSmH 147890
   Verse: "A Valediction: forbidding mourning," pp. 36, 38; *T*"A Valediction: forbidding mourning," pp. 37, 39; "Hero and Leander," p. 38; "Hero and Leander" (heading only), p. 39; *T*" Hero and Leander," p. 39; "A licentious person," p. 40; *T*"A licentious person," p. 41

1658:6a

Author: Izaak Walton

Title [within ornamental border]: THE LIFE | OF | *JOHN DONNE*, [swash *J N, D, N, N, E*] | Dr. in Divinty, | AND | Late Dean of Saint | *PAVLS* Church [swash *P*] | *LONDON*. | [rule] | The ſecond impreſſion cor- | rected and enlarged. | [rule] | Ecclus. 48.14. | *He did wonders in his life, and at his | death his works were marvelous.* [swash *k*] | [rule] | *LONDON,* | Printed by *J. G.* for *R. Marriot*, and [swash *J*] | are to be ſold at his ſhop under | S. *Dunſtans* Church in [swash *D*] | Fleet-ſtreet. 1658.

Collation: 12°. A–G¹² ($5: A1, blank, unsigned; A1v, portrait; A2, title, unsigned; A5, unsigned)

Wing:¹ W668; Keynes: 193

Copy: CSmH 148356

Verse: "A Hymne to God the Father," p. 77; "To Mʳ George Herbert, with one of my seals" (ll. 1–3), p. 83; *T*"To Mʳ George Herbert, with one of my seals" (ll. 3–24),² pp. 83–84; "Hymne to God my God, in my sicknesse" (heading only), p. 85; "Ioannes Donne Sac: Theol: Profess," pp. 113–14

----

1. The earliest version of Walton's *The Life of John Donne* appears in 1640:2a.

2. The English translation remains anonymous.

1659:1a

Author: John Suckling

Title: THE LAST | REMAINS | OF | Sʳ *JOHN SVCKLING.* [swash *J, N, K, N, G*] | [rule] | Being a Full | COLLECTION | Of all his | Poems and Letters | which have been ſo long expected, | and never till now Publiſhed. | WITH | The *Licence* and *Approbation* of his | Noble and Deareſt | FRIENDS. | [rule] | *LONDON:* | Printed for *Humphrey Moſeley* at the Prince's | Arms in St. *Pauls* Churchyard. 1659.

Collation: 8°. A–G⁸ ($4: A1, title, unsigned; a⁴, with a1 and a2 signed, inserted between A1v and A2; A3, unsigned; E1, separate title, unsigned; G2, missigned F2)

Wing: S6130

Copy: L 643.C.70.(2)

Verse: "The Storme" (ll. 3–5), sig. a3v

The Thomason copy (L, shelfmark: E.1768.[2]) is dated "June" 1659.

1660:1a
Author: William Winstanley
Title [typeset within ornamental border]: England's | WOR-
THIES. | Select LIVES of the moſt | Eminent Perſons from *Conſtan-
tine* the | Great, to the death of *Oliver Cromwel* | late Protector. | [rule]
Polib. *Hiſtorici eſt, ne quid falſi, audeat dicere; ne quid | veri, non audeat.*
| [rule] | By WILLIAM WINSTANLEY, Gent. | [rule] | [printer's device]
| [rule] | *London,* Printed for *Nath. Brooke,* at the Sign of [swash *k*] |
the Angel in *Cornhill,* 1660.
    Collation: 8°. A⁸ a⁸ B–2R⁸ 2S⁴ ($4: A1, blank, unsigned; A1v,
engraved title; A2, title, unsigned; 2R3, unsigned; 2S3, unsigned;
2S4, unsigned)
    Wing: W3058
    Copy: L E.1736.(1)
    Verse: "A Hymne to God the Father," p. 305
    This, the Thomason copy, is dated "ffeb. 2 1659."

Additional seventeenth-century edition:

1660:1b 1684 (Wing: W3059): p. 384

1661:1a
Author: Thomas Forde
Title [within double rules]: A | THEATRE | OF | WITS, | Ancient
and Modern. | *Attended with ſeverall other inge-* | *nious Pieces from the
ſame PEN.* |

	I. *Fæneſtra in Pectore,* or a Century of Familiar *LETTERS.*
	II. *Loves Labyrinth:* A Tragi-comedy.
Viz.	III. *Fragmenta Poetica:* Or Poetical Diverſions.
	IV. *Virtus Rediviva,* a Panegyrick on our late King *CHARLES* of ever bleſſed Memory.

| Concluding, with | A PANEGYRICK on His | Sacred Majeſties moſt
happy | Return. | [rule] | By *T. F.* | [rule] | *Varietas delectat.* | [rule] |
LONDON | Printed by *R. & W. Leybourn,* for *Thomas Baſſet,* | in St.
Dunſtans Church-yard in *Fleet-ſtreet.* | 1661.
    Collation: 8°. π¹ A–2B⁸ 2C⁴ ($4: π1, collective title; A1, separate
title, unsigned; C3, unsigned; G4, unsigned; H4, unsigned; K3,
unsigned; K4, unsigned; N4, unsigned; P3, unsigned; Q3, un-
signed; R3, unsigned; T3, unsigned; V1, separate title, unsigned;
V3, unsigned; 2C3, missigned C3)

Wing: F1548A
Copy: O Douce F 303
Separate title: A | THEATRE | OF | WITS, | Ancient and Modern. | *Reprefented in a Collection of* | Apothegmes. | *Pleafant and Profitable.* | [rule] | By Tho. Forde. | [rule] | *Omne tulit punctum, qui mifcuit utile dulci.* | *Habent enim Apothegmata peculiarem quandam* [swash A] | *rationem, & indolem fuam, ut breviter, argutè, falsè,* | *& urbanè cujufq; ingenium exprimant.* Erafmus. | [rule] | *LONDON,* | Printed by R. and W. Leybourn, for *William* | *Grantham* at the Black Bear in St. *Pauls* | Church-yard, neer the little | North Door. 1660.

Verse: "Satyre II" (ll. 21–22), sig. D1

Separate title: *Fæneftra in Pectore.* | OR, | FAMILIAR LETTERS. | [rule] | By Tho. Forde. | [rule] | *Quid melius defidiofus agam!—* [swash Q] | [rule] | [ornament] | *LONDON,* | Printed by R. and W. *Leybourn,* for *William* | *Grantham* at the Black Bear in St. *Pauls* | Church-yard, neer the little | North Door, 1660.

Verse: "Satyre II" (ll. 23–24), sig. K1v

The sheets of this collection were issued with three different and independently printed collective title pages that were stitched in: the present version with *A Theatre of Wits* as the featured work; two others with *Virtus Rediviva* as the featured work constitute 1661:2a and 1661:2b. Although the works do appear individually (e.g. *A Theatre of Wits*, O, shelfmark: Harding E.245[2]), the sequence of signatures (*Virtvs Rediviva* [A1–C3], *A Theatre of Wits* [C7–I6v], *Fænestra in Pectore* [I7–T8v], *Love's Labyrinth* [V1–2A7], and *Fragmenta Poetica* [2A8–2C4]) suggests that the volume was printed as a collection and not intended for piecemeal distribution.

1661:2a

Author: Thomas Forde

Title [within single rules]: *Virtus Rediviva* | A | Panegyrick | On our late | King Charles the I. *&c.* | of ever bleffed Memory. | ATTENDED, | *with feverall other Pieces from the* | *fame PEN.* |

Viz. {
I. A Theatre of Wits: Being a Col-
lection of *APOTHEGMS.*
II. *Fæneftra in Pectore*: or a Century of
Familiar *LETTERS.*
III. *Loves Labyrinth*: A Tragi-comedy.
IV. *Fragmenta Poetica*: Or Poeticall
Diverfions.
}

| Concluding, with | A Panegyrick on His | Sacred Majefties moft happy | Return. | [rule] | By T. F. | [rule] | *Varietas delectat.* | [rule] |

Printed by *R. & W. Leybourn, for William Gran-* | *tham,* at the Sign of the Black Bear in St. *Pauls* | Church-yard neer the little North door; | and *Thomas Baʃʃet,* in Sᵗ. *Dunʃtans* Church- | yard in *Fleet-ʃtreet.* 1661

Collation: 8°. π² A–2B⁸ C⁴ ($4: π1v, portrait of Charles I; π2, collective title; A1, separate title, unsigned; C3, unsigned; G4, unsigned; H4, unsigned; K3, unsigned; K4, unsigned; N4, unsigned; P3, unsigned; Q3, unsigned; R3, unsigned; T3, unsigned; V1, separate title, unsigned; V3, unsigned; 2C3, missigned C3; 2C4, unsigned)

Wing: F1550

Copy: L G.12805

Separate title: A | THEATRE | OF | WITS, | Ancient and Modern. | *Repreʃented in a Collection of* | Apothegmes. | *Pleaʃant and Profitable.* | [rule] | By Tho. Forde. | [rule] | *Omne tulit punctum, qui miʃcuit utile dulci.* | *Habent enim Apothegmata peculiarem quandam* [swash A] | *rationem, & indolem ʃuam, ut breviter, argutè, falsè,* | *& urbanè cujuʃq; ingenium exprimant.* Eraʃmus. | [rule] | *LONDON,* | Printed by *R.* and *W. Leybourn,* for *William* | *Grantham* at the Black Bear in St. *Pauls* | Church-yard, neer the little | North Door. 1660.

Verse: "Satyre II" (ll. 21–22), sig. D1

Separate title: *Fæneʃtra in Pectore.* | OR, | FAMILIAR LETTERS. | [rule] | By Tho. Forde. | [rule] | *Quid melius deʃidioʃus agam!—* [swash Q] | [rule] | [ornament] | *LONDON,* | Printed by *R.* and *W. Leybourn,* for *William* | *Grantham* at the Black Bear in St. *Pauls* | Church-yard, neer the little | North Door, 1660.

Verse: "Satyre II" (ll. 23–24), sig. K1v

The Thomason copy (L, shelfmark: E.1806) is dated "Octob: 1660."

Additional seventeenth-century issue:

1661:2b 1661 (Wing: F1550A): sigs. D1, K1v

Title [within single rules]: *Virtus Rediviva* | A | Panegyricke | On our late | King Charles the I. *&c.* | of ever bleʃʃed Memory. | ATTENDED, | *With ʃeverall other Pieccs from the* | *ʃame PEN.*

Viz. {

I. A Theatre of Wits: Being a Collection of *APOTHEGMS.*

II. *Fæneʃtra Pectore:* or a Century of
Familiar *LETTERS.*

III. *Loves Labyrinth:* A Tragi-comedy.

IV. *Fragmenta Poetica:* Or Poeticall
Diverʃions.

}

| Concluding, with | A PANEGYRICKE on His | Sacred Majeſties moſt happy | Return. | By *T. F.* | *Varietas delectat.* | LONDON: | Printed by *R.* and *W. Leybourn*, for *William* | *Grantham*, and are to be ſold at the Sign of the [swash G] | Black Bear in St. *Pauls* Church-yard neer | the little North door, 1661.

The priority of 1661:2a and 1661:2b is uncertain; however, their collation and typesettings of "Satyre II" (ll. 21–22, 23–24) are identical (see discussion of 1661:1a).

1662:1a

Author: Aston Cokayne

Title: Poems. | With the Obſtinate | LADY, | AND | TRAPOLIN | A ſuppoſed PRINCE. | BY | Sir ASTON COKAIN, Baronet. | Whereunto is now Added | The TRAGEDY | OF | OVID | Intended to be Acted ſhortly. | [rule] | *LONDON,* | Printed for *Phil. Stephens* junior, at the Kings- | Arms over againſt Middle Temple Gate | in *Fleet-ſtreet.* 1662.

Collation: 8°. π¹ A–2L⁸ ²A⁶ ²B–²I⁸ ²K⁶ ($4: π1v, portrait; A1, title, unsigned; A2, separate title, unsigned; A4, unsigned; B3, unsigned; T7, blank; T8, blank; V1, separate title, unsigned; V3, missigned X3; 2A3, missigned A3; ²A1, title, unsigned; ²A4, unsigned; ²K4, unsigned)

Wing: C4897

Copy: L 238.b.32

Verse: "The second Anniversarie" (l. 65), sig. R3 (ll. 25–28)

A reissue of the sheets of 1658:2a with a preliminary general title page and the addition of *The Tragedy of Ovid* with a separate title page dated 1662 and an independent sequence of signatures. The Wing entry C4897A showing another 1662 edition of 1662:1a printed *"For Francis Kirkman"* with a unique copy at L cannot be confirmed.

1662:2a

Author: Newcastle, Margaret Cavendish, Duchess of

Title: PLAYES | Written by the | *Thrice NOBLE, ILLUSTRIOUS* [swash N, B, R] | AND | Excellent Princeſs, | THE | LADY MARCHIONESS | OF | NEWCASTLE. | [rule] | [printer's device] | [rule] | *LONDON,* [swash N, D, N] | Printed by *A. Warren,* for *John Martyn, James* [swash J, J] | *Alleſtry,* and *Tho. Dicas,* at the Bell in [swash D] | Saint *Pauls* Church Yard, 1662. [swash P]

Collation: 2º. A¹⁴ B–8I² ($2: A1, title, unsigned; A3–7, signed; A14, wanting; L2, unsigned; X1, unsigned; 2G2, unsigned; 3D2, unsigned; 3G2, unsigned; 3Q2, unsigned; 6G2, missigned, 5G2; 6M2, unsigned; 7X1, unsigned; 8D2, unsigned; 8I2, unsigned)¹
Wing: N868
Copy: L C.102.k.9
Verse: "The Storme" (ll. 35–36), p. 219

---

1. The catchwords "To" (sig. A6v), "An" (sig. A8), and "*A*" (sig. A9) suggest that "*A General Prologue to all my Playes*" (sigs. A7–8) should follow present sig. A13v.

1664:1a
Author: George Etherege
Title: THE | Comical Revenge; | OR, | LOVE | IN A | TUB. | Acted at His Highneſs the Duke of *YORK*'s [swash R, K] | Theatre in *Lincolns-Inn-Fields.* | [rule] | LICENSED, | *July* 8. | 1664. *Roger L'Eſtrange.* | [double rule] | *LONDON,* | Printed for *Henry Herringman,* and are to be ſold at his Shop | at the *Blew-Anchor,* in the Lower Walk of the | New-Exchange. 1664.
Collation: 4º. A–N⁴ ($2: A1, blank?, wanting; A2, title, unsigned; A3, signed; N4, blank?, wanting)
Wing: E3367
Copy: L C.71.e.10
Verse: "Twicknam garden" (l. 1), p. 61
H. F. B. Brett-Smith, ed., *The Dramatic Works of Sir George Etherege* (Oxford: Basil Blackwell, 1927), argues for the priority of this 1664 edition over 1664:1b (1:xcvii–xcviii).

Additional seventeenth-century editions/issues:

1664:1b 1664 (Wing: E3368): p. 48

1664:1c 1667 (Wing: E3369): p. 48

1664:1d 1669 (Wing: E3370): p. 48

1664:1e 1689 (Wing: E3371): p. 48

1664:1f 1690 (Wing: E3372): p. 48

1664:1g 1697 (Wing: E3373):[1] p. 45

---

1. C. D. W. Sheppard, sub-librarian of the Brotherton Collection at Leeds University Library, informs me that their copy of the 1697 edition listed by Wing as E3373A is actually a copy of 1664:1g.

1664:2a
Author: Thomas Killigrew
Title: COMEDIES, | AND | TRAGEDIES. | [rule] | WRITTEN BY | Thomas Killigrew, | Page of Honour to King *CHARLES* the Firſt. [swash *R, E*] | AND | Groom of the Bed-Chamber to King | *CHARLES* the Second. [swash *R, E*] | [rule] | [ornament] | [double rule] | *LONDON,* [swash *N, D, N*] | Printed for *Henry Herringman,* at the Sign of the *Anchor* in [swash *A*] | the Lower Walk of the *New-Exchange.* 1664. [swash *N*]
Collation: 2°. π¹ [*]² A–4C⁴ [a]–[k]⁴ ($2: π1v, portrait; [*]1, title, unsigned; A1, separate title, unsigned; V2, separate title, unsigned)
Wing: K450
Copy: CSmH 144710
Separate title: THE | Parſons Wedding, | A | COMEDY. | The Scene *LONDON.* [swash *N, D, N*] | [rule] | WRITTEN AT | Baſil in Switzerland: | BY | *THOMAS KILLIGREW.* [swash *K, G, R*] | [rule] | DEDICATED | TO THE | LADY *VRSVLA BARTV,* [swash *R, B, R*] | WIDOW. | [rule] | [ornament] | [rule] | *LONDON:* | Printed by *J. M.* for *Henry Herringman,* and are to be [swash *J*] | ſold at his Shop at the ſign of the *Blew Anchor,* in | the lower Walk of the *New-Exchange.* 1663.
Verse: "A Lecture upon the Shadow" (l. 26), p. 88; "Breake of day" (l. 13), p. 88; "Loves Alchymie" (l. 3), p. 122

1668:1a
Author: Abraham Cowley
Title: THE | WORKS | OF | Mʳ Abraham Cowley. | Conſiſting of | *Thoſe which were formerly Printed*: [swash *P*] | AND | *Thoſe which he Deſign'd for the Preſs,* [swash *D, P*] | Now Publiſhed out of the Authors | *ORIGINAL COPIES.* [swash *R, G, N, P*] | [rule] | [ornament] | [double rule] | *LONDON,* | Printed by *J.M.* for *Henry Herringman,* at the Sign of the [swash *J*] | *Blew Anchor* in the Lower Walk of the *New* | *Exchange.* 1668.

Collation: 2º. π² A² a–e² B–3C⁴ 3D² ²A–²S⁴ ²T² ($2: π1, blank; π1v, portrait; π2, title; π2v, blank; A2, unsigned; a2, unsigned; b2, unsigned; c2, unsigned; d2, unsigned; e2, unsigned; 3D2, unsigned; ²T2, unsigned)

Wing: C6649; Perkin:[1] B1

Copy: CT H.15.41

Verse: "The Will" (l. 51), sig. C1

The two issues of the 1668 1st ed. have identical title pages and texts of "The Will" (l. 51), and their order is uncertain. 1668:1a has the errata list pasted on sig. C4v and has the uncorrected state of the text.

Additional seventeenth-century issues/editions:

1668:1B 1668 (Wing: C6649. L, shelfmark: Eve.b.28): sig. C1

Large-paper copy (307 × 184 mm) with the uncorrected state of the text and the errata list printed on sig. ²T2v.

1668:1b 1668 (Wing: C6649; Perkin: B1. C, shelfmark: Syn.4.66.8): sig. C1

Small-paper copy (293 × 183 mm).

1668:1C 1668 (Wing: C6649; Perkin: B2. O, shelfmark: Antiq.c.E.1668[1]): sig. C1

Large-paper (318 × 192 mm) resetting of 1668:1a with 1668 title pages throughout; sheet E signed sig. E1, E3, E4 unsigned, and E2; the errata sheet (distinguished from that in 1668:1a by having double, swash italic "R" in its "*ERRATA*") printed on sig. ²T2v; and the corrected state of the text.[2]

1668:1D 1668 (Wing: C6649; Perkin: none. CSmH, shelfmark: 120865): sig. C1

Large-paper (306 × 190 mm) copy of another issue of 1668:1C with 1668 title pages throughout, sheet E correctly signed, the errata sheet printed on ²T2v, and the corrected state of the text.

1668:1e 1669 (Wing: C6650; Perkin: B3. L, shelfmark: 641.l.4): sig. C1

There are four issues of this edition, all with identical texts of the Donne verse. 1668:1e has the general title page dated 1668, section titles dated 1669, and lacks the list of errata usually printed on sig. ²T2v. The small-paper size is approximately 289 × 177 mm (OME, shelfmark: 34.k.16).

1668:1f 1669 (Wing: C6650; Perkin: B3. ICN, shelfmark: Case Y 185.C8267): sig. C1

A variant issue of 1668:1e with the general title page dated 1668, section titles dated 1669, and the list of errata printed on sig. ²T2v.

1668:1g 1669 (Wing: C6650; Perkin: B3. LG, shelfmark: AN.4.6.6): sig. C1

A variant issue of 1668:1e with all titles dated 1669, the list of errata printed on sig. ²T2v, and the uncorrected state of the text.

1668:1h 1669 (Wing: C6650; Perkin: B3. C, shelfmark: Y.7.38): sig. C1

A variant issue of 1668:1e with all titles dated 1669, no list of errata, but the corrected state of the text.

1668:1i 1672 (Wing: C6651; Perkin: B4): sig. C1

1668:1j 1674 (Wing: C6652; Perkin: B5): sig. C1

1668:1k 1678 (Wing: C6653; Perkin: B6): sig. C1

1668:1l 1680 (Wing: C6654; Perkin: B7. TxU, shelfmark: Aj C839 +C680): sig. C1

Title: THE | WORKS | OF | Mʳ Abraham Cowley. | Conſiſting of | *Thoſe which were formerly Printed:* | AND | *Thoſe which he Deſign'd for the Prefs,* | Now publiſhed out of the Authors | ORIGINAL COP-IES. | [rule] | 𝕿𝕳𝖊 𝕾𝖎𝖝𝖙𝖍 𝕰𝖉𝖎𝖙𝖎𝖔𝖓. | [rule] | [ornament] | [double rule] | *LONDON,* | Printed by *J. M.* for *Henry Herringman,* at the Sign of the [swash J] | *Blue Anchor* in the Lower Walk of the [swash B] | *New Exchange.* 1680.

The priority of variant issues 1668:1l and 1668:1m is uncertain. Their texts of "The Will" (l. 51) are identical and derive directly from that in 1668:1k.

1668:1m 1680 (Wing: C6654; Perkin: B7. O, shelfmark: fol.Δ.721): sig. C1

Title: THE | WORKS | OF | Mʳ. Abraham Cowley. | Conſiſting of · | *Thoſe which were formerly Printed:* [swash P] | AND | *Thoſe which he Deſign'd for the Prefs,* [swash D, P] | Now Publiſhed out of the Authors | *ORIGINAL COPIES.* [swash R, G, N, C, P] | [rule] | 𝕿𝖍𝖊 𝕾𝖎𝖝𝖙 𝕰𝖉𝖎𝖙𝖎𝖔𝖓. | [rule] | [ornament] | [double rule] | *LONDON,* | Printed by *J. M.* for *Henry Herringman*, at the Sign of the [swash *J*] | *Bluew Anchor* in the Lower Walk of the [swash *B, A*] | *New Exchange.* 1680.

1668:1n 1681 (Wing: C6655; Perkin: B8): sig. C1

1668:1o 1681 (Wing: C6656; Perkin: B9): sig. C2v

1668:1p 1684 (Wing: C6657; Perkin: B12. L, shelfmark: 12272.m.7.[1]): sig. C1
    Title: THE | WORKS | OF | Mr Abraham Cowley. | Confifting of | *Thofe which were formerly Printed:* | AND | *Thofe which he Defign'd for the Prefs,* | Now publifhed out of the Authors | ORIGINAL COP-IES. | [rule] | 𝕿𝖍𝖊 𝕰𝖎𝖌𝖍𝖙𝖍 𝕰𝖉𝖎𝖙𝖎𝖔𝖓. | [rule] | [ornament] | [double rule] | *LONDON,* | Printed by *J. M.* for *Henry Herringman*, at the Sign of the [swash *J*] | *Blue Anchor,* in the Lower Walk of the [swash *B*] | *New-Exchange.* 1684.
    The texts of "The Will" (l. 51) in variant issues 1668:1p and 1668:1q are identical and derive directly from that in 1668:1n. The priority of the issues is uncertain, though Perkin notes that "from the few copies recorded with title 1) it seems likely that title 2), adding the names of the booksellers Charles Harper and Abel Swalle, who produced the *Second part of the works* usually bound with this edition, was substituted quite soon after printing had started" (p. 66).

1668:1q 1684 (Wing: C6657; Perkin: B12. TxU, shelfmark: Aj C839 +C684): sig. C1
    Title: THE | WORKS | OF | Mr Abraham Cowley. | Confifting of | *Thofe which were formerly Printed*: [swash *P*] | AND | *Thofe which he Defign'd for the Prefs*: [swash *D, P*] | Now publifhed out of the Authors | ORIGINAL COPIES. | [rule] | 𝕿𝖍𝖊 𝕰𝖎𝖌𝖍𝖙𝖍 𝕰𝖉𝖎𝖙𝖎𝖔𝖓. | [rule] | [ornament] | [double rule] | *LONDON*: [swash *N, D, N*] | Printed by *J. M.* for *Henry Herringman*, and are to be fold [swash *J*] | by *Charles Harper* at the Flower-de-luce over againft S. *Dunftan's* | Church in *Fleetftreet*, and *Abel Swalle* at the Unicorn at the | Weft End of S. *Paul's.* 1684.

1668:1r 1688 (Wing: C6658; Perkin: B14): sig. C1

1668:1s 1693 (Wing: C6659; Perkin: B16): sig. C1

1668:1t 1700 (Wing: C6660; Perkin: B17): sig. C3v

1. According to Perkin's account of the publication of the B1 states of Cowley's *Works* (p. 57) and his lists of copies consulted (p. 59), copies of the 1st ed. should exist with the uncorrected state of the text and without the errata list either printed on sig. ²T2v or pasted in (usually on sig. C4v); however, I am unable to confirm the existence of such a copy.

2. Perkin (p. 60) lists a copy of 1668:1C with the uncorrected state of the text at NcD; however, Linda McCurdy, head of public services at NcD, informs me that their only copy has the corrected state.

1669:1a

Author: Aston Cokayne

Title: CHOICE | POEMS | Of SEVERAL SORTS. | WITH THREE | New Plays: | VIZ. | *The Obſtinate Lady.* A Comedy | *Trappolin, ſuppos'd a Prince.* [swash P] | A Tragi-Comedy. | *The Tragedie of* Ovid. | [rule] | All written | By Sir *Aston Cokain.* [swash k] | [rule] | *London:* Printed for *Francis Kirkman;* and are [swash k] | to be ſold at his ſhop under S. *Ethelboroughs* | Church in *Biſhops-gate-ſtreet.* 1669.

Collation: 8°. π¹ A² χ² A³⁻⁸ B–2L⁸ ²A² ²B–²I⁸ ²K⁶ ($4: π1v, portrait; A1, title, unsigned; X1, "To the Author"; A4, unsigned; B3, unsigned; T7, blank; T8, blank; V1, separate title, unsigned; V3, missigned X3; 2A3, missigned A3; ²A1, blank; ²A1v, portrait of Ovid; ²A2, separate title, unsigned; ²A2v, blank)

Wing: C4895

Copy: O Douce C.120

Verse: "The second Anniversarie" (l. 65), sig. R3 (ll. 25–28)

A reissue of the sheets of 1662:1a with a new title and title page, the addition of "To the Author," and updated separate title pages.

1670:1a

Author: Izaak Walton

Title: THE LIFE | OF | Mr. *GEORGE HERBERT.* | [rule] | Written by *Izaack Walton.* | [rule] | To which are added ſome | LETTERS | Written by | Mr. *George Herbert,* at his being in | *Cambridge:* with others to his Mother, | the Lady *Magdalen Herbert:* Written | by *John Donne,* afterwards Dean of St. | *Pauls.* | [rule] | Wiſdom of Solom. 4. 10. | *He pleaſed God, and was beloved of him:* | *ſo that whereas he lived among ſinners,* | *he tranſlated him.* | [rule] | *LONDON,* | Printed by *Tho: Newcomb,* for *Rich: Marriott,* | Sold by moſt Bookſellers. M.DC.LXX.

Collation: 8°. A–I⁸ K² ($4: A1, blank, unsigned, portrait on verso, misbound between B1v and B2; A2, title, unsigned; A3, missigned A2; H3, missigned F3; H4, unsigned)
Wing: W669
Copy: L 702.b.10.(1)
Verse:¹ "Elegy: The Autumnall" (ll. 1–2), p. 22; "Elegy: The Autumnall" (ll. 23–24), p. 22; "Elegy: The Autumnall" (heading only), p. 22; "To the Lady Magdalen Herbert: of St. Mary Magdalen," pp. 25–26

---

1. Earliest printing of "To the Lady Magdalen Herbert: of St. Mary Magdalen."

1670:2a
Author: Izaak Walton
Title [within double rules]: THE | LIVES |
Of | Dʳ· *John Donne,*
Sir *Henry Wotton,*
Mʳ· *Richard Hooker,*
Mʳ· *George Herbert.* [swash *J, D, R, k, G*]
| [rule] | Written by Iᴢᴀᴀᴋ Wᴀʟᴛᴏɴ. | [rule] | To which are added ſome Letters written by | Mr. *George Herbert,* at his being in *Cam-* | *bridge:* with others to his Mother, the | Lady *Magdalen Herbert,* written by *John* [swash *J*] | *Donne,* afterwards Dean of St. *Pauls.* | [rule] | Eccleſ. 44. 7. | *Theſe were honourable men in their Generations.* | [rule] | *LONDON,* | Printed by *Tho. Newcomb* for *Richard Marriott.* | Sold by moſt Bookſellers. 1670.
Collation: 8°. A–F⁸ G⁴ χ¹ ²A⁴ ²B–²E⁸ ²F⁴ 2χ¹ ³A⁴ ³B–³H⁸ 3χ¹ ⁴A– ⁴F⁸ ⁴G⁴ ($4: A1, blank, unsigned; A1v, portrait of Donne; A2, title, unsigned; A8, wanting; D4, unsigned; χ1, blank; χ1v, portrait of Wotton; ²A1, separate title, unsigned; ²A2, missigned ²B2; ²A4, unsigned; ²F3, unsigned; ²F4, unsigned; 2χ1, blank; 2χ1v, portrait of Hooker; ³A1, separate title, unsigned; ³H2, missigned ³F2; ³H4 missigned F4; 3χ1, blank; 3χ1v, portrait of Herbert; ⁴A1, separate title, unsigned; ⁴A2, unsigned; ⁴F2, separate title, unsigned; ⁴G3, unsigned; ⁴G4, unsigned)
Wing: W671
Copy: L 615.b.1
Verse: "A Hymne to God the Father," pp. 54–55; "To Mʳ George Herbert, with one of my seals" (ll. 1–3), p. 58; *T*"To Mʳ George

Herbert, with one of my seals"[1] (ll. 3–22), pp. 58–59; "Hymne to God my God, in my sicknesse" (ll. 1–8, 26–30), p. 60; "Ioannes Donne Sac: Theol: Profess," p. 76

Separate title: THE | LIFE | OF | Sr HENRY WOTTON, | SOME-TIME | *Provoſt* of *Eaton Colledge.* [swash *P*] | [rule] | [ornament] | [rule] | There are them that have left a name behinde them; ſo that | their praiſe ſhall be ſpoken of: *Eccluſ.* 44. 8. | [rule] | *LONDON,* | Printed by *Thomas Newcomb,* for *Richard Marriot,* | and ſold by moſt Bookſellers. 1670.

Verse: "To Sir H. W. at his going Ambassador to Venice," pp. 30–31

Separate title: The LIFE | OF | Mr. *GEORGE HERBERT.* | [rule] | Wiſdom of Salom. 4. 10. | *He pleaſed God, and was beloved of him: ſo* | *that whereas he lived among ſinners, he tran-* | *ſlated him.* | [rule] | [ornament] | [rule] | *LONDON,* | Printed by *Tho: Newcomb,* for *Richard Marriott,* | ſold by moſt Bookſellers. M.DC.LXX.

Verse: "Elegy: The Autumnall" (ll. 1–2), p. 15; "Elegy: The Autumnall" (ll. 23–24), p. 15; "Elegy: The Autumnall" (heading only), p. 15; "To the Lady Magdalen Herbert: of St. Mary Magdalen," p. 18

Additional seventeenth-century edition:

1670:2b 1675

Title [within double rules]: THE | LIVES |

Of $\left\{\begin{array}{l}\text{D}^r \text{ } \textit{John Donne,} \\ \text{Sir } \textit{Henry Wotton,} \\ \text{M}^r \text{ } \textit{Richard Hooker,} \\ \text{M}^r \text{ } \textit{George Herbert.}\end{array}\right.$

[swash *J,k*] | [rule] | Written by *IZAAK WALTON.* | [rule] | 𝕿𝖍𝖊 𝕱𝖔𝖚𝖗𝖙𝖍 𝕰𝖉𝖎𝖙𝖎𝖔𝖓. | [rule] | Eccleſ. XLIV. 7. | *Theſe were Honourable Men in their* *Generations.* | [rule] | *LONDON,* | Printed by *Tho. Roycroft* for *Richard Marriot* | Sold by moſt Bookſellers. 1675.

Collation: 8°. A–Z⁸ 2A⁴ ($4: A1, blank, unsigned; A1v, portrait of Donne; A2, title, unsigned; G3, blank, unsigned; G4, separate title, unsigned; S4, blank, unsigned; Z3, separate title, unsigned; 2A3, unsigned; 2A4, unsigned)

Wing: W672

Copy: L C.71.bb.18

Verse: "A Valediction: forbidding mourning," pp. 33–34; "A Hymne to God the Father," p. 53; "To Mr George Herbert, with one of my seals" (ll. 1–3), p. 56; *T*"To Mr George Herbert, with one of my seals" (ll. 3–24), pp. 56–57; "Hymne to God my God, in my sicknesse" (ll. 1–8, 26–30), p. 58; "Ioannes Donne Sac: Theol: Profess," p. 73

Separate title: THE | LIFE | OF | Sir *HENRY WOTTON,* | LATE | PROVOST | OF | *EATON COLLEGE.* | [rule] | Eccleſ. 44. | *Theſe were Honourable Men in their Generation.* | [rule] | *LONDON,* | Printed in the Year 1675.

Verse: "To Sir H. W. at his going Ambassador to Venice," pp. 109–10

Separate title: THE | LIFE | OF | Mr. *GEORGE HERBERT.* | [rule] | *Wiſdom of Salom. 4. 10.* | *He pleaſed God, and was beloved of him: ſo that* | *whereas he lived among ſinners, he tranſlated* | *him.* | [rule] | [ornament] | [rule] | *LONDON,* | Printed in the Year 1675.

Verse: "Elegy: The Autumnall" (ll. 1–2), p. 267; "Elegy: The Autumnall" (ll. 23–24), p. 267; "Elegy: The Autumnall" (heading only), p. 267; "To the Lady Magdalen Herbert: of St. Mary Magdalen," p. 269

---

1. The English translation remains anonymous.

1673:1a

Author: Andrew Marvell

Title: THE | REHEARSALL | TRANSPROS'D : | [rule] | The SECOND PART. | [rule] | *Occaſioned by Two Letters: The firſt* | *Printed, by a nameleſs Author,* | *Intituled,* A Reproof, *&c.* | *The Second Letter left for me at a* | *Friends Houſe, Dated* Nov. 3. | *1673. Subſcribed* J. G. *and* | *concluding with theſe words;* If | thou dareſt to Print or Publiſh | any Lie or Libel againſt Doctor | *Parker,* By the Eternal God I [swash *k*] | will cut thy Throat. | [rule] | *Anſwered by* ANDREW MARVEL | [rule] | *LONDON,* | *Printed for* Nathaniel Ponder *at the* Peacock *in* | Chancery Lane *near* Fleet-Street, 1673.

Collation: 8°. π³ A–2C⁸ χ¹ ($4: π1, blank; π2, blank; π3, title; χ1, blank)

Wing: M882

Copy: L 1019.e.13

Verse: "The Progresse of the Soule" (ll. 61–62, 66–69), p. 63; "The Progresse of the Soule" (ll. 148–50), p. 64; "The Progresse of the Soule" (ll. 193–94), p. 64; "The Progresse of the Soule" (l. 331), p. 65; "The Progresse of the Soule" (ll. 318–19), p. 65; "The Progresse of the Soule" (ll. 379–80), p. 65; "The Progresse of the Soule" (l. 387), p. 65; "The Progresse of the Soule" (ll. 404–6), p.

56[66]; "The Progresse of the Soule" (ll. 444–46), p. 56[66]; "The Progresse of the Soule" (ll. 449–50), p. 67

Additional seventeenth-century edition and issue:

1673:1b 1673

Title [within double rules]: THE | REHEARSALL | TRANS-PROS'D : | [rule] | The SECOND PART. | [rule] | *Occafioned by Two Letters: The firft Print-* | *ed, by a namelefs Author, Intituled* A | Reproof, *&c.* | *The Second Letter left for me at a Friends* | *Houfe, Dated* Nov. 3. 1673. *Subfcri-* | *bed* J.G. *and concluding with thefe words,* | If thou dareft to Print or Publifh any | Lie or Libel againft Doctor *Parker,* By [swash *k*] | the Eternal God I will cut thy Throat. | [rule] | *Anfwered by* ANDREW MARVEL | [rule] | *LONDON,* | *Printed for* Nathaniel Ponder *at the* Peacock *in* | Chancery-Lane *near* Fleet-Street, 1673.

Collation: 12°. π^2 A–P^{12} Q^6 ($5: π1, blank; π2, title; E3, both "E" and "3" reversed; G3, missigned G5; G5, unsigned; L5, unsigned; M3, missigned M1; P6, signed; Q4, unsigned; Q5, unsigned)

Wing: M882A

Copy: L C.115.n.27

Verse: "The Progresse of the Soule" (ll. 61–62, 66–69), p. 57; "The Progresse of the Soule" (ll. 148–50), p. 58; "The Progresse of the Soule" (ll. 193–94), p. 58; "The Progresse of the Soule" (l. 331), p. 59; "The Progresse of the Soule" (ll. 318–19), p. 59; "The Progresse of the Soule" (ll. 379–80), p. 59; "The Progresse of the Soule" (l. 387), p. 59; "The Progresse of the Soule" (ll. 404–6), p. 60; "The Progresse of the Soule" (ll. 444–46), p. 60; "The Progresse of the Soule" (ll. 449–50), p. 61

D. I. B. Smith, editor of *Andrew Marvell: The Rehearsal Transpros'd and The Rehearsal Transpros'd the Second Part* (Oxford: Clarendon Press, 1971), does not mention 1673:1b; however, his textual introduction (pp. xxv–xxxiv) establishes that 1673:1c, a reissue of the sheets of 1673:1b with a cancel title page, is a substantial rewriting of 1673:1a.

1673:1c 1674 (Wing: M883): pp. 57, 58, 58, 59, 59, 59, 59, 60, 60, 61

1674:1a

Author: George Herbert

Title [within double rules]: THE | TEMPLE. | [rule] | SACRED POEMS | AND PRIVATE | EJACULATIONS. | [rule] | By Mr *George*

Herbert, [swash *G*] | Late ORATOUR of the | Univerſity of *CAM-BRIDGE.* | [rule] | *Together with his* LIFE. *with* | *ſeveral Additions.* [swash *A*] | [rule] | PSAL. 29. | *In his Temple doth every man ſpeak of his honour.* [swash *k*] | [rule] | *The Tenth Edition, with an Alphabetical* | *Table for ready finding out the chief places.* | [rule] | *LONDON,* | Printed by W. *Godbid,* for *R.S.* and are to | be Sold by *John Williams* Junior, in *Croſs-* | *Key* Court in *Little-Britain,* 1674. [swash *K*]

Collation: 12°. π⁶ [*]⁶ A–B¹² C⁶ ($5: π2v, portrait; π3, title; [*]1, unsigned; [*]3, missigned [*]4; A5, missigned I5; C4, unsigned; C5, unsigned) A–I¹² K⁶ ($5: B4, missigned B2; K4, unsigned; K5, unsigned)

Wing:[1] H1521

Copy: C Adams.8.67.17

Verse: "Elegy: The Autumnall" (ll. 1–2), p. 6; "Elegy: The Autumnall" (ll. 23–24), p. 6; "Elegy: The Autumnall" (heading only), p. 6; "To the Lady Magdalen Herbert: of St. Mary Magdalen," p. 8

Additional seventeenth-century editions:

1674:1b 1678 (Wing: H1522): pp. 6, 8

1674:1c 1679 (Wing: H1523): pp. 6, 8

1674:1d 1695 (Wing: H1524): pp. 6, 8

---

1. For the initial publication of Izaak Walton's *The Life of Mr. George Herbert,* see 1670:1a. This 1674 edition of *The Temple* is the first to contain Walton's *Life.*

1676:1a

Authors: Izaak Walton, Charles Cotton, and Robert Venables

Title [within double rules]: THE | UNIVERSAL | ANGLER, | Made ſo, by | Three BOOKS | OF | FISHING. | The *Firſt* | Written by Mr. *IZAAK WALTON;* | The *Second* | By *CHARLES COTTON* Eſq; | The *Third* | By Col. *ROBERT VENABLES.* | [rule] | All which may be bound together, or ſold | each of them ſeverally. | [rule] | *LONDON,* | Printed for *Richard Marriott,* and ſold by | moſt Bookſellers. MDCLXXVI.

Collation: 8°. π² A–T⁸ V⁴ ²A⁴ ²B–²H⁸ ³A–³G⁸ ³H⁴ ($4: π1v, engraved title; π2, title; A1, separate title, unsigned; A4, unsigned; V3, unsigned; V4, unsigned; ²A1, wanting; ²A2, title, unsigned; ²A4, unsigned; ²F3, missigned B3; ³A1, blank, unsigned; ³A2, title,

unsigned; sheet ³A misfolded so that ³A3 and ³A4 as well as ³A4 and ³A6 are interchanged; ³H3, unsigned; ³H4, blank, unsigned)
Wing:[1] W674
Copy: L C.31.a.7
Separate title [lacks engraving]: PART. I. | BEING A | DIS-COURSE | OF | Rivers, Fiſh-ponds, Fiſh & Fiſhing. | [rule] | Written by *IZAAK WALTON.* | [rule] | *The Fifth Edition, much corrected and enlarged.* | [rule] | *London,* Printed for *R. Marriot,* and are to be ſold by | *Charles Harper* at his Shop, the next door to the | *Crown* near *Sergeants-Inn* in *Chancery Lane,* 1676.
Verse: "The Baite," pp. 194–95

Additional seventeenth-century issues:

1676:1b 1676 (Wing: W674. CSmH, shelfmark: 138284): pp. 194–95
The general title page, collation, and text of "The Baite" are identical to those of 1676:1a; 1676:1b can be distinguished by its half title.[2]
Half title [engraved and typeset]: *The* | *Compleat Angler* | *or the* | *Contemplative Man's* | *Recreation.* | *The first part.* | PART. I. | BEING A | DISCOURSE | OF | *Rivers, Fiſh-ponds, Fiſh* and *Fiſhing.* | [rule] | Written by *IZAAK WALTON.* | [rule] | *The Fifth Edition much corrected and enlarged.* | [rule] | *LONDON,* | Printed for *Richard Marriott,* 1676.

1676:1c 1676 (Wing: W674. CSmH, shelfmark: 148257): pp. 194–95
Collation: 8°. A–T⁸ V⁴ ²A–²H⁸ ($4: A1, title, unsigned; A4, unsigned; V3, unsigned; V4, blank, unsigned; ²A1, blank, unsigned; ²A2, title, unsigned; ²A4, unsigned; ²F3, missigned ²B3)
This copy contains the works by Walton and Cotton in a single contemporary binding without the general title page.[3] The text of "The Baite" is identical to that of 1676:1a.

---

1. 1676:1a contains the 5th ed. of Izaak Walton's *The Compleat Angler* (1653:3a). Bevan mistakenly lists (p. 51) the L copy (shelfmark: C.31.a.7) among those of the 2d issue.
2. For reproductions of the general, separate, and half title pages of the two issues, see Bevan (pp. 46–48).
3. According to Bernard S. Horne (*The Compleat Angler 1653–1967: A New Bibliography* [Pittsburgh: University of Pittsburgh Press, 1970], p. 20), the combinations of Walton and Venable or Venable and Cotton do not exist independently in contemporary bindings.

1677:1a

Author: William Winstanley

Title [within single rules]: Poor *ROBIN'S* [swash *R, B, N*] | VI-
SIONS: | Wherein is Defcribed, | The prefent Humours of | the
TIMES; the VICES | and Fafhionable Fopperies thereof; | And after
what manner Men are | Punifhed for them hereafter. | *Difcovered in
a Dream.* [swash *D, D*] | [rule] |———— *Fatebere tandem* | *Nec* Surdum,
nec Tirefiam *quenquam effe Deorum* | [rule] | Licenfed *May* 17. 1677. |
ROGER L'ESTRANGE. | [rule] | *LONDON,* | Printed for, and fold by
Arthur Boldero | Stationer at the *Mitre* in *Mitre-Court* | near the *Inner
Temple* in *Fleet-ftreet,* 1677.

Collation: 8°. A–H⁸ I⁴ ($4: A1, title, unsigned; I3, unsigned; I4,
unsigned)

Wing: H1598

Copy: CSmH 401195

Verse:[1] "The Storme" (ll. 71–72), p. 4

---

1. Winstanley's text derives from 1607:1a.

1678:1a

Compiler: S. N.

Title: THE | LOYAL GARLAND, | Containing choice Songs and
Sonnets of | our late unhappy Revolutions. | [rule] | *Very delightful
and profitable, both to this prefent,* | *and future Ages.* | [rule] | Publifhed
by *S. N.* A Lover of Mirth. | *The fourth Edition, with Additions.* |
[within ornamental garland] Fear God, Honor the | King, 1 *Pet.* 2.
17. | My fon, fear thou the | LORD, and the King: | and meddle not
with | them that are given to | change, *Prov.* 24.21. | [below gar-
land] *London,* Printed by *T. Johnfon,* for *T. Paffenger* at the [swash *J*]
| Three Bibles on *London*-Bridge. 1678.

Collation: 8°. A–H⁸ ($4: A1, title, unsigned)

Wing:[1] M70; Case: 475(d)

Copy: O Douce.H.80[2]

Verse: *D*"Breake of day" (ll. 1–6), sig. C6v; "Breake of day" (ll.
1–2), sig. C6v; "Breake of day" (l. 4), sig. C6v; "Breake of day" (ll.
5–6), sig. C7

Additional seventeenth-century edition:

1678:1b 1686 (Wing: none; Case: 475[e]. O, shelfmark: Douce S 23):
sigs. D6v, D7, D7, D7

1. Wing listings of 1671, 1673, and 1685 editions at O are incorrect. The copy (O, shelfmark: Douce.H.80[2]) dated 1673 and filmed on Wing reel 643 is probably 1678: the "8" in what I read as "1678" has significantly deteriorated. The volume, dated "1673" on its spine, contains, in order, a 1670 edition of *Robin Hoods Garland*, *The Loyal Garland*, and a 1678 edition of *The Garland of Good-will*.

1680:1a
Author: Nathaniel Lee
Title: THEODOSIUS: | OR, | 𝕿𝔥𝔢 𝕱𝔬𝔯𝔠𝔢 𝔬𝔣 𝕷𝔬𝔳𝔢, | A | TRAGEDY. | ACTED BY | Their ROYAL HIGHNESSES Servants, | AT THE | Duke's Theatre. | [rule] | Written by *NAT. LEE.* | [rule] | WITH THE | MUSICK betwixt the ACTS. | [rule] |————*Nec minus periculum ex magna* | *Fama quam ex mala.* Tacit. | [rule] | *LONDON,* | Printed for *R. Bentley* and *M. Magnes*, in *Ruſſel-ſtreet*, | near *Covent-garden.* 1680.
Collation: 4°. A–I⁴ χ⁵ ($2: A1, title, unsigned; χ1–5, musical score)
Wing:[1] L877
Copy: CSmH 146644
Verse: "The first Anniversary" (ll. 112–14, 117–20), sig. A2; "The second Anniversarie" (ll. 244–46), sig. A2v; "To the Countesse of Bedford. Honour is so" (ll. 22–24), sig. A2v

Additional seventeenth-century editions:

1680:1b 1684 (Wing: L878): sigs. A2, A2v, A2v

1680:1c 1692 (Wing: L879): sigs. A2, A2v, A2v

1680:1d 1697 (Wing: L880): sigs. A2, A2v, A2v

1. The MH copy of the 1680 edition (Wing: L877) filmed for the Wing microfilm collection (reel 639:3) is actually a copy of 1680:1d with a title page from 1680:1a.

1681:1a
Author: Anonymous
Title: A | PARADOX | Againſt LIFE. | [rule] | Written | By the LORDS in the | TOWER. | [rule] | 𝔄𝔫 𝕳𝔢𝔯𝔬𝔦𝔠𝔨 𝔓𝔬𝔢𝔪. | [rule] |
————*Beatus* | ·*Ante Obitum Nemo*———— — | [rule] | *LON-*

DON, | Printed for *James Vade* at the Cock and Sugar-Loaf in *Fleet=Street,* | 1681.

Collation: 2°. A–D² ($1: A1, title, unsigned; A2, signed; B2, signed)

Wing: P331

Copy: L 163.m.61

Verse: "A nocturnall upon S. Lucies day" (ll. 5–6), p. 6; "A nocturnall upon S. Lucies day" (l. 16), p. 6; "A nocturnall upon S. Lucies day" (l. 15), p. 6; "The first Anniversary" (ll. 97–98), p. 9

1681:2a

Author: Thomas Barlow

Title: PAPISMUS | Regiæ Poteſtatis Everſor: | SIVE | TRAC-TATUS | In quo oſtenditur | Eccleſiæ Romanæ Principia | Eſſe Regibus, & Principibus univerſis, | præcipuè verò Proteſtantibus, | Tum Periculoſa, tum Pernicioſa. | [rule] | Reverendus admodum in Chriſto Pater | *THOMAS BARLOVIUS* Epiſc. Linc. [swash *B, R*] | Anglicè ſcripſit. | *Robertus Grovius* S. T. B. [swash *R, G*] | De Anglicano Latinum fecit; | JUSTITIAM BRITANNICAM | & alia quædam adjici curavit. | [rule] | *LONDINI,* | Veneunt apud Bibliopolas. 1681.

Collation: 8°. π⁴ (a)⁸ B–Q⁸ ($4: π1, blank; π2, blank; π3, title; (a)1, separate title, unsigned; K1, separate title, unsigned; P1, unsigned) A–O⁸ ($4: A1, separate title, unsigned; I3, unsigned; I4, unsigned; O8, blank?, wanting)

Wing: B836; Keynes: 11

Copy: O 8° A.1.Linc.

Separate title [within double rules]: LUCII CORNELII | EURO-PÆI | Monarchia | SOLIPSORUM. | ET | CONCLAVE | IGNATII: | SIVE | Ejus in Nuperis Inferni Co- | mitiis Inthroniſatio. | [rule] | *LONDINI,* | Proſtat venalis apud JACOBUM | COLLINS, in Vico vulgò | vocato 𝕰𝖘𝖘𝖊𝖝-𝕾𝖙𝖗𝖊𝖊𝖙. | 1680.

Separate title: CONCLAVE | IGNATII: | SIVE | Ejus in nuperis Inferni Co- | mitiis Inthroniſatio. | UBI VARIA |

De { Jeſuitarum Indole, | Novo inferno creando, | Eccleſia Lunatica Inſtituenda,

| *PER SATYRAM* | CONGESTA SUNT. | Acceſſit & Apologia pro | JESUITIS. | Omnia | *Duobus Angelis Adverſariis, qui con*= [swash *D*] | *ſiſtorio Papali, & Collegio Sorbonæ* [swash *P*] | *præſident, dedicata.* | *LONDINI,* | Anno Domini, 1680.

Verse: "Aversâ facie *Janum* referre," p. 1; "Operoso tramite scandent," pp. 2–3; "Tanto fragore boatuque," p. 22; "Aut plumam, aut paleam, quae fluminis innatat ori," p. 48; "Qualis hesterno madefacta rore," pp. 75–76

Even though it has an independent sequence of signatures, the *Lucii Cornelii Europæi Monarchia Solipsorum* does not appear to have been published independently in 1680.

Additional seventeenth-century issue:

1681:2b 1682 (Wing: B837; Keynes: 11): pp. 1, 2–3, 22, 48, 75–76
A reissue with a collective title page as follows:
Title [within double rules]: PAPISMUS | Regiæ Poteʃtatis | EVERSOR. | Reverendus admodum Epiʃcopus | *Lincoln. Anglicè* ʃcripʃit. [swash *A*] | *Robertus Grovius* S. T. B. De *An=* | *glicano Latinum* fecit: | Juʃtitiam *Britannicam,* & alia quæ- [swash *B*] | dam, adjici curavit. | [rule] | Quibus ab alio adjunguntur | MONARCHIA SOLIPSORUM | ET | CONCLAVE IGNATII. | [rule] | *LONDINI,* | Proʃtant venales apud *Jacobum Collins,* & [swash *J*] | *Samuelem Lown-des,* in vico vulgò vocato | 𝕿𝖍𝖊 𝕾𝖙𝖗𝖆𝖓𝖉, è Regione 𝕰𝖝𝖊𝖙𝖊𝖗 | 𝕰𝖝𝖈𝖍𝖆𝖓𝖌𝖊. 1682.

This issue replaces the two initial blank leaves of 1681:2a with an engraving of Ignatius Loyola and the collective title page. The texts of its Donne verse are identical with those in 1681:1a.

1683:1a
Author: John Shirley
Title [within single rules]: THE | 𝕮𝖔𝖒𝖕𝖑𝖊𝖆𝖙 𝕮𝖔𝖚𝖗𝖙𝖎𝖊𝖗: | OR, | *CVPID's* Academy. [swash *V*] | Containing | An Exact and excellent Collec-tion of all | the neweʃt and choiceʃt Songs, Poems, Epigrams, | Satyrs, Elegant Epiʃtles, Ingenious Dialogues, | Quaint Expreʃʃions, Complemental Ceremonies, | Amorous Addreʃʃes and Anʃwers, in a moʃt plea- | ʃant and pathetick ʃtrain, fitted and prepared | for all capacities. And humbly recommended to | the peruʃal of all young Gentlemen, Ladies, and | others, who are incliuable to recreate themʃelves | with harmleʃs mirth. | [rule] | By *J. SHURLY,* Gent. [swash *R*] | [rule] | *LONDON,* | Printed for W. T. and are to be ʃold | by *Joʃhua Conyers,* at the *Black* | *Raven* in *Duck lane.* 1683.
Collation: 12º. A⁶ B–G¹² H⁶ ($5: A1, wanting; A2, title, un-signed; A4, unsigned; A5, unsigned; H4, unsigned; H5, unsigned)
Wing: S3503; Case: 168
Copy: O Mal.350(2)
Verse: "Womans constancy" (ll. 1, 3, 2, 5, 7, 8, 11, 9–10, 12–13,

17), pp. 45–46; "The broken heart" (ll. 1–3), p. 62; "The broken heart" (ll. 7–8), p. 62

1684:1a
Author: Payne Fisher
Title: THE | Tombes, Monuments, | And Sepulchral Inſcriptions, | Lately Viſible in | St. Pauls Cathedral, | And St. FAITH'S under it. | Compleatly Rendred | In LATIN and ENGLISH, | With Several Hiſtorical Diſcourses, | On Sundry Perſons Intombed therein. | A WORK | Never yet Performed by any Author | OLD or NEW. | [rule] | By P. F. Student in Antiquities, Batchelor of Arts and heretofore [swash P] | One of His late Majeſties Majors of Foot, | To the late Honorable Sir *Patricius Curwen* c. Cumb. Baronet. | [rule] | *LONDON*, [swash *N, D, N*] | Printed for the Author, | And properly Preſented to the kind Encouragers, | Of ſo Worthy a Work.
Collation: 4º. A–X⁴ [A]⁴ ($2: A1, title, unsigned; P3, signed; Q3, signed)
Wing: F1041
Copy: L 577.c.6
Verse: "Ioannes Donne Sac: Theol: Profess," p. 56; *T*"Ioannes Donne Sac: Theol: Profess," p. 56
No publisher's name appears; the date "*MDCLXXXIV*" appears on the final page, sig. [A]4v. The L copy (shelfmark: 577.c.6), evidently a presentation copy, has a note on the upper right corner of the recto of a leaf tipped in before the title: "E. B. 15.º die Sept. An.º 1684. / Ex dono Authoris." and "Payne Fisher" in the same hand above "*P. F.*" on the title page.

Additional seventeenth-century editions:[1]

1684:1b 1684 (Wing: F1041. O, shelfmark: Wood 534[7]): pp. 55–56
The same title page and typesetting of "Ioannes Donne Sac: Theol: Profess" and *T*"Ioannes Donne Sac: Theol: Profess" as 1684:1a; however, an additional quarto sheet, a, is inserted between leaves A2 and A3 as well as two additional unsigned leaves following X4. The O copy (shelfmark: Wood 534[7]) lacks sheets C and [A].

1684:1c 1684 (Wing: F1042. O, Shelfmark: B.16.12.Linc.): pp. 55–56
Title: THE | Tombes, Monuments, | And Sepulchral Inſcrip-

tions, | Lately Viſible in | St. Pauls Cathedral, | Compleatly Rendred | In LATIN and ENGLISH. | With Several Hiſtorical Diſcourſes, | On Sundry Perſons Intombed therein. | A WORK | Never yet Performed by any Author | OLD or NEW. | By Major *P. Fiſher* Student in Antiquities, Grandchild to the late Sir | *William Fiſher*, and that Moſt Memorable Kt. Sir *Thomas Neale* by [swash *N*] | his Wife *Elizabeth*, Siſter to that ſo publick-ſpirited Patriot the late [swash *z*] | Sir *Thomas Freke. &c.* vide the laſt ſheet. [swash *k*] | From the FLEET, | Under the generous Juriſdiction of *Richard Manlovs* Esq; [swash *M*] | The Worthy Warden thereof.

Collation: A–X⁴ [A]⁴ χ²

The texts of "Ioannes Donne Sac: Theol: Profess" and T"Ioannes Donne Sac: Theol: Profess" in 1684:1a, 1684:1b, and 1684:1c are identical; and the priority of 1684:1a, 1684:1b, and 1684:1c is uncertain (the Wing numbers are arbitrary in this instance).

---

1. No record exists of the copies of a 1688 edition (Wing: F1043) listed at C and O; and G. Blacker Morgan, in his edition *THE Tombs, Monuments, &c., Visible in S. Paul's Cathedral (AND S. FAITH'S BENEATH IT) Previous to its Destruction by FIRE A.D. 1666* (1885), does not mention a 1688 printing.

1687:1a
Author: William Winstanley
Title [within double rules]: THE | LIVES | Of the moſt Famous | Engliſh Poets, | OR THE | Honour of *PARNASSVS*; [swash *V*] | In a Brief | ESSAY | OF THE | WORKS and WRITINGS | of above Two Hundred of them, from the | Time of K. *WILLIAM* the Conqueror, | To the Reign of His Preſent Majeſty | King JAMES II. | [rule] | *Marmora* Mæonij *vincunt Monumenta Libelli;* | *Vivitur ingenio, cætera Mortis erunt.* | [rule] | Written by *WILLIAM WINSTANLEY*, Author of | the *Engliſh Worthies.* | [rule] | 𝕷𝖎𝖈𝖊𝖓𝖘𝖊𝖉, *June* 16, 1686. Rob. Midgley. [swash *J*] | [rule] | *LONDON,* | Printed by *H. Clark,* for 𝕾amuel 𝕸anſhip at the [swash *k*] | Sign of the *Black Bull* in *Cornhil,* 1687. [swash *k*]

Collation: 8°. π¹ A⁸ a⁴ B–P⁸ ($4: π1v, portrait bust; A1, title, unsigned; a4, unsigned; L4, unsigned; N4, unsigned; P4, unsigned; P8, blank)
Wing: W3065
Copy: L 1477.aa.26
Verse: "A Hymne to God the Father," p. 120

1688:1a
Author: Jane Barker
Title [within double rules]: POETICAL | RECREATIONS: | Conſiſting of | ORIGINAL POEMS, | SONGS, ODES, &c. | With ſeveral | New *TRANSLATIONS*. | [rule] | In Two PARTS. | [rule] | PART I. | Occaſionally Written by Mrs. *JANE BARKER*. [swash J, K] | PART II. | By ſeveral Gentlemen of the UNIVERSITIES, | and Others. | [rule] |————pulcherrima Virgo | Incedit, magnâ Juve-num ſtipante catervâ. Virg. [swash J] | [rule] | *LONDON*, | Printed for *Benjamin Crayle*, at the *Peacock* [swash k] | and *Bible*, at the Weſt-end of St. *Pauls*. 1688.
    Collation: 8°. A⁸ a⁴ B–H⁸ 2A⁴ 2B–2T⁸ ($4: A1, blank, unsigned; A1v, printer's device and license; A2, title, unsigned; a3, unsigned; a4, unsigned; 2A1, separate title, unsigned; 2A3, unsigned; 2A4, unsigned; 2M2, missigned M2)
    Wing: B770; Case: 186
    Copy: CSmH 58018
    Separate title [within double rules]: MISCELLANEA: | OR, | THE | **Second Part** | OF | POETICAL RECREATIONS. | [rule] | Com-pos'd by ſeveral Authors. | [rule] |————*Non, ubi plura nitent in carmine, paucis | Offendi maculis, quas aut incuria ſudit | Aut humana parum cavit Natura.*———— Hor. | [rule] | *LONDON*, | Printed for *Benjamin Crayle*, at the *Peacock* [swash k] | and *Bible*, at the Weſt-end of St. *Pauls*. 1688.
    Verse: "The Will" (ll. 1–6, 10–11, 14–15, 23–24, 28–33, 37–42, 7–9, 17–18), sigs. 2I1v–2

1688:2a
Compiler: Henry Playford
Title [within double rules]: <Harmonia Sacra;> | OR, | DIVINE HYMNS | AND | <DIALOGUES:> | WITH | A THOROW-BASS for the *Theorbo-Lute*, | *Baſs-Viol, Harpſichord*, or *Organ*. | [rule] | <Com-poſed by the Beſt Maſters of the Laſt and Preſent Age.> [swash <B, P>] | [rule] | The WORDS by ſeveral Learned and Pious Perſons. | [rule] | *Cannon a 3, in the Fifth and Eighth below, riſing a Note every time.* | [musical score] | *Laudate Dominum de Cæ——lis, lau-da——te e—um in ex—cel—ſis.* | [rule] |
                              IMPRIMATUR,
Ex Ædib. Lamb.   *Guil. Needham RR. in Chriſto P. ac D.*
Nov.7.1687.   *D. Wilhelmo Archiep. Cant. à Sacr.*
                         Domeſt.

| [double rule] | *In the SAVOY:* | Printed by <*Edward Jones,*> for <*Henry Playford,*> at his Shop near the *Temple* Church. | [rule] | MDCLXXXVIII.

Collation: 2°. π^2 a^2 B–X^2 ($2: π1v, engraving; π2, title; a2, unsigned; B2, missigned B3; X2, unsigned)

Wing: P2436; Keynes: 110

Copy: O Mus.54.c.3.(1)

Verse:[1] "A Hymne to God the Father," pp. 51–52

––––––––

1. For musical setting, see plate 4.

1691:1a

Author: Thomas Pope Blount

Title [within double rules]: ESSAYS | On Several | SUBJECTS. | [rule] | Written By | Sir *Tho. Pope Blount.* [swash *T*] | [rule] | *Conamur Tenues Grandia.* | Hor. Lib. I. Ode. 6. | [rule] | *LONDON,* | Printed for *Richard Bently,* | in *Ruſſel-ſtreet* in *Covent-* | *Garden.* MDCXCI.

Collation: 8°. A^4 B–M^8 N^2 ($4: A1, title, unsigned; A1v, blank; A4, wanting; F3, missigned E3; N2, unsigned)

Wing: B3348

Copy: DFo B3348

Verse:[1] "The Will" (l. 51), p. 61

Additional seventeenth-century editions:

1691:1b 1692 (Wing: B3349): p. 61

1691:1c 1697 (Wing: B3350): p. 100

––––––––

1. Keynes (p. 301) notes the parallel to Abraham Cowley's quotation of the same line—see 1656:1a.

1691:2a

Author: John Dryden

Collective title [within double rules]: THE | WORKS | OF | Mr. John Dryden, | *Containing as follows,* |

ESSAY on Dramatick Po- etry.	*Oedipus.*
Wild Gallant.	*Troilus* and *Creſſide.*
Rival Ladies.	*Spaniſh*-Fryar.
	Duke of *Guiſe.*

Indian Emperour.
Maiden Queen.
Sir Martin Marr-all.
The Tempest.
Evening Love.
Royal Martyr.
Conquest of *Granada*.
Marriage A-la-mode.
Love in a Nunnery.
Amboyna.
State of Innocence.
Aurenzebe.
All for Love.
Limberham.

Vindication of the Duke of *Guiſe*
Don *Sebaſtian*.
Amphitryon.
King *Arthur*.
Annus Mirabilis.
Poem on the Return of K. *Ch*. II.
—On the Coronation of K. *Ch*. II.
A Poem to the L. Chancellor *Hide*.
Abſalom and *Achitophel*.
The Medall, a Poem.
Religio Laici, a Poem.
Elegy on the Death of K *Charles* II.
The *Hind* and *Panther*.
Poem on the Birth of the Prince.

| [rule] | *LONDON*, | Printed, and are to be Sold by *Jacob Tonſon*, at the Sign [swash *J* | of the *Judge's Head* in *Chancery-Lane*, near *Fleet-ſtreet*, 1691. [swash *J*]

Wing: D2207; MacDonald: 106a

Volume title [within double rules]: *ANNVS MIRABILIS*. [swash *A, N, N, M, R, B*] | The YEAR of | WONDERS, | M. DC. LXVI. | AN | Hiſtorical Poem. | [rule] | ALSO | A *POEM* on the Happy RESTORA-TION and RETURN of | His Late *Sacred MAJESTY* [swash *J*] | 𝕮𝖍𝖆𝖗𝖑𝖊𝖘 𝖙𝖍𝖊 𝕾𝖊𝖈𝖔𝖓𝖉. | LIKEWISE | A PANEGYRICK on His *CORONATION*. [swash *T, N*] | TOGETHER | With a POEM to My LORD CHANCELLOR | Preſented on *New-Years-Day*. 1662. | [rule] | By *JOHN DRYDEN*, Eſq; [swash *J, N, D, R, Y, D*] | [rule] | *LONDON*, Printed for *Henry Herringman*, and ſold by | *Jacob Tonſon* at the *Judges-Head* in *Chancery-Lane*. 1688. [swash *J, J*]

Collation: 4°. a⁴ ✳✳✳⁴ †††² B–P⁴ Q² ²A–²D⁴ ²E² ³A⁴ ²a² ³B–³C⁴ ³D² ⁴A⁴ ³a⁴ ($2: A1, title, unsigned; ✳✳2, unsigned; F3, missigned †1; N1, separate title, unsigned; P2, separate title, unsigned; Q2, unsigned; ²A1, separate title, unsigned; ²E2, unsigned; ³A1, separate title, unsigned; ²a2, unsigned; ³D2, unsigned; ⁴A1, separate title, unsigned) B–D⁴ E² ($3: D3, unsigned; E2, unsigned) A–C⁴ D² ($2: A1, separate title, unsigned; D2, unsigned) A–T⁴ χ¹ ²A–²C⁴ †⁴ ³A–³C⁴ ($2: A1, blank; A2, separate title, unsigned; ²A1, separate title, unsigned; †1, separate title, unsigned)

Copy:[1] OW Shelfmark not for publication

Separate title [within double rules]: Eleonora: | [rule] | A PAN-EGYRICAL | POEM: | Dedicated to the | MEMORY | Of the Late | COUNTESS | OF | *ABINGDON*. | [rule] | Written by Mr. *DRYDEN*. | [rule] |——— ——— *Superas evadere ad auras*, | *Hoc opus, hic labor*

PLATE 4. Musical setting of "A Hymne to God the Father" (1688:2a).
Reproduced by permission of the Bodleian Library, Oxford.
Shelfmark: Mus.54.c.3.(1), pp. 51–52.

Wilt thou forgive that Sin, by which I've won o—thers to sin, and made my Sin their

dore? Wilt thou forgive that Sin, which I did fhun a Year or two, yet wallow'd in a

fcore? When thou haft done, thou haft not done, for I have more. I have a Sin of

Fear, that when I've fpun my laft Thread, I fhall perifh on the Shore; but fwear by thy felf that art my

Death, thy Sun fhall fhine, as he fhines now and heretofore, and having done

that thou haft done, I fear no more.

eſt. Pauci, quos æquus amavit | *Juppiter, aut ardens evexit ad æthera virtus;* [swash J] | *Diis geniti potuere.* Virgil Æneid. 1. 6. | [rule] | LONDON: | Printed for *Jacob Tonſon,* at the *Judges Head* in *Chancery-* [swash J, J] | *Lane,* near *Fleetſtreet.* 1692. | Where compleat Sets of Mr. *Dryden's* Works are Sold: The Plays being put | in the order they were Written.

Verse: "Obsequies to the Lord Harrington" (ll. 5–6), p. 22; A"Elegie. Death" (ll. 61–62), p. 23

Additional seventeenth-century editions:[2]

1691:2b 1693 (Wing: D2208; Macdonald: 106b): IV, 22, 23

1691:2c 1694 (Wing: D2209; Macdonald: 106c): IV, 22, 23

1691:2d 1695 (Wing: D2210; Macdonald: 106e): IV, 22, 23

---

1. Hugh Macdonald, in *John Dryden: A Bibliography of Early Editions and of Drydeniana,* notes that the four-volume OW set has "a copy of *Eleonora,* 29, the title of the poem ["Eleonora:"] being added in manuscript to the others on the title page" (p. 146). The described OW volume title page (this volume lacks the collective title page) also has "Albion" added in the identical hand (probably that of George Clarke, who purchased the volume and who signed his initials on the title page) after "Don *Sebastion.*"

2. Another edition containing *Eleonora* may exist: the title page of the 1695 edition published by Bentley (Wing: D2210; Macdonald: 106f) states that the edition consists of *"Three Volumes"*; however, Macdonald observes that "Sometimes a fourth volume containing sets of the poems, without a general title, is found with the above volumes" (p. 148). I am unable to confirm the existence of this fourth volume.

1692:1A

Author: John Dryden

Title [within double rules]: Eleonora: | [rule] | A PANEGYRICAL | POEM: | Dedicated to the | MEMORY | Of the Late | COUNTESS | OF | *ABINGDON.* | [rule] | Written by Mr. *DRYDEN.* | [rule] |——— ——— *Superas evadere ad auras,* | *Hoc opus, hic labor eſt. Pauci, quos æquus amavit* | *Juppiter, aut ardens evexit ad æthera virtus;* [swash J] | *Diis geniti potuere.* Virgil Æneid. 1. 6. | [rule] | LONDON: | Printed for *Jacob Tonſon,* at the *Judges Head* in *Chancery-* [swash J, J] | *Lane,* near *Fleetſtreet.* 1692. | Where compleat Sets of Mr. *Dryden's* Works are Sold: The Plays being put | in the order they were Written.

Collation: 4°. †⁴ A–C⁴ ($2: †1, title, unsigned)
Wing: D2270; Macdonald: 29
Copy: OW Shelfmark not for publication
Verse: "Obsequies to the Lord Harrington" (ll. 5–6), p. 22; *A*"Elegie. Death" (ll. 61–62), p. 23

Large-paper (277 × 216 mm) copy with the same typesetting of "Obsequies to the Lord Harrington" (ll. 5–6) and *A*"Elegie. Death" (ll. 61–62) as in 1691:2a.

Additional seventeenth-century issue:

1692:1a 1692 (Wing: D2270. CLU-C, shelfmark: *PR 3419 E21): pp. 22, 23

Small-paper (217 × 155 mm) copy with the same typesetting of "Obsequies to the Lord Harrington" (ll. 5–6) and *A*"Elegie. Death" (ll. 61–62) as in 1691:2a.

1696:1a
Author: Mary de la Riviere Manley
Title [within double rules]: LETTERS | Writen by | Mrs. *MAN-LEY.* | To which is Added | A Lᴇᴛᴛᴇʀ from a ſuppoſed | Nᴜɴ in *Portugal*, to a | Gᴇɴᴛʟᴇᴍᴀɴ in *France*, in | Imitation of the Nᴜɴ's Five | Lᴇᴛᴛᴇʀs in Print, by Co- | lonel *Pack.* [swash *k*] | [double rule] | *LONDON,* | Printed for *R. B.* and Sold by the | Book-Sellers of *London* and *Weſt-* | *minſter,* 1696.
Collation: 8°. A⁴ B–F⁸ G⁴ ($4: A1, title, unsigned; A3, unsigned; A4, unsigned; G3, unsigned; G4, unsigned)
Wing: M434
Copy: L 1086.b.7
Verse: "The Will" (l. 51), p. 2

Works Containing Translations Only

T1641:1a

    Author: Georg Rodolf Weckherlin

    Title [engraved]: 𝕲𝖊𝖔𝖗𝖌 𝕽𝖔𝖉𝖔𝖑𝖋 | 𝖂𝖊𝖈𝖐𝖍𝖊𝖗𝖑𝖎𝖓𝖘 | 𝕲𝖆𝖎𝖘𝖙𝖑𝖎𝖈𝖍𝖊 | 𝖚𝖓𝖉 | 𝖂𝖊𝖑𝖙𝖑𝖎𝖈𝖍𝖊 | 𝕲𝖊𝖉𝖎𝖈𝖍𝖙𝖊. | AMSTERDAM | *Bey* Iohan Ianſſon *A°. 1641.* [swash *B*]

    Collation: 8°. A–T⁸ ($5: A1, title, unsigned; B6, signed; E6, signed; T8, blank)

    Wing: none

    Copy: L 1460.b.16

    Verse: *T*"Niobe" (l. 1), sig. A7v; *T*"A licentious person" (l. 1), sig. A8; *T*"Phryne" (l. 1), sig. A8; *T*"Antiquary" (l. 1), sig. A8; *T*"Hero and Leander" (l. 1), sig. A8v; *T*"Niobe," p. 178; *T*"Hero and Leander," p. 178; *T*"Antiquary," p. 187; *T*"A licentious person," p. 187; *T*"Phryne," p. 190

    Epigram number 1 is dated 1615 (p. 177); thus, the translations could date from much earlier than 1641 and could derive from manuscripts.

Additional seventeenth-century edition:[1]

T1641:1b 1648

    Title [typeset]: 𝕲𝖊𝖔𝖗𝖌-𝕽𝖔𝖉𝖔𝖑𝖋 | 𝖂𝖊𝖈𝖐𝖍𝖊𝖗𝖑𝖎𝖓𝖘 | 𝕲𝖆𝖎𝖘𝖙𝖑𝖎𝖈𝖍𝖊 𝖚𝖓𝖉 𝖂𝖊𝖑𝖙𝖑𝖎𝖈𝖍𝖊 | 𝕲𝖊𝖉𝖎𝖈𝖍𝖙𝖊. | [ornament] | 𝕬𝖒𝖘𝖙𝖊𝖗𝖉𝖆𝖒/ | [rule] | 𝕭𝖊𝖞 𝕵𝖆𝖓 𝕵𝖆𝖓𝖘𝖘𝖔𝖓. | 1648.

    Collation: 12°. A⁶ B–P¹²)(⁶ Q–2O¹² 2P–2Q⁶ ($6: A1, engraved title, unsigned; A2, typeset title, unsigned; A6, unsigned; P12, torn out;)(1, separate title, unsigned;)(6, unsigned; 2P4, unsigned; 2P6, unsigned; 2Q1, wanting; 2Q6, unsigned)[2]

    Wing: none

    Copy: L 11517.b.33

    Separate title: 𝕲𝖊𝖔𝖗𝖌-𝕽𝖔𝖉𝖔𝖑𝖋 | 𝖂𝖊𝖈𝖐𝖍𝖊𝖗𝖑𝖎𝖓𝖘 | 𝖂𝖊𝖑𝖙𝖑𝖎𝖈𝖍𝖊 𝕲𝖊𝖉𝖎𝖈𝖍𝖙𝖊/ | 𝕺𝖉𝖊𝖗 | 𝕺𝖉𝖊𝖓 𝖚𝖓𝖉 𝕲𝖊𝖘ä𝖓𝖌𝖊. | 𝕯𝖆𝖘 𝕰𝖗𝖘𝖙𝖊 𝕭𝖚𝖈𝖍. | [ornament] | 𝕬𝖒𝖘𝖙𝖊𝖗𝖉𝖆𝖒/ | [rule] | 𝕭𝖊𝖞 𝕵𝖆𝖓 𝕵𝖆𝖓𝖘𝖘𝖔𝖓. | 1648.

    Verse: *T*"Niobe," p. 799; *T*"Hero and Leander," p. 799; *T*"A licentious person," p. 808; *T*"Antiquary," pp. 808–9; *T*"Phryne," pp. 825–26; *A*"A lame begger,"[3] pp. 829–30; *T*"Niobe" (heading only), sig. 2Q4v; *T*"Hero and Leander" (heading only), sig. 2Q4v; *T*"A licentious person" (heading only), sig. 2Q5; *T*"Antiquary" (heading only), sig. 2Q5; *T*"Phryne" (heading only), sig. 2Q5v; *A*"A lame begger" (heading only), sig. 2Q6

---

1. O has an independently bound copy (shelfmark: 8°.G.84.Linc.) of the second section of T1641:1b, with the identical separate title page on

sig.)(1; however, neither its pagination (sig.)(6v is paginated 336) nor its collation ()(⁶ Q–2O¹² 2P–2Q⁶) suggests a deliberate separate printing.

2. The catchword on sig. P11v, "Georg-", is correct for sig.)(1; thus, leaf P12 was likely deliberately removed. The stub remains in the described copy.

3. Bohm first pointed out the similarity between "An die schöne Marina" and "A lame begger": "Das Wortspiel mit 'liegen' findet sich, wie A 829 no 112, auch bei Donne (Engl. poets V S 142): *A lame beggar*" (p. 75).

T1657:1a

Compiler: Henrik Rintjus

Title: *KLIOOS* | KRAAM, | *VOL* | VERSCHEIDEN GEDICHT-EN. | *De Tweede Opening*. | [ornament] | Gedrukkt te Leeuwarden, | By Henrik Rintjus, Boekdrukker in de Pe- | perſtraat, in den Zaadzaaijer. cIɔ Iɔc lvii.

Collation: 8°. *⁸ A–Z⁸ ($5: *1, title, unsigned; *3, unsigned; A1, unsigned; K5, unsigned; N5, unsigned; R5, unsigned; Y5, missigned Y9)

Wing:[1] none

Copy: CSmH bound with 404592

Verse: T"A Valediction: of weeping" (heading only), sig. *5v; T"Breake of day" (heading only), sig. *5v; T"The Legacie" (heading only), sig. *5v; T"The triple Foole" (heading only), sig. *5v; T"The Blossome" (heading only), sig. *5v; T"Song. 'Go, and catch a falling star'" (heading only), sig. *5v; T"A Valediction: of weeping," pp. 360–61; T"Breake of day," pp. 361–62; T"The Legacie," p. 362; T"The triple Foole," pp. 362–63; T"The Blossome," pp. 363–65; T"Song. 'Go, and catch a falling star,'" p. 365

---

1. The 1656 *Klioos Kraam, vol Verscheiden Gedichten. D'Eerste Opening* lacks Donne verse. Daley, who dates Huygens' translations of these poems between "August 18 and October 17, 1633" (p. 165), does not mention T1657:1a. If Rintjus' 1626 date is correct (see Introduction) Huygens must have had access to one or more Donne manuscripts.

A1613:1a

Author: Daniel Price

Title [within single rules top, left, and bottom; double rule on right]: PRINCE HENRY | His | FIRST ANNIVERSARY. | Heb. 11.38. | *Of whom the world was not worthy.* | By | Daniel Price *Doctor in Divinity, one of | his Highneffe Chaplaines.* | [printer's device] | *AT OXFORD,* [swash *A*] | Printed by Jofeph Barnes. 1613.

Collation: 4°. *² A–D⁴ ($3: *1, title, unsigned)

STC: 20299

Copy: CSmH 23673

Verse: *A*"The second Anniversarie" (ll. 68–69), p. 4; *A*"The second Anniversarie" (l. 70), p. 4; *A*"The second Anniversarie" (ll. 222–23), p. 4

A1613:2a

Author: Daniel Price

Title [within single rules]: SPIRITVALL | ODOVRS TO THE | MEMORY OF PRINCE | *HENRY* [swash *R*] | IN FOVRE OF THE | LAST SER- | mons preached in St James after his High- | neffe death, the laft being the Sermon be- | fore the body, the day before | the Funerall. | By | Daniel Price *then Chaplaine in Attendance.* | Ecclvs. 49.1. | *The remembrance of Iofias is like the compofition of the per-* [swash *k*] | *fume made by the Apothecary.* | [printer's device] | *AT OXFORD* [swash *A*] | *Printed by Iofeph Barnes and are to be fold by Iohn Barnes | dwelling neere Holborne Conduit.* 1613. [swash *C*]

Collation: 4°. π² A–O⁴ P² ($3: π1, title; G3, separate title, unsigned; L3, unsigned; P2, unsigned)

STC: 20304

Copy: O Antiq.e.E.110

Verse: *A*"The second Anniversarie" (ll. 222–23), sig. B4v; *A*"The second Anniversarie" (ll. 361–64), sig. B4v; *A*"The second Anniversarie" (ll. 223–24), sig. B4v; *A*"The second Anniversarie" (ll. 465–67), sig. B4v; *A*"The second Anniversarie" (ll. 491–94), sig. B4v; *A*"The second Anniversarie" (ll. 345–46), sigs. B4v–C1

Separate title [within single rules]: TEARES | SHED OVER AB-NER. | *THE* | SERMON PREACHED ON THE | Sunday before the Prince his fu- | nerall in St. James Chappell | *before the body.* | By | Daniel Price *then Chaplaine in Attendance.* | Seneca. | *Hectora flemus.* | [printer's device] | *AT OXFORD* [swash *A*] | *Printed by*

Iofeph Barnes and are to be fold by Iohn Barnes | dwelling neere Holborne Conduit. 1613. [swash C]

Verse: *A*"The first Anniversary" (refrain line), sig. P2r–v

Additional seventeenth-century edition:

A1613:2b 1613 (STC: 20304.5. O, shelfmark: Vet.A2 e.418)

Title [within single rules]: SPIRITVALL | ODOVRS TO THE | MEMORY OF PRINCE | HENRY. | IN FOVRE OF THE LAST | Sermons preached in S^t· IAMES after his High- | neffe death, the laft being the Sermon be- | fore the bodie, the day before | the Funerall. | By DANIEL PRICE *then Chaplaine in Attendance.* | ECCLVS 49.1. | *The remembrance of Iofias is like the compofition of the perfume* [swash k] | *made by the Apothecary.* | [printer's device] | *AT OXFORD* [swash A, D] | *Printed by Iofeph Barnes and are to be fold by Iohn Barnes* [swash P, B, B] | *dwelling neere Holborne Conduit.* 1613.

Collation: 4º. π² A–O⁴ P² ($3: π1, title; F3, unsigned; G3, separate title, unsigned; L3, unsigned; M3, unsigned; P2, unsigned)

Verse: *A*"The second Anniversarie" (ll. 222–23), sig. B4v; *A*"The second Anniversarie" (ll. 361–64), sig. B4v; *A*"The second Anniversarie" (ll. 223–24), sig. B4v; *A*"The second Anniversarie" (ll. 465–67), sig. B4v; *A*"The second Anniversarie" (ll. 491–94), sig. B4v; *A*"The second Anniversarie" (ll. 345–46), sigs. B4v–C1

Separate title [within single rules]: TEARES | SHED OVER | ABNER. | THE SERMON PREACHED ON | the Sunday before the *Prince* his funerall | in S^t. IAMES Chappell before | *the BODIE.* | By | DANIEL PRICE *then Chaplaine in Attendance.* | SENECA. | *Hectora flemus.* | [printer's device] | *AT OXFORD* [swash A] | *Printed by Iofeph Barnes and are to be fold by Iohn Barnes* | *dwelling neere Holborne Conduit.* 1613. [swash C]

Verse: *A*"The first Anniversary" (refrain line), sig. P2r–v

The priority of A1613:2a and A1613:2b is uncertain; the STC numbers are arbitrary.

A1613:3a

Author: Cyril Tourneur

Title [xylographic, within double rules]: *Three Elegies | on | the moft lamented | DEATH | of | PRINCE HENRIE,* [swash R, N, N, R] |

The first	⎫		⎧	*Cyril Töurneur.*
The fecond	⎬	*written by*	⎨	*John Webster.*
The third	⎭		⎩	*Tho: Heywood.*

| London | Printed for William Welbie. | 1613.

Collation: 4°. A⁴ B–C⁴ ²A–²C⁴ ³A–³C⁴ ($3: C2, unsigned; C3, unsigned; ²A1, black, unsigned; ²A2, separate title, unsigned; ²C2, unsigned; ²C3, black, unsigned; ²C4, black; ³A1, separate title, unsigned; ³A2, unsigned)

STC: 24151; Case: 42

Copy: CSmH 69680

Separate title: A | MONVMENTAL | COLVMNE, | Erected to the liuing Memory of | the euer-glorious Henry, late | *Prince of Wales.* [swash P] | Virgil. *Oftendent terris hunc tantum fata* | By Iohn Webster. | [rule] | [ornament] | [rule] | *LONDON,* | Printed by *N. O.* for *William Welby,* dwelling in | Pauls Church-yard at the ſigne of the | Swan. 1613.

Verse: A"The first Anniversary" (l. 115), sig. ²B2

A1613:4a

Author: John Webster

Title: A | MONVMENTAL | COLVMNE, | Erected to the liuing Memory of | the euer-glorious Henry, late | *Prince of Wales.* [swash P | Virgil. *Oftendent terris hunc tantum fata* | By Iohn Webster. | [rule] | [ornament] | [rule] | *LONDON,* | Printed by *N. O.* for *William Welby,* dwelling in | Pauls Church-yard at the ſigne of the | Swan. 1613.

Collation: 4°. A–C⁴ ($3: A1, black, unsigned; A2, title, unsigned; C2, unsigned; C3, black, unsigned; C4, black)

STC: 25174

Copy: DFo STC 25174

Verse: A"The first Anniversary" (l. 115), sig. B2

Also appears as part of A1613:3a, and A"The first Anniversary" (l. 115) is in the same typesetting as that in A1613:3a.

A1623:1a

Author: John Webster

Title: THE | TRAGEDY | *OF THE DVTCHESSE* [swash D, C] | *Of Malfy.* | *As it was Preſented priuatly, at the Black-* [swash P, B, k] | *Friers; and publiquely at the Globe, By the* | Kings Maieſties Seruants. | The perfect and exact Coppy, with diuerſe | *things Printed, that the length of the Play would* | not beare in the Preſentment. | VVritten by *John Webſter.* [swash J] | Hora.————*Si quid———* |————*Candidus Imperti ſi non his vtere mecum.* | [rule] | *LONDON:* | Printed by

Nicholas Okes, for Iohn | Waterson, and are to be ſold at the | ſigne of the Crowne, in *Paules* [swash *P*] | Church-yard, 1623.
Collation: 4°. A–N⁴ ($3: A1, blank, unsigned; A2, title, unsigned; H3, unsigned)
STC: 25176
Copy: CLU-C *PR 3184 T71
Verse: A"The first Anniversary" (ll. 156–57), sig. H3v; A"The second Anniversarie" (ll. 181–82), sig. H4; A"The first Anniversary" (l. 356), sig. L3v

Additional seventeenth-century issues/editions:

A1623:1b 1640 (STC: 25177): sigs. F3v, F4, I1v

A1623:1c 1640 (STC: 25177a): sigs. F3v, F4, I1v

A1623:1d 1660 (Wing: W1222): sigs. F3v, F4, I1v
The sheets of A1623:1b with a cancel title page.

A1623:1e 1678 (Wing: W1223): pp. 45, 45, 65

A1629:1a
Author: Francis Quarles
Title [engraved]: ARGALVS and PARTHENIA | The Argument of yᵉ Hiſtory | *Written by Fra: Quarles.* [swash *W, F, Q*] | *Luſit Anacreon* [swash *L, A*] | London Printed for Iohn Marriott in Sᵗ Dunſtons Church: [swash *L*] | *yard fleetſtreet.* 1629. *Tho: Cecill ſculp*
Collation: 4°. A–X⁴ ($3: title mounted on guard in examined copy; A1, blank, unsigned; A2, unsigned; K3, unsigned; L3, unsigned)
STC: 20526; Horden:[1] VI.1
Copy: O 4°.W.2.(6)Jur.
Verse:[2] A"A licentious person" / A"A Hymne to God the Father," p. [162]

Additional seventeenth-century issues/editions:

A1629:1b 1630 (STC: 20526.5; Horden: VI.2): p. 154

A1629:1c 1632 (STC: 20527; Horden: VI.3): p. 154
Several issues of *Argalus and Parthenia* were printed in 1632. Book III, l. 1 in A1629:1c ends "ouerblowne".

A1629:1d 1632 (STC: 20527.5; Horden: VI.4): p. 154
In A1629:1d, book III, l. 1 ends "overblowne".

A1629:1e 1632 (Horden: VI.4a. L, shelfmark: C.57.e.5):[3] p. 154
A reissue of the sheets of A1629:1d with the undated title leaf of A1629:1f.

A1629:1f 1632? (STC: 20528; Horden: VI.5): p. [153]
The dates and order of A1629:1f–i are indeterminate. Horden lists them as "1632?"; the *STC*, as "c. 1635"; the *National Union Catalog of Pre-1956 Imprints* dates A1629:1g "ca. 1634" and A1629:1j, "ca. 1636"; and Freeman describes A1629:1a–c and collates A1629:1a–f, h, i, but does not date A1629:1f–i. Descriptions of the title pages are provided in Horden. Book II, l. 1 of 1629:1f ends "cleare,"; book III, l. 2 reads "showrs".

A1629:1g 1632? (STC: 20528.5): p. [153]
Book II, l. 1 ends "cleare,"; book III, l. 2 has "show'rs".

A1629:1h 1632? (STC: 20528a; Horden: VI.6): p. [153]
Book II, l. 1 reads "clear,".

A1629:1i 1632? (STC: 20528a.5; Horden: VI.7): p. [153]
Book II, l. 1 ends "clar,".

A1629:1j 1647 (Wing: Q39; Horden: VI.8): p. [153]

A1629:1k 1651 (Wing: Q40; Horden: VI.9): p. [153]

A1629:1l 1654 (Wing: Q41; Horden: VI.10): pp. 131–32

A1629:1m 1656 (Wing: Q41A): pp. 131–32

A1629:1n 1656 (Wing: Q42; Horden: VI.11): p. 166

A1629:1o 1659 (Wing: Q42A): pp. 131–32

A1629:1p 1659 (Wing: Q43; Horden: VI.12): pp. 131–32

A1629:1q 1664 (Wing: Q43A; Horden: VI.13): pp. 131–32

A1629:1r 1668 (Wing: Q44; Horden: VI.14): pp. 131–32

A1629:1s 1669 (Wing: Q44A; Horden: VI.15): p. 166

A1629:1t 1671 (Wing: Q45; Horden: VI.16): pp. 131–32

A1629:1u 1677 (Wing: Q46; Horden: VI.17): pp. 131–32

A1629:1v 1677 (L, shelfmark: 1482.aaa.10.):[4] p. 215

A1629:1w 1684 (Wing: Q47; Horden: VI.18): p. 215

A1629:1x 1687 (Wing: Q48; Horden: VI.19): p. [139]

A1629:1y 1687 (Wing: Q48A; Horden: VI.20): p. [139]

A1629:1z 1690 (Wing: Q48B; Horden: VI.21): p. 215

A1629:1aa 1692 (STC: Q49; Horden: VI.22): p. 215

---

1. John Horden, *Francis Quarles (1592–1644): A Bibliography of His Works to the Year 1800.*

2. Milgate (*Satires*, p. 199) feels that "Francis Quarles adapts the epigram ["A licentious person"] as part of one of his own . . . in *Divine Fancies* . . . 1632, p. 97 ('On Sinnes,' Bk. ii, no. 66)." The epigram in *Divine Fancies* (see A1632:1a) is a reprinting of stanza 1 of "The Authors Dreame"; stanzas 2 and 3 of "The Authors Dreame" become epigrams 69 and 71 respectively in book II of *Divine Fancies* but do not resemble any Donne poem closely enough to receive separate notice. David Freeman (*Argalus and Parthenia: Francis Quarles*) observes that "such a serious penitential poem is without earlier precedent in Quarles's canon" and suggests that "it recalls Donne's 'A Hymne to God the Father'" (p. 223).

3. The *British Museum General Catalogue of Printed Books* speculatively dates this copy 1630.

4. On the basis of information on the title pages of A1629:1w, A1629:1z, and A1629:1aa, Horden (p. 27) postulated the existence of this edition and placed it between A1629:1u and A1629:1w, though he did not number it and was unable to locate a copy.

A1632:1a

Author: Francis Quarles

Title [within double rules]: DIVINE | FANCIES: | Digeſted into | EPIGRAMMES, | MEDITATIONS, | AND | OBSERVATIONS. | [rule] | *By* Fra: Qvarles. [swash *B*] | [rule] | [ornament] | [rule] |

LONDON, | Printed by *M. F.* for Iohn Marriot, | and are to be ſold at his Shop in Sᵗ. *Dunſtanes* | Church-yard in *Fleet-ſtreet*. | 1632.

Collation: 4°. q⁴ A–2D⁴ ($3: q1, blank?, wanting; q2, title, un-signed; B3, missigned A3; G3, unsigned; L3, unsigned; O3, un-signed; P3, unsigned; 2D4, blank?, wanting)

STC: 20529; Horden: IX.1

Copy: CSmH 69003

Verse:[1] *A*"A licentious person," p. 97

Additional seventeenth-century issues /editions:

A1632:1b 1633 (STC: 20530; Horden: IX.2): p. 97

A1632:1c 1636 (STC: 20531; Horden: IX.3): p. 97

A1632:1d 1638 (STC: 20532; Horden: IX.4): p. 95

A1632:1e 1641 (Wing: Q62; Horden: IX.5): p. 95

A1632:1f 1652 (Wing: Q63; Horden: IX.6): p. 85

A1632:1g 1657 (Wing: Q64; Horden: IX.7): p. 85

A1632:1h 1660 (Wing: Q65; Horden: IX.8): p. 85

A1632:1i 1664 (Wing: Q66; Horden: IX.9): p. 81

A1632:1j 1671 (Wing: Q67; Horden: IX.10): p. 81

A1632:1k 1675 (Wing: Q68; Horden: IX.11): p. 81

A1632:1l 1687 (Wing: Q69; Horden: IX.12): p. 81

---

1. For the epigram as it appears earlier as the first stanza of "The Authors Dreame," see A1629:1a.

A1634:1a

Author: William Habington

Title: CASTARA. | [rule] | The firſt part. | [rule] |—*Carmina non prius* | *Audita, Muſarum ſacerdos* [swash *A, M*] | *Virginibus.*——| [rule] | [ornament] | [rule of decorations] | LONDON, | Printed by

Anne Griffin for *William Cooke*, [swash G, k] | and are to bee *fold* at his *fhop* neare | *Furnivals Inne* gate in Holburne: [swash v] | 1634.

Collation: 4°. A–L⁴ ($2: A1, title, unsigned; B3, signed; L4, errata sheet, bound between A1 and A2)

STC: 12583

Copy: CSmH 61226

Separate title: CASTARA. | [rule] | The *fecond* part. | [rule] | *Vatumque lafcivos triumphos,* [swash v] | *Calcat Amor, pede conjugali.* [swash C, A] | [rule] | [ornament] | [rule of decorations] | LON-DON, | Printed by *Anne Griffin* for *William Cooke,* [swash G, k] | and are to be *fold* at his *fhop* neare | *Furnivals Inne* Gate in Holburne. [swash v] | 1634.

Verse: *A*"Song. 'Go, and catch a falling star'" (ll. 5, 1), p. 73; *A*"Song. 'Go, and catch a falling star'" (l. 18), p. 73; *A*"Song. 'Go, and catch a falling star'" (l. 11), p. 74; *A*"The Sunne Rising" (l. 24), p. 74

Additional seventeenth-century issues/editions:

A1634:1b 1635 (STC: 12584): pp. 112, 112, 113, 113

A1634:1c 1635 (STC: 12584a): pp. 112, 112, 113, 113

A1634:1d 1639 (STC: 12585): pp. 112, 112, 113, 113

A1638:1a

Compiler: Anonymous

Title: JUSTA | EDOVARDO KING | naufrago, | ab | Amicis mœrentibus, | amoris | & | μνείας χάριν. | [double rule] | *Si rectè calculum ponas, ubique naufragium eft.* | Pet. Arb. | [double rule] | *CANTABRIGIÆ:* | Apud *Thomam Buck,* & *Rogerum Daniel,* celeberrimæ | Academiæ typographos. 1638.

Collation: 4°. A–D⁴ E⁶ F–H⁴ I² ($3: A1, title, unsigned; A2, unsigned; E4, signed; F1, separate title, unsigned; F3, unsigned; G3, unsigned; I2, unsigned)

STC: 14964; Shawcross:[1] 41

Copy: L 239.k.36

Separate title [within triple frame]: Ob*fequies* to | the memorie | of | M*ʳ* EDWARD [swash M] | KING, | *Anno Dom.* [swash A, D, m] | 1638. | [rule] | [ornament] | [rule] | Printed by *Th. Buck,* and *R. Daniel,* | printers to the *Vniverfitie* of | *Cambridge.* 1638.

Verse:[2] *A*"A Funerall Elegie" (ll. 45–46), sig. H3

Shawcross informs me that the title page of A1638:1b as described in item 41 (*Milton*) is incorrect, and I am unable to confirm any second state even though a cursory examination of several copies indicates that there were a number of stop-press corrections in the printing (l. 15 of "Lycidas" is not indented in L copy C.131.c.15, and CT copy VI 11 10[1] has "MDCXXXVIII" in the last line on sig. A2), the English poems exist bound separately (though signed as usual: L copy C.21.c.42), and the normal Latin-English order of poems has been reversed in at least one copy (though signed as usual: L copy G.11474).

---

1. John T. Shawcross, *Milton: A Bibliography for the Years 1624–1700*.
2. Lewalski (p. 320) notes the adaptation.

A1640:1a
Author: Francis Beaumont
Title: POEMS: | BY | *FRANCIS BEAVMONT,* | Gent. |

$$Viz. \begin{cases} \text{The Hermaphrodite.} \\ \text{The Remedie of Love.} \\ \text{Elegies.} \\ \text{Sonnets, with other Poems.} \end{cases}$$

| [rule] | *LONDON,* | Printed by *Richard Hodgkinſon* for W. W. [swash *k*] | and *Laurence Blaikelocke* and are [swash *k, k*] | to be ſold at the ſigne of the | Sugar-loafe next Temple | Bar in Fleet-ſtreet. | 1640.
Collation: 4º. A–K⁴ ($3: A1, title, unsigned; A3, unsigned; E2, missigned D2; F1, unsigned; K2v, missigned K3; K3, unsigned)
STC: 1665
Copy: CSmH 60332
Verse: *A*"Song. 'Go, and catch a falling star,'" sig. I1v

A1640:2a
Author: Thomas Carew
Title: POEMS. | *By* [swash *B*] | Thomas Carevv [second "v" is inverted "a"] | Eſquire. | One of the Gentlemen of the | Privie-Chamber, and Sewer in | Ordinary to His Majeſty. | [two rules] | LONDON, | Printed by *I. D.* for *Thomas Walkley,* | and are to be ſold at the ſigne of the | flying Horſe, between Brittains | Burſe, and York-Houſe. | 1640.

Collation: 8°. *A*² B–R⁸ S⁴ ($4: *A*1, title; *A*2, errata; B4, missigned A4; E4, missigned F4; S3, missigned S5)
STC: 4620
Copy: CSmH 80753
Verse: *A*"The Dampe," p. 16

Additional seventeenth-century editions /issues:

A1640:2b¹ 1640 (STC: 4620. L, shelfmark: C.71.a.9): p. 16
Leaf G7 is a cancel: its l. 4 of "*Epitaph on the Lady* S. *Wife to Sir* W.S." reads "To crown one Soveraigne beauty lies confind."

A1640:2c 1642 (Wing: C564): p. 15[16]

A1640:2d 1651 (Wing: C565. O, shelfmark: 8° T 9 2 Art B.S.[2]): p. 12
Title: POEMS. | With a | MASKE, | BY | *THOMAS CAREW* Eſq; | One of the Gent. of the privie- | Chamber, and Sewer in Ordinary | to His late Majeſty. | The *Songs* were ſet in *Muſick* by | Mr. Henry Lawes Gent: of the | Kings Chappell, and one of his late | Majeſties Private Muſick. | [rule] | *The third Edition reviſed and enlarged.* | [rule] | LONDON, | Printed for Humphrey Moseley | and are to be ſold at his Shop at the | ſigne of the Princes Armes in St. | *Pauls*-Church-yard. 1651.

A1640:2e 1651 (Wing: C565. L, shelfmark: 643.a.17): p. 12
This second 1651 issue has the following cancel title page: POEMS, | With a | MASKE, | BY | *THOMAS CAREW* Eſq; | One of the Gent. of the Privy- | Chamber, and Sewer in Ordi- | nary to his late Majeſtie. | The *Songs* were ſet in *Muſick* by [swash *k*] | Mr. Henry Lawes Gent. of the | Kings Chappell, and one of his late | Majeſties Private Muſick. | [rule] | *The third Edition reviſed and en- | larged.* | [rule] | LONDON | Printed for *H. M.* and are to be ſold | by *J: Martin*, at the ſigne of the | Bell in St. *Pauls*-Church- | Yard. 1651.

A1640:2f 1670 (Wing: C566): p. 13

A1640:2g 1671 (Wing: C567): p. 13

---

1. A third issue of the 1640 1st ed. may exist: Dunlap notes a copy belonging to David Nichol Smith having a title page with a comma after the initial "POEMS" (p. lxiv).

A1641:1a[1]
Compiler: John Mennes
Title: WITS | Recreations. | *CONTAINING,* | 630. Epigrams. |
160: Epitaphs, |
$$\left\{\begin{array}{l}\text{Fancies}\\\textit{and}\\\text{Fanta}\textit{ſ}\text{ticks,}\end{array}\right.$$
Variety of
| Good for melancholly humours. | [rule] | *Mart. Non cuique datur
habere naſum.* | [rule] | *LONDON,* | Printed by *Thomas Cotes,* for
Humphry | *Blunden* at the Caſtle in | *Corn-Hill.* 1641.
Collation: 8°. *A*⁴ B–Y⁸ Z⁴ ($4: *A,* wanting; *A*2v, engraved title
page; *A*3, title; C4, unsigned; E4, unsigned; L4, unsigned; Z3,
unsigned; Z4, blank?, wanting)
Wing: M1720; Case: 95(b)
Copy: CSmH 148543
Verse: *A*"Song. 'Go, and catch a falling star,' "[2] sig. D7; *A*"A
lame begger," sig. G2v; *A*"Song. 'Go, and catch a falling star,' " sig.
N3v; *A*"A Valediction: forbidding mourning,"[3] sig. V3v

Additional seventeenth-century editions /issues:

A1641:1b 1645
Title [within ornamental border]:[4] RECREATION | FOR | *Inge-
nious Head-peeces.* | OR, | A Pleaſant Grove for their Wits | to walke
in, |
$$\left\{\begin{array}{l}\textit{Epigrams,}\text{—630.}\\\textit{Epitaphs,}\text{—180.}\\\textit{Fancies,}\text{ a number.}\\\textit{Fanta}\textit{ſ}\text{ticks, abundance.}\end{array}\right.$$
Of
[swash *k*] | [rule] | Good for Melancholy Humours. | [rule] | Mart.
Non cuique datur habere naſum. | [rule] | *LONDON,* | Printed by
R. Cotes for *H. B.* at the Caſtle | in *Cornehill,* 1645.
Collation: 8°. *A*⁴ B–Z⁸ 2*A*⁴ ($4: *A*1, wanting; *A*2, blank; *A*3,
engraved title; *A*4, title; S1, unsigned; S2, unsigned; V3, unsigned;
X4, missigned V4)
Wing: M1712; Case: 95(c)
Copy: L 11623.aa.33
Verse: *A*"A Valediction: forbidding mourning," sig. T4v;
A"Song. 'Go, and catch a falling star,' " sig. V7v

A1641:1c 1650 (Wing: M1713; Case: 95[d]): sigs. Q8r–v, T6

A1641:1d 1654 (Wing: M1714; Case: 95[e]): sigs. Q8r–v, T6

A1641:1e 1663 (Wing: M1715; Case: 95[f]. L, shelfmark: 1076.i.39): sigs. Q8r–v, T6

Title [typeset, within single rules]: RECREATION | FOR | Ingenious Head-peeces. | OR A | Pleaſant Grove | FOR THEIR | WITS TO VVALK IN. |

$$Of \begin{cases} \textit{Epigrams, 700.} \\ \textit{Epitaphs, 200.} \\ \textit{Fancies, a number.} \\ \textit{Fantaſticks, abundance.} \end{cases}$$

[swash k] | [rule] | With their new Addition, Multipli- | cation and Diviſion. | [rule] | Mart. *Non cuique datur habere naſum.* | [rule] | LONDON, *Printed by* S. Simmons, *in* | Alderſgate-Street. 1663.

The order of the two 1663 issues is uncertain: the engraved and typeset titles of A1641:1e are dated 1663; the engraved title page of A1641:1f is dated 1663, but its typeset title page is undated. The typesettings for the adapted Donne verses are identical. As the engraved title pages are identical, I give the typeset title pages.

A1641:1f 1663 (Wing M1715. CSmH, shelfmark: 147489): sigs. Q8r–v, T6

Title [typeset, within single rules]: RECREATION | FOR | Ingenious Head-Peeces: | OR A | Pleaſant Grove | FOR THEIR [swash R] | WITS TO WALK IN. |

$$Of \begin{cases} \textit{Epigrams, 700.} \\ \textit{Epitaphs, 200.} \\ \textit{Fancies, a number.} \\ \textit{Fantasticks, abundance.} \end{cases}$$

| [rule] | With their new Addition, Multipli- | cation and Diviſion. | [rule] | Mart. *Non cuique datur habere naſum.* | [rule] | LONDON, Printed for *John Stafford*, living in [swash 2d N, J] | *George*-Yard near *Fleet-Bride.*

A1641:1g 1665 (Wing: M1715A): sigs. Q8r–v, T6

Another issue of A1641:1e/f, having the 1663 engraved title page and a cancel, typeset title page dated 1665.

A1641:1h 1667 (Wing: M1716; Case: 95[g]): sigs. Q8r–v, T6

A new edition "Printed by *S. Simmons*." with the 1663 engraved title page.

A1641:1i 1667 (Wing: M1717; Case: 95[h]): sigs. Q8r–v, T6

Another issue of A1641:1h "Printed by S. *Simmons*, and are to be *fold* by *Thomas Helder*," having the 1663 engraved title page and a cancel, typeset title page.

A1641:1j 1683 (Wing: M1718; Case: 95[i]): pp. 173, 203

---

1. For the 1st ed. of *Wits Recreations*, see 1640:3a.
2. The poem is Francis Beaumont's "Womans Mutability."
3. The poem is Thomas Carew's "An Excuse of absence."
4. The title of the 3d and later editions of *Wits Recreations*.

A1646:1a

Author: Henry Vaughan

Title: POEMS, | WITH | The tenth Satyre of | IVUENAL | EN-GLISHED. | [rule] | By *Henry Vaughan*, Gent. | [rule] |————*Tam nil, nullâ tibi vendo* | *Illiade*———— | [rule] | *LONDON*, | Printed for *G. Badger*, and are to be *fold* at his | *fhop* under Saint *Dunftans* Church in | Fleet-*ftreet*. 1646.

Collation: 8°. §⁴ A–E⁸ F⁴ ($4: §1, wanting; §2, title, unsigned; §4, unsigned; A1, wanting; A3, unsigned; F4, unsigned)

Wing: V124

Copy: CSmH 105602

Verse: *A*"A Valediction: forbidding mourning," pp. 33–35

Additional seventeenth-century issue:

A1646:1b 1646 (Wing: V124. L, shelfmark: E.1178.[3]): pp. 33–35

The priority of A1646:1a and A1646:1b is uncertain, though A1646:1b would seem to have the corrected state of the title page, collation, and text for the poem.

Title: POEMS, | WITH | The tenth Satyre of | IVUENAL | EN-GLISHED. | [rule] | By *Henry Vaughan*, Gent. | [rule] |— *Tam nil, nullâ tibi vendo* | *Illiade*—— | [rule] | *LONDON*, | Printed for *G. Badger*, and are to be *fold* at his | *fhop* under Saint *Dunftans* Church in | Fleet-*ftreet*. 1646.

The described copy has sig. A3 signed and its l. 16 reads "Eyes." for "Eyes:". This, the Thomason copy, has no manuscript date on its title page.

A1659:1a

Contributor: John Wilson

Title [within double rules]: *SELECT | AYRES | AND | DIA-LOGUES* | For One, Two, and Three Voyces; | TO THE | *THEORBO-LUTE* or *BASSE-VIOL.* | [rule] |

Compoſed by
{
John Wilſon
Charles Colman
} Doctors in *Muſick.*
{
Henry Lawes
William Lawes
Nicholas Laneare
William Webb
}
Gentlemen and Servants to his late Majeſty in his Publick and Private Muſick.

And other Excellent Maſters of Muſick.

[swash *J, k, k*] | [rule] | [ornament] | [rule] | *LONDON,* | Printed by *W. Godbid* for *John Playford*, and are to be ſold at his Shop [swash *J*] | in the *Inner Temple,* neer the Church dore. 1659.

Collation: 2°. π² *A*² B–2F² ($1: π1v, illustration; π2, title; C1, unsigned)

Wing: W2909

Copy: L E.1078

Verse: *A*"Song. 'Go, and catch a falling star'"[1] (l. 1), sig. *A*1v; *A*"The Dampe"[2] (l. 1), sig. *A*2; *A*"Song. 'Go, and catch a falling star,'"[3] p. 11; *A*"The Dampe," p. 102; *A*"The Dampe," p. 102; *A*"The Dampe,"[4] p. 102

This, the Thomason copy, is dated "Decemb: 2ᵈ."

---

1. The poem is Francis Beaumont's "Womans Mutability."
2. The poem is Thomas Carew's "Secresie protested."
3. For musical setting, see plate 5.
4. For musical setting, see plate 6.

A1669:1a

Author: Henry Lawes

Title [within double rules]: The Treaſury of Muſick: | *CON-TAINING* | AYRES | AND | DIALOGUES | To Sing to the | THEORBO-LUTE | OR | BASSE-VIOL. | [rule] | *COMPOSED* | By Mʳ· *HENRY LAWES*, late Servant to His Majeſty | in His Publick and Private MUSICK: | *And other Excellent MASTERS.* | [rule] | *In Three* Books. | [rule] | [ornament] | [rule] | *LONDON,* | Printed by *William Godbid* for *John Playford*, and are to be Sold at his Shop [swash *J*] | in the *Temple,* near the Church Dore. 1669.

On Womens Inconstancy.

Catch me a Star that's fal--ling from the Skie, Cause an Immortall creature for to die; Stop with thy hand the Current of the Seas, Peirce the earths Center to th' Antipodies; Cause Time return, and call back Yesterday, Cloath Ja-nu-a-ry like the moneth of May; Weigh me an ounce of Flame, Blow back the wind; Then hast thou found Faith in a Womans mind.

John Playford.

PLATE 5. Musical setting of A "Song. 'Go, and catch a falling star' " (A1659:1a). Reproduced by permission of The Huntington Library, San Marino, California.

PLATE 6. Musical setting of *A*"The Dampe" (A1659:1a). Reproduced by permission of The Huntington Library, San Marino, California.

Collation: 2⁰. π² A² B–2F² ($1: π1, blank; π1v, engraved illustration of "Musick"; π2, title, unsigned; A1, unsigned; C1, unsigned) A⁴ ($3: A1, separate title, unsigned) B–2F² ($2: N2, unsigned; O2, missigned M2; leaves containing *"Italian* Ayrs" and signed 2A1, 2B2, 2B1, and 2B2, inserted between 2B2 and 2C1; 2D2, missigned 2D1) χ¹ A² B–O² ($1: χ1, separate title; G1, missigned F1; O2, wanting)

Wing: L645

Copy: L K.3.m.19

Verse: A"Song. 'Go, and catch a falling star'"¹ (l. 1), sig. A1v; A"The Dampe"² (l. 1), sig. A2; A"Song. 'Go, and catch a falling star,'"³ p. 11; A"The Dampe," p. 102; A"The Dampe," p. 102; A"The Dampe,"⁴ p. 102

Book I is a reissue of A1659:1a. The "Table of the Songs and Dialogues in this Book [II]" which lists "*A Table of* Italian *AYRS in this Book*" (without page numbers—pp. 97–104 are reserved for them) and the pagination sequence (p. 96 on sig. 2B2v and p. 105 on sig. 2C1) suggest that the insertion of the *"Italian* Ayrs" was planned for pages 97–104, though the pagination within the insertion runs 89, 94, 95, 92, 93, 94, 95, 96. The CLU-C copy (shelfmark: *fM1549 L41) also has the insertion.

---

1. The poem is Francis Beaumont's "Womans Mutability."
2. The poem is Thomas Carew's "Secresie protested."
3. For musical setting, see plate 7.
4. For musical setting, see plate 8.

A1672:1a

Compiler: Anonymous

Title [within double rules]: 𝔚𝔦𝔫𝔡𝔰𝔬𝔯=𝔇𝔯𝔬𝔩𝔩𝔢𝔯𝔶. | [rule] | Being a more Exact | COLLECTION | Of the Neweſt | *Songs, Poems, and Catches,* | Now in Uſe, | Both in CITY and COUNTRY, | then any yet Extant. | [rule] | 𝔚𝔦𝔱𝔥 𝔄𝔡𝔡𝔦𝔱𝔦𝔬𝔫𝔰. | [rule] | *Collected by a Perſon of Quality.* [swash Q] | [rule] | *LONDON,* | Printed for J. M. and are to be ſold [swash J] | by the Book-Sellers of *London* and | *Weſtminſter,* 1672.

Collation: 12⁰. π¹ A–G¹² H⁷ I⁵ ($5: π1, title; F3, unsigned; F4, unsigned; F5, unsigned; H5, unsigned; I3, unsigned; I4, unsigned; I5, unsigned)

Wing: W2980; Case: 154

Copy: CSmH 148513

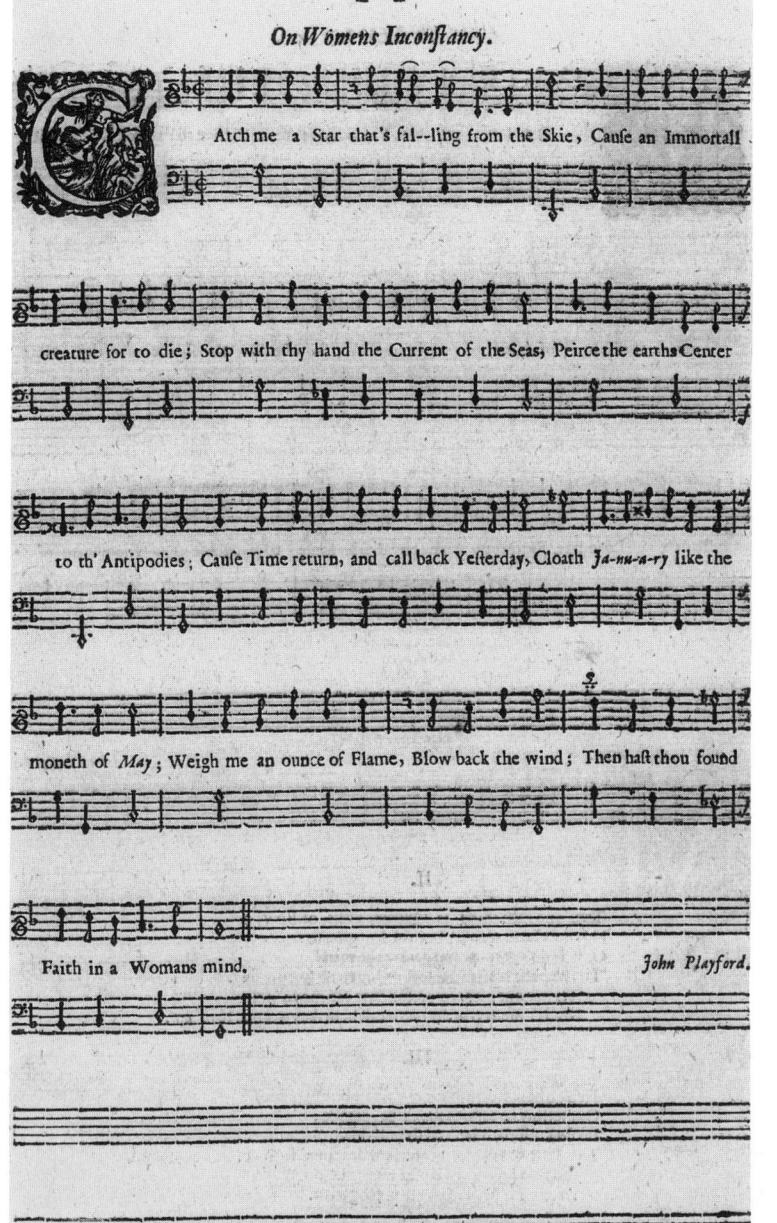

PLATE 7. Musical setting of A "Song. 'Go, and catch a falling star'"
(A1669:1a). Reproduced by permission of the William Andrews
Clark Memorial Library, University of California, Los Angeles.

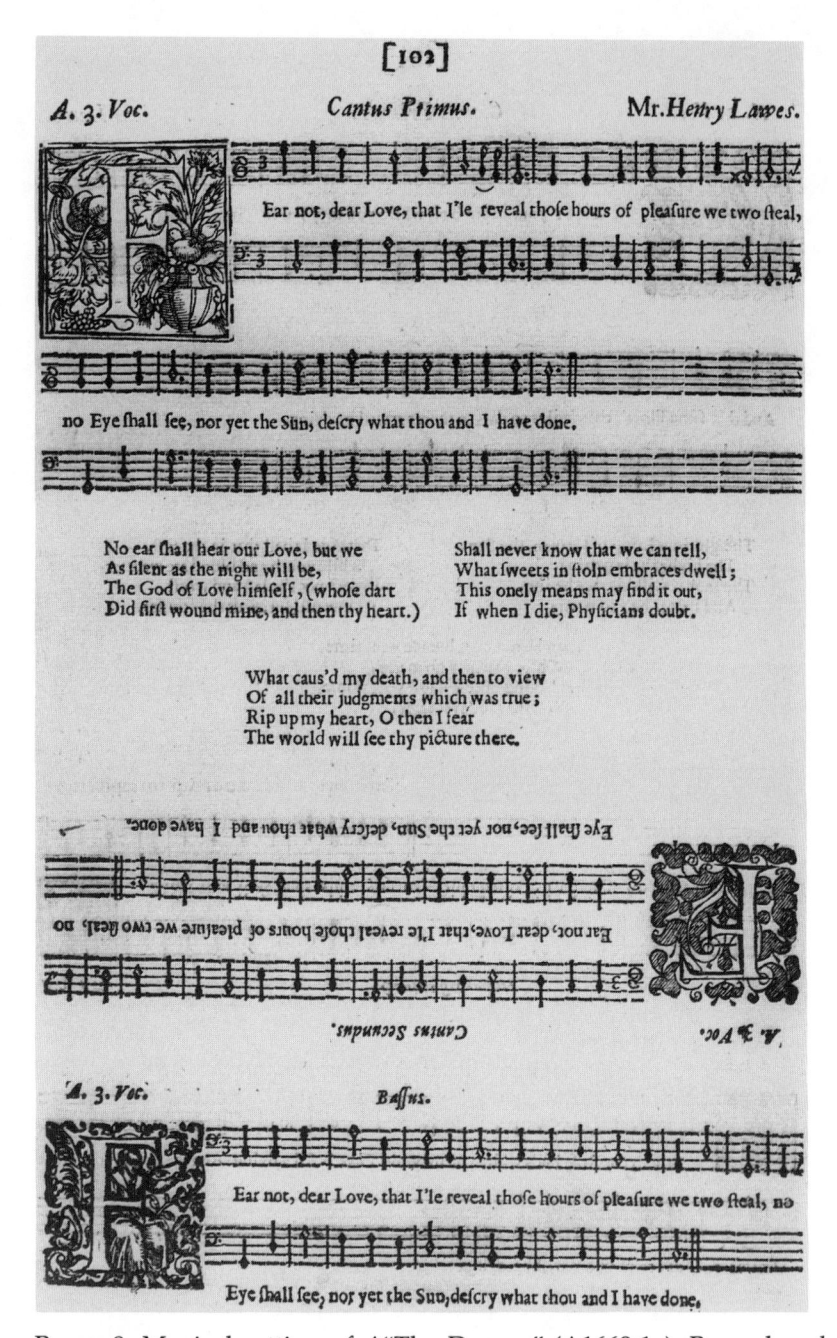

A. 3. Voc.   *Cantus Primus.*   Mr. *Henry Lawes.*

Ear not, dear Love, that I'le reveal thofe hours of pleafure we two fteal,

no Eye fhall fee, nor yet the Sun, defcry what thou and I have done.

No ear fhall hear our Love, but we   Shall never know that we can tell,
As filent as the night will be,   What fweets in ftoln embraces dwell;
The God of Love himfelf, (whofe dart   This onely means may find it out,
Did firft wound mine, and then thy heart.)   If when I die, Phyficians doubt.

What caus'd my death, and then to view
Of all their judgments which was true;
Rip up my heart, O then I fear
The world will fee thy picture there.

(inverted text) Eye fhall fee, nor yet the Sun, defcry what thou and I have done.

(inverted text) Ear not, dear Love, that I'le reveal thofe hours of pleafure we two fteal, no

(inverted text) *Cantus Secundus.*   *A. 3. Voc.*

A. 3. Voc.   *Baffus.*

Ear not, dear Love, that I'le reveal thofe hours of pleafure we two fteal, no

Eye fhall fee, nor yet the Sun, defcry what thou and I have done.

PLATE 8. Musical setting of *A*"The Dampe" (A1669:1a). Reproduced by permission of the William Andrews Clark Memorial Library, University of California, Los Angeles.

Verse: *A*"Song. 'Go, and catch a falling star,'" pp. 151–52; *A*"Song. 'Go, and catch a falling star'" (l. 1), sig. I2

A1697:1a
Author: Daniel Baker
Title: POEMS | UPON | Several Occaſions. | [rule] | By Daniel Baker, M.A. | Sometimes of *Gonvil* and *Caius* Coll. | in Cambridge. | [rule] | Virgil. Eclog. 9. |— ———— ——— *Me quoque dicunt* | *Vatem Paſtores; ſed non ego credulus illis.* [swash P] | [double rule] | *LONDON,* [swash N, D, N] | Printed for *J. Jones,* at the *Dolphin* and *Crown* [swash J, J, D] | in S. *Paul's* Church-yard. 1697. [swash P]
Collation: 8°. *A*⁴ B–L⁸ ($4: *A*1, blank?, wanting; *A*2, title; C4, unsigned; K3, unsigned)
Wing: B489A
Copy: O Harding c 465
Verse: *A*"A Valediction: forbidding mourning," pp. 34–35

Additional seventeenth-century issue:

A1697:1b 1697 (Wing: B489A. O, shelfmark: 280 n.659): pp. 34–35
A1697:1a and A1697:1b have the same collation and text of *A*"A Valediction: forbidding mourning," even in the obviously erroneous "Aud" (l. 16). A1697:1b has the following cancel title page pasted onto the stub conjugate with sig. *A*2:
Title: POEMS | UPON | Several Occaſions. | [rule] | By Daniel Baker, M. A. | Sometimes of *Gonvil* and *Caius* Coll. | in Cambridge. | [rule] | Virgil. Eclog. 9. |——— ——— ——— *Me quoque dicunt* | *Vatem Paſtores; ſed non ego credulus illis.* [swash P] | [double rules] | *LONDON,* [swash N, D, N] | Printed for *J. Jones,* and are to be ſold by [swash J, J] | *Joſeph Wilde,* at the *Elephant* near *Charing-* [swash J] | *Croſs,* 1697.

Works Containing Dubia Only

D1612:1a

Author: John Dowland

Title [within ornamental border]: A Pilgrimes Solace. | [rule] | VVherein is contained Muſicall | Harmonie of 3. 4. and 5. parts, to be | ſung and plaid with the Lute | and Viols. | By *John Douland*, Batchelor of Muſicke in [swash *J*] | both the Vniuerſities: and Lutteniſt to the | Right Honourable the | Lord Walden. | 1612 [within ornament] | *LONDON:* | Printed for *M. L. J. B.* and *T. S.* [swash *J*] | by the Aſſignment of | *William Barley.* [swash *B*]

Collation: 2°. *A*² B–M² ($2: A1, title, unsigned; A1v, blank; B1, The Table, unsigned)

STC: 7098

Copy: CSmH 59103

Verse: *D*"Breake of day" (l. 1), sig. B1; *D*"Breake of day,"[1] sig. B2v; *D*"Breake of day," sig. C1; *D*"Breake of day," sig. C1; *D*"Breake of day,"[2] sig. C1

---

1. The first stanza was prefixed to "Breake of day" in Donne's *Poems* (1669). Grierson prints the stanza in his "Appendix B. Poems Which Have Been Attributed to John Donne in the Old Editions and the Principal MS. Collections, Arranged According to Their Probable Authors" (p. 432) as by "John Dowlands"; Gardner prints the stanza as "Dubia" (*Elegies*, p. 108); and Keynes regards the stanza as Dowland's, not Donne's (p. 207). Beal notes the textual significance of this verse: "the *Song* 'Stay, O sweet, and do not rise' . . . which, although perhaps written by John Dowland, has special textual interest because of its frequent association with *Breake of day*" (1:259). For musical setting, see plate 9.

2. For musical setting, see plate 10.

D1612:2a

Author: Orlando Gibbons

Title [within ornamental border]: {CANTVS.} | THE | *FIRST SET* [swash *R, E*] | OF | MADRIGALS | AND MOTTETS | of 5. Parts: apt for | Viols and Voyces. | *NEWLY COMPOSED* [swash *N, Y, P, E, D*] | by *Orlando Gibbons*, Batche- [swash *G*] | ler of Muſicke, and Organiſt of | his Maieſties Honourable Chappell | in *Ordinarie*. | *LONDON:* | Printed by Thomas Snodham, | the Aſſigne of *W. Barley.* | 1612.

Collation: 4°. A–C⁴ ²A–²C⁴ ³A–³C⁴ ⁴A–⁴C⁴ ⁵A–⁵C⁴ ($3: A1, title, unsigned; A2, unsigned; ²A1, separate title, unsigned; ²A2,

PLATE 9. Musical setting of D"Breake of day" (D1612:1a).
Reproduced by permission of The Huntington Library, San Marino,
California.

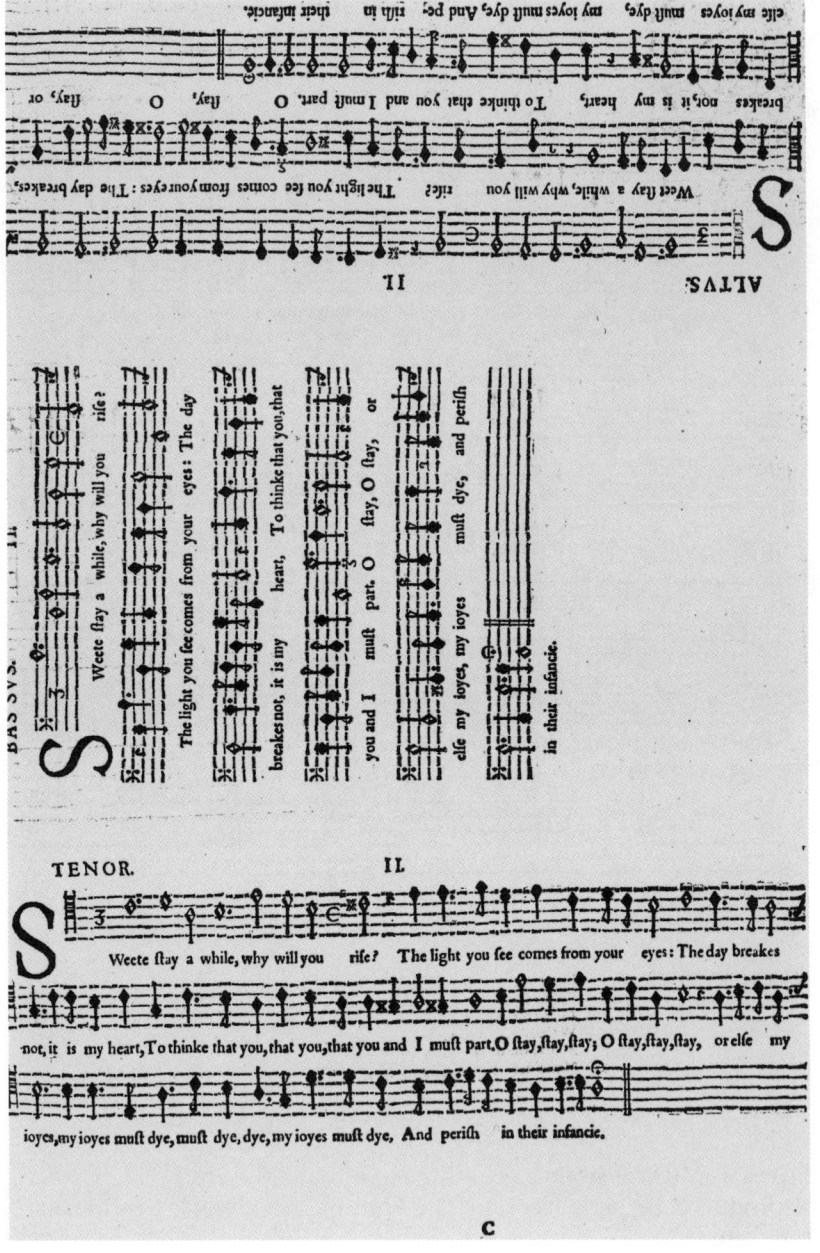

PLATE 10. Musical setting of D"Breake of day" (D1612:1a).
Reproduced by permission of The Huntington Library, San Marino,
California.

unsigned; [3]A1, separate title, unsigned; [3]A2, unsigned; [4]A1, separate title, unsigned; [4]A2, unsigned; [5]A1, separate title, unsigned; [5]A2, unsigned)

STC: 11826

Copy: CSmH 13103

Verse:[1] D"Breake of day" (l. 1), sig. A2v; D"Breake of day,"[2] sig. C2

Separate title [within ornamental border]: {ALTVS.} | THE | *FIRST SET* [swash *R, E*] | OF | MADRIGALS | AND MOTTETS | of 5. Parts: apt for | Viols and Voyces. | *NEWLY COMPOSED* [swash *N, Y, P, E, D*] | by *Orlando Gibbons,* Batche- [swash *G*] | ler of Muſicke, and Organiſt of | his Maieſties Honourable Chappell | *in Ordinarie.* | *LONDON:* | Printed by THOMAS SNODHAM, | the Aſſigne of *W. Barley.* | 1612.

Verse: D"Breake of day" (l. 1), sig. [2]A2v; D"Breake of day,"[3] sig. [2]C2

Separate title [within ornamental border]: {TENOR.} | THE | *FIRST SET* [swash *R, E*] | OF | MADRIGALS | AND MOTTETS | of 5. Parts: apt for | Viols and Voyces. | *NEWLY COMPOSED* [swash *N, Y, P, E, D*] | by *Orlando Gibbons,* Batche- [swash *G*] | ler of Muſicke, and Organiſt of | his Maieſties Honourable Chappell | *in Ordinarie.* | *LONDON:* | Printed by THOMAS SNODHAM, | the Aſſigne of *W. Barley.* | 1612.

Verse: D"Breake of day" (l. 1), sig. [3]A2v; D"Breake of day,"[4] sig. [3]C2

Separate title [within ornamental border]: {QVINTVS.} | THE | *FIRST SET* [swash *R, E*] | OF | MADRIGALS | AND MOTTETS | of 5. Parts: apt for | Viols and Voyces. | *NEWLY COMPOSED* [swash *N, Y, P, E, D*] | by *Orlando Gibbons,* Batche- [swash *G*] | ler of Muſicke, and Organiſt of | his Maieſties Honourable Chappell | *in Ordinarie.* | *LONDON:* | Printed by THOMAS SNODHAM, | the Aſſigne of *W. Barley.* | 1612.

Verse: D"Breake of day" (l. 1), sig. [4]A2v; D"Breake of day,"[5] sig. [4]C2

Separate title [within ornamental border]: {BASSVS.} | THE | *FIRST SET* [swash *R, E*] | OF | MADRIGALS | AND MOTTETS | of 5. Parts: apt for | Viols and Voyces. | *NEWLY COMPOSED* [swash *N, Y, P, E, D*] | by *Orlando Gibbons,* Batche- [swash *G*] | ler of Muſicke, and Organiſt of | his Maieſties Honourable Chappell | *in Ordinarie.* | *LONDON:* | Printed by THOMAS SNODHAM, | the Aſſigne of *W. Barley.* | 1612.

Verse: *D*"Breake of day" (l. 1), sig. [5]A2v; *D*"Breake of day,"[6] sig. [5]C2

---

1. For the connection of *D*"Breake of day" to Donne, see D1612:1a, n. 1.

2. For musical setting, see plate 11.

3. For musical setting, see plate 12.

4. For musical setting, see plate 13.

5. For musical setting, see plate 14.

6. For musical setting, see plate 15.

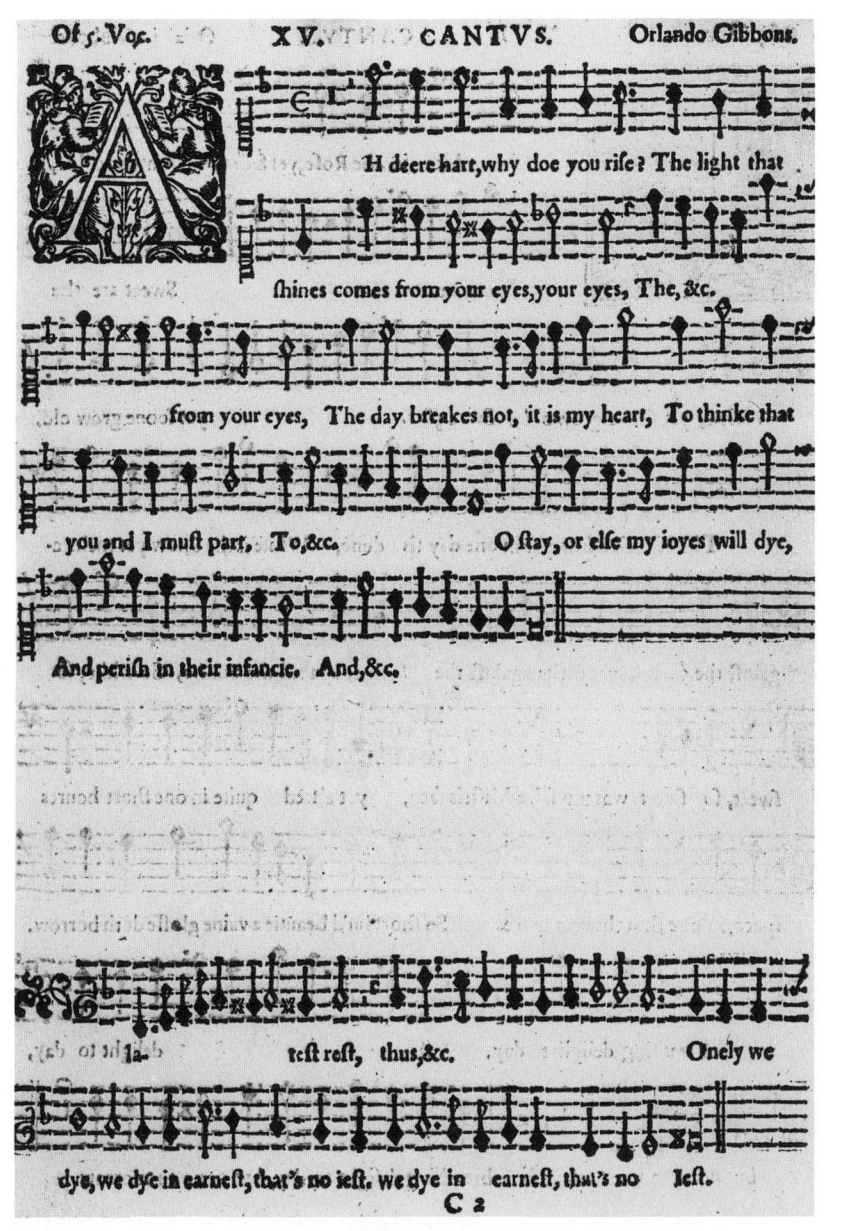

PLATE 11. Musical setting of *D*"Breake of day" (D1612:2a).
Reproduced by permission of The Huntington Library, San Marino,
California.

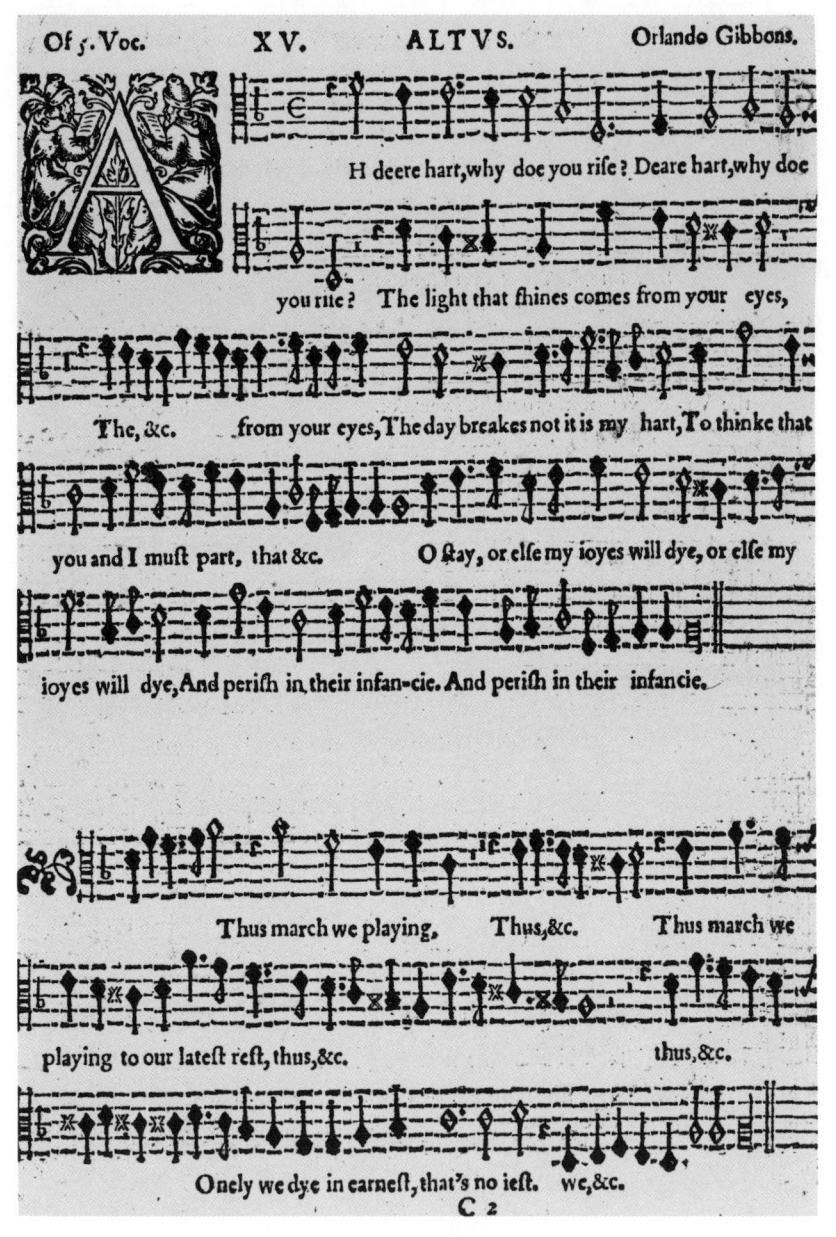

Plate 12. Musical setting of *D*"Breake of day" (D1612:2a).
Reproduced by permission of The Huntington Library, San Marino,
California.

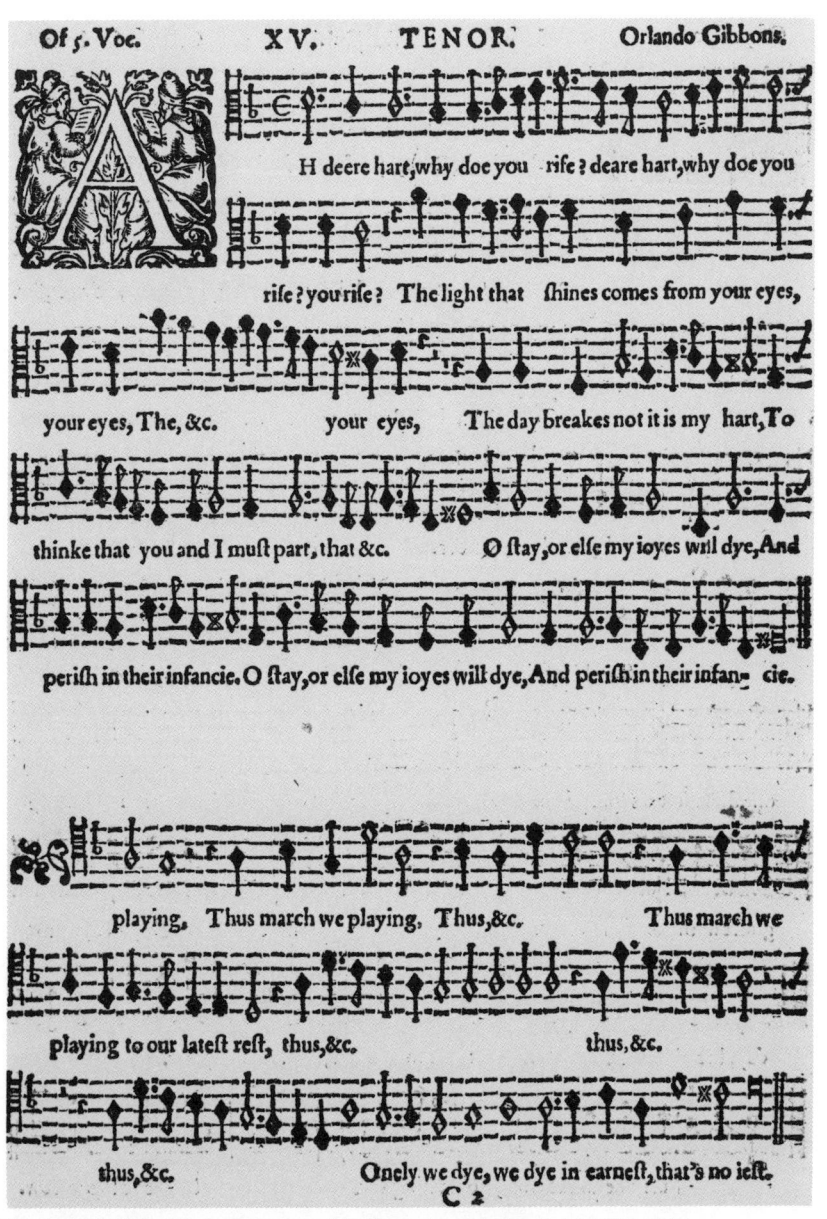

PLATE 13. Musical setting of D"Breake of day" (D1612:2a).
Reproduced by permission of The Huntington Library, San Marino,
California.

PLATE 14. Musical setting of D"Breake of day" (D1612:2a).
Reproduced by permission of The Huntington Library, San Marino,
California.

PLATE 15. Musical setting of D"Breake of day" (D1612:2a).
Reproduced by permission of The Huntington Library, San Marino,
California.

CHRONOLOGY OF PRINTINGS

1607: 1607:1a, 1607:2a, 1607:3a
1609: 1609:1a, 1609:2a
1611: 1611:1a, 1611:2a, 1611:3a, 1611:4a, 1611:4b, 1611:5a
1612: 1611:3b, 1612:1a, D1612:1a, D1612:2a
1613: 1613:1a, 1613:1b, 1613:1c, 1613:1d, 1613:1e, 1613:1f,
    1613:1g, 1613:1h, 1613:1i, 1613:1j, A1613:1a, A1613:2a,
    A1613:2b, A1613:3a, A1613:4a
1614: 1614:1a
1616: 1616:1A, 1616:1a, 1616:1b, 1616:1C, 1616:1c
1617: 1617:1a
1618: 1618:1a
1619: 1619:1a, 1619:2a
1620: 1618:1b, 1619:1b
1621: 1611:3c, 1619:1c, 1621:1a
1623: 1619:1d, 1623:1A, 1623:1a, 1623:1B, 1623:1C, A1623:1a
1624: 1624:1a, 1624:1b, 1624:1c
1625: 1611:3d
1626: 1611:5b, 1624:1d
1627: 1619:1e, 1624:1e
1628: 1619:1f
1629: 1619:1g, A1629:1a
1630: 1619:1h, 1621:1b, 1623:1D, 1623:1d, 1623:1E, 1623:1e,
    A1629:1b
1631: 1619:1i
1632: 1632:1a, A1629:1c, A1629:1d, A1629:1e, A1629:1f,
    A1629:1g, A1629:1h, A1629:1i, A1632:1a
1633: 1614:1b, 1632:1b, 1632:1c, 1632:1d, 1633:1a, 1633:1b,
    1633:2a, A1632:1b
1634: 1611:5c, 1624:1f, 1633:1c, A1634:1a
1635: 1611:5d, 1619:1j, 1635:1a, A1634:1b, A1634:1c
1636: 1619:1k, A1632:1c
1638: 1619:1l, 1624:1g, A1632:1d, A1638:1a
1639: A1634:1d
1640: 1616:1D, 1616:1d, 1616:1e, 1616:1F, 1616:1f, 1616:1g,
    1619:1m, 1633:2b, 1640:1a, 1640:1b, 1640:2a, 1640:3a,
    A1623:1b, A1623:1c, A1640:1a, A1640:2a, A1640:2b
1641: 1616:1h, 1616:1I, 1616:1i, T1641:1a, A1632:1e, A1641:1a

1642: A1640:2c
1643: 1635:1b
1644: 1635:1c
1645: 1645:1a, A1641:1b
1646: 1645:1b, A1646:1a, A1646:1b
1647: A1629:1j
1648: 1619:1n, T1641:1b
1650: 1645:1c, 1645:1d, 1650:1a, 1650:2a, A1641:1c
1651: 1651:1a, 1651:2a, A1629:1k, A1640:2d, A1640:2e
1652: 1652:1a, 1652:1b, A1632:1f
1653: 1653:1a, 1653:1b, 1653:2a, 1653:2b, 1653:3a
1654: 1619:1o, 1645:1e, 1653:2c, 1654:1a, 1654:2a, 1654:2b,
    1654:3a, 1654:4a, A1629:1l, A1641:1d
1655: 1650:2b, 1653:3b, 1655:1a, 1655:2a, 1655:3a
1656: 1656:1A, 1656:1a, 1656:2a, 1656:3a, A1629:1m, A1629:1n
1657: 1657:1a, 1657:1b, T1657:1a, A1632:1g
1658: 1645:1f, 1658:1a, 1658:2a, 1658:3a, 1658:4a, 1658:5a, 1658:6a
1659: 1658:2b, 1659:1a, A1629:1o, A1629:1p, A1659:1a
1660: 1651:1b, 1653:1c, 1660:1a, A1623:1d, A1632:1h
1661: 1653:3c, 1656:2b, 1661:1a, 1661:2a, 1661:2b
1662: 1655:1b, 1662:1a, 1662:2a
1663: 1619:1p, 1645:1g, A1641:1e, A1641:1f
1664: 1653:3d, 1664:1a, 1664:1b, 1664:2a, A1629:1q, A1632:1i
1665: 1635:1d, A1641:1g
1667: 1619:1q, 1664:1c, A1641:1h, A1641:1i
1668: 1653:3e, 1668:1a, 1668:1B, 1668:1b, 1668:1C, 1668:1D,
    A1629:1r
1669: 1664:1d, 1668:1e, 1668:1f, 1668:1g, 1668:1h, 1669:1a,
    A1629:1s, A1669:1a
1670: 1635:1e, 1645:1h, 1670:1a, 1670:2a, A1640:2f
1671: 1655:1c, A1629:1t, A1632:1j, A1640:2g
1672: 1654:3b, 1658:4b, 1668:1i, A1672:1a
1673: 1673:1a, 1673:1b
1674: 1668:1j, 1673:1c, 1674:1a
1675: 1670:2b, A1632:1k
1676: 1653:3f, 1676:1a, 1676:1b, 1676:1c
1677: 1657:1c, 1677:1a, A1629:1u, A1629:1v
1678: 1657:1d, 1668:1k, 1674:1b, 1678:1a, A1623:1e
1679: 1651:2b, 1674:1c
1680: 1668:1l, 1668:1m, 1680:1a
1681: 1668:1n, 1668:1o, 1681:1a, 1681:2a
1682: 1619:1r, 1681:2b

1683: 1683:1a, A1641:1j
1684: 1645:1i, 1645:1j, 1660:1b, 1668:1p, 1668:1q, 1680:1b, 1684:1a, 1684:1b, 1684:1c, A1629:1w
1685: 1654:3c
1686: 1678:1b
1687: 1687:1a, A1629:1x, A1629:1y, A1632:1l
1688: 1668:1r, 1688:1a, 1688:2a
1689: 1664:1e
1690: 1664:1f, A1629:1z
1691: 1691:1a, 1691:2a
1692: 1616:1j, 1680:1c, 1691:1b, 1692:1A, 1692:1a, A1629:1aa
1693: 1668:1s, 1691:2b
1694: 1691:2c
1695: 1674:1d, 1691:1d
1696: 1696:1a
1697: 1664:1g, 1680:1d, 1691:1c, A1697:1a, A1697:1b
1698: 1635:1f
1700: 1668:1t

SELECTED BIBLIOGRAPHY

The following list includes works (other than those assigned a siglum) cited more than once in the preceding pages; the short forms used after the initial citation appear in brackets preceding the full bibliographical entry.

[Beal] Beal, Peter. *Index of English Literary Manuscripts.* Vol. 1, pts. 1, 2. London and New York: Mansell Publishing, 1980.

[Bevan] Bevan, Jonquil, ed. *Izaak Walton: The Compleat Angler 1653–1676.* Oxford: Clarendon Press, 1983.

[Bohm] Bohm, Wilhelm. *Englands Einfluss auf Georg Rudolf Weckherlin.* Göttingen, 1893.

[Carey] Carey, John, ed. *John Donne.* Oxford: Oxford University Press, 1990.

[Case] Case, Arthur E. *A Bibliography of English Poetical Miscellanies 1521–1750.* Oxford: Oxford University Press, 1935 (for 1929).

[Chambers] Chambers, E. K., ed. *Poems of John Donne.* 2 vols. London: Lawrence & Bullen, 1896.

[Daley] Daley, Koos. *The Triple Fool: A Critical Evaluation of Constantijn Huygens' Translations of John Donne.* Nieuwkoop: De Graff Publishers, 1990.

[Dunlap] Dunlap, Rhodes, ed. *The Poems of Thomas Carew with His Masque Coelum Britannicum.* Oxford: Clarendon Press, 1949.

[Flynn, "Epigrams"] Flynn, Dennis. "Jasper Mayne's Translation of Donne's Latin Epigrams." *John Donne Journal* 3 (1984): 121–30.

[Flynn, "Ignatius"]———. "Donne's *Ignatius His Conclave* and Other Libels on Robert Cecil." *John Donne Journal* 6 (1987): 163–83.

[Freeman] Freeman, David, ed. *Argalus and Parthenia: Francis Quarles.* The Renaissance English Text Society. London: Associated University Presses, 1986.

[Gardner, *Divine*] Gardner, Helen, ed. *John Donne: The Divine Poems.* 2d ed. Oxford: Clarendon Press, 1978.

[Gardner, *Elegies*]———. *John Donne: The Elegies and The Songs and Sonnets.* Oxford: Clarendon Press, 1965.

[Greg] Greg, W. W. *A Bibliography of the English Printed Drama to the Restoration.* Vol. 3. Rpt., London: The Bibliographical Society, 1970.

[Grierson] Grierson, Herbert J. C., ed. *The Poems of John Donne*. 2 vols. Oxford: Oxford University Press, 1912.

[Healy] Healy, T. S., ed. *John Donne: Ignatius His Conclave*. Oxford: Clarendon Press, 1969.

[Herford and Simpson] Herford, C. H., and Percy Simpson, eds. *Ben Jonson*. Vol. 1. Oxford: Clarendon Press, 1925.

[Horden] Horden, John. *Francis Quarles (1592–1644): A Bibliography of His Works to the Year 1800*. Oxford Bibliographical Society. N.S. 1953 (for 1948).

[Johnson] Johnson, Samuel. "Cowley." In *The Lives of the Most Eminent English Poets*, vol. 1. London, 1781.

[Kastner] Kastner, L. E., ed. *The Poetical Works of William Drummond of Hawthornden with a Cypresse Grove*. 2 vols. Edinburgh: William Blackwood and Sons, 1913. Also printed as volumes 5 and 6 of the English Series. Manchester: University of Manchester Press, 1913.

[Keynes] Keynes, Geoffrey. *A Bibliography of Dr. John Donne*. 4th ed. Oxford: Clarendon Press, 1973.

[Lewalski] Lewalski, Barbara Kiefer. *Donne's Anniversaries and the Poetry of Praise*. Princeton: Princeton University Press, 1973.

[Macdonald] Macdonald, Hugh. *John Dryden: A Bibliography of Early Editions and of Drydeniana*. Oxford: Clarendon Press, 1939.

[Mann] Mann, Francis Oscar, ed. *The Works of Thomas Deloney*. Rpt., Oxford: Clarendon Press, 1967.

[Marotti] Marotti, Arthur F. *John Donne: Coterie Poet*. Madison: University of Wisconsin Press, 1986.

[Martin] Martin, L. C., ed. *The Works of Henry Vaughan*. 2d ed. Oxford: Clarendon Press, 1957.

[Milgate, *Epithalamions*] Milgate, Wesley, ed. *John Donne: The Epithalamions Anniversaries and Epicedes*. Oxford: Clarendon Press, 1978.

[Milgate, *Satires*]————. *John Donne: The Satires, Epigrams and Verse Letters*. Oxford: Clarendon Press, 1967.

[Perkin] Perkin, M. R. *Abraham Cowley: A Bibliography*. Folkestone, Kent, England: Wm Dawson & Sons, 1977.

[Quaranta] Quaranta, Stephanus. *Summa Bullarii*. Venice, 1609.

[Raspa] Raspa, Anthony, ed. *John Donne: Devotions upon Emergent Occasions*. Montreal: McGill-Queen's University Press, 1975.

[Sellin] Sellin, Paul. *So Doth, So Is Religion: John Donne and Diplomatic Contexts in the Reformed Netherlands, 1619–1620*. Columbia: University of Missouri Press, 1988.

[Shawcross, *Donne*] Shawcross, John T., ed. *The Complete Poetry of John Donne*. Garden City, N.Y.: Doubleday & Company, 1967.

[Shawcross, *Milton*]————. *Milton: A Bibliography for the Years 1624–1700*. Binghamton, N.Y.: Medieval & Renaissance Texts & Studies, 1984.

[Smith] Smith, A. J. *John Donne: The Critical Heritage*. London: Routledge & Kegan Paul, 1975.

[STC] Pollard, A. W., and G. R. Redgrave. *A Short-Title Catalogue of Books Printed in England, Scotland, & Ireland and of English Books Printed Abroad 1475–1640*. 2d ed. rev. and enl. by W. A. Jackson, F. S. Ferguson, and Katharine F. Pantzer. 2 vols. London: Bibliographical Society, 1976–1986.

[Sullivan] Sullivan, Ernest W., II, ed. *The Harmony of the Muses*. Hants, England: Scolar Press, 1990.

[Thomason] British Library collection of the pamphlets, books, newspapers, and manuscripts relating to the Civil War, the Commonwealth, and Restoration, collected by George Thomason, 1640–1661. Cataloged in *Catalogue of the Pamphlets, Books, Newspapers, and Manuscripts Relating to the Civil War, the Commonwealth, and Restoration, Collected by George Thomason, 1640–1661*. 2 vols. London, 1908.

[Wing] Wing, Donald. *Short-Title Catalogue of Books Printed in England, Scotland, Ireland, Wales, and British America and of English Books Printed in other Countries 1641–1700*. 2d ed. rev. and enl. by John J. Morrison. 3 vols. New York: Modern Language Association of America, 1972–1988.

[Worp] Worp, J. A., ed. *Gedichten*. Vol. 2. Groningen: Wolters, 1893.

INDEX OF VERSE,
TRANSLATIONS,
ADAPTATIONS,
AND DUBIA

Entries preceded by an asterisk indicate printings of the entire poem.

201

TRANSLATIONS

ADAPTATIONS

INDEX OF AUTHORS, COMPILERS, CONTRIBUTORS, AND TRANSLATORS

This index lists the persons under whom each work is usually cataloged; thus, more than one person may be listed for a single work.

INDEX OF SHORT TITLES
OF WORKS

INDEX OF FIRST LINES

Indexing Donne verse by first line requires an arbitrary choice of text. The first lines in this index are modernized and regularized first lines from Grierson or from the earliest printing for verses (including dubia) not in Grierson. For translations, the index gives the first line from the earliest printing in each language. For adaptations in verse, the index gives the first line of the earliest printing of each different adaptation. Lines in this index are keyed to the verse short titles or are the first lines (when the verse is identified only by its first line) used in my Index of Verse, Translations, Adaptations, and Dubia.